LEVELS OF ABSTRACTION IN LOGIC AND HUMAN ACTION

A theory of discontinuity in the structure of mathematical logic, psychological behaviour, and social organization

Editor: Elliott Jaques

with

R. O. Gibson

and

D. J. Isaac

Heinemann · London

Heinemann Educational Books Ltd

LONDON   EDINBURGH   MELBOURNE   AUCKLAND
TORONTO   HONG KONG   SINGAPORE
KUALA LUMPUR   NEW DELHI   NAIROBI
JOHANNESBURG   LUSAKA   IBADAN
KINGSTON

ISBN 0 435 82280 2

Published by
Heinemann Educational Books Ltd
48 Charles Street, London W1X 8AH

Printed in Great Britain by
Butler & Tanner Ltd, Frome and London

Preface and Acknowledgments

This book is a combination of original papers and reprints. The reprints and their sources are as follows:

Chapter 4: 'Experimental Treatment of Discontinuity Theory of Human Development': D. J. Isaac and B. M. O'Connor, *Human Relations*, Vol. 22, No. 5, 1969, pp. 427–55.

Chapter 5: 'Use of Loss of Skill under Stress, to Test a Theory of Psychological Development': D. J. Isaac and B. M. O'Connor, *Human Relations*, Vol. 26, No. 4, 1973, pp. 488 ff.

Chapter 6: 'Separation of Two Adult Populations': D. J. Isaac and B. M. O'Connor, *Human Relations* (to be published).

Chapter 7: 'Discontinuity Theory of Psychological Development': D. J. Isaac and B. M. O'Connor, *Human Relations*, Vol. 29, No. 1, 1975, pp. 41–61.

Chapter 16: 'Stratification of Work and Organizational Design': Ralph Rowbottom and David Billis, *Human Relations*, Vol. 30, No. 1, 1977.

Chapter 15: 'Stratified Depth Structure of Bureaucracy': Elliott Jaques; and
Chapter 19: 'Levels of Abstraction in Mental Activity': Elliott Jaques; both in *A general theory of bureaucracy*, Elliott Jaques; Heinemann Educational Books/Halsted Press, 1976.

The quotations from G. A. Miller's *Psychology, the science of mental life*, are included by permission of Hutchinson Publishing Group Limited.

Various parts of the manuscript have been typed by Mrs C. Borg-Skelton, Miss R. Fowler, Mrs M. Lewis, Mrs C. S. Sparks and Miss M. Stevens.

Contents

Introduction

1

Structure of the Book

Elliott Jaques

The fact that qualitative changes may occur in the state of material things, and that those changes may occur suddenly, is an ordinary part of everyday experience: falling snow may change to a water droplet as it touches the ground; a stationary object moves when touched; a dark wire lights up when electrically activated. The natural sciences take such changes for granted, it being expected that at certain critical points changes in quality will occur with changes in the quantity of given properties of a substance – its temperature, velocity, electrical resistance, and so on. In short, continuous change in quantity may be accompanied at certain decisive points by discontinuity in state.

The most commonly used examples are, of course, quantum theory on the one hand, and on the other hand changes in state of water, from ice to water to steam to super-heated steam: with continuous change in quantity in temperature sudden rapid changes occur in density at critical temperatures, the qualitative changes in density being manifested in change in appearance.

In the social sciences, discontinuity in state with change in quantity has been far less taken for granted. It is, indeed, only in the Marxist theory of dialectical materialism that the notion of change in quality with change in quantity appears in any systematic way – although unfortunately linked to a highly improbable historical materialistic view of the development of one type of society from another. Apart from that attempt at an explanation of social history, there have been occasional references from time to time to the possibility of discontinuity in so-called levels of abstraction. Little in the way of systematic work has been done, however; the results which are available are summarized by Gillian Stamp in Chapter 17.

The most familiar quantitative expression of continuity theory in the social sciences is the normal distribution curve. It is this normal distribution which is usually looked for in systematic studies. What is less commonly recognized is that the normal distribution curve implies a single-parameter, or single-property, description of psychological and social phenomena. It is precisely this single-parameter notion which dominates the outlook in the social sciences.

The less common outlook – that of multiple parameters, or discontinuity – would express itself in multi-modality of distribution. Multi-modality has never been a very popular interpretation of distribution arrays. There has been a marked tendency to smooth out the peaks and valleys so as to get a uni-modal normal distribution. A useful example is that of the many rat-learning experiments in which, despite the fact that the data point to two different populations of rats in the sense that one group seems to be using a higher level of abstraction in solving the maze-running problem, the interpretation is stated in terms of higher ability only, rather than in terms of higher ability having led to a change in quality to a different type or quality of ability in the 'smarter' group of rats.[1]

It will be argued in this book that multiple parameters are as ordinary a feature of human phenomena as they are of all other natural phenomena, and that, under ordinary conditions, discontinuity will characterize the properties and development of human characteristics. This idea is generally accepted in the notion of stages in individual development as in the extensive work of Piaget and other developmental psychologists. We shall try to show, however, that these discontinuities are manifest also in individual differences which divide populations into multi-modally distributed groups. This manifestation of discontinuities in individual differences has extensive implications for the analysis of psychological and social processes.

---

[1] *See*, for example, Tolman, E. C. (1951) 'Cognitive Maps in Rats and Men', in *Behaviour and Psychological Man*: University of California Press, pp. 256–9.

Background

The present work began in 1961 and came about through a chance meeting and discussion between John Isaac and myself. At that time he had been working with the idea that significant discontinuities showed up in levels of abstraction in mathematics and in scientific theory. His concern was with the education of science students; he had become aware of possible discontinuities in levels of abstraction, through such observations as the fact that some students were so concretely orientated that they could never quite encompass the fact that a triangle was a mental construct and not a physical thing.

At the time he had already worked out with Roland Gibson a preliminary analysis of geometry in terms of six discrete levels (later changed to five), ranging from primitive behaviour in a three-dimensional space to the development of the highly abstract hodological geometries. This work is reported in Gibson's article in Chapter 10. At the same time I had become interested in the idea of an underlying structure of discrete levels of managerial organization, and we were aware of a strong commonality in our approach – his to teaching and science and mine to organization structure.

Since that time we have continued to exchange views and ideas. Isaac has pursued a programme of experimental work with Brian O'Connor, and latterly has generalized his results in collaboration with Gibson through an analysis of the structure of mathematical logic. A series of publications has resulted from this work, and it is the collection of these publications which forms the centre-piece of this book.

Structure of the Book as a Statement of Scientific Methods

The book falls into five main parts – A to E – which are systematically connected as shown in the accompanying diagram. The circular five-stage process which is represented gives a picture of scientific methodology in its most general sense *in action*; that is to say, it contains *all* the components of scientific method, in contrast to many theories of method which concentrate on only one or a few components.

This general statement of scientific methodology comprises: the interaction between initial hunches, hypotheses, theories (B) and the data collected in the context of those ideas (A);

then the conversion of the elaborated theory and data (C) into logical terms (D) where they can be systematically and rigorously examined for logical consistency. This logical testing is reinforced by practical testing and application (E), processes D and E interacting in the same way as A and B. Probability statements may be derived from the D–E interaction, linking again with empirical data in A.

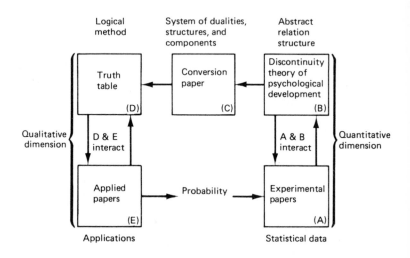

The organization of the book reflects this general methodology. It begins with the A–B empirical–theoretical interaction. For clarity of presentation, and not for reasons of empiricist philosophy, it presents first the purely statistical data in Part A, reprinting a series of experimental papers by Isaac and O'Connor. From these raw data an abstract relation structure is derived in Part B, described in the Isaac and O'Connor 'Discontinuity Theory of Psychological Development'. The relationship between Parts A and B is that of empirical data and an abstraction within which those data were sought and found, and the abstraction further elaborated. It is a quantitative dimension.

Part C takes the material from A and B and puts it through a conversion process. It introduces a system of dualities, structure, and components, which allows the experimental material to be converted to the general system of mathematical logic.

In Part D the logical systematic testing is carried through by means of a systematic analysis of truth table logic. The use of truth tables is the methodology for the analysis, from which is constructed an internally coherent system of five levels of abstraction. These five levels, derived from independent logical analysis, are found to match the levels which were demonstrated experimentally.

From Part D to Part E the two-way movement is between the abstract and the concrete (but at a higher level of generalization), mirroring the two-way movement between A and B which also connects data and abstraction. D and E constitute a qualitative dimension, as a counterpart to the quantitative character of the A and B interaction. In Part E are presented a number of different examples of how the experimentally and logically derived levels of abstraction are manifested in the structure of mental capacity and in hierarchical social organization. Logically the relation is between universal principle and the specific instance, a relationship which introduces the notion of probability. It is via probability that Part E returns to Part A, in the sense that probability provides the general context for the empirical statistical analysis of data.

This movement through Parts A, B, C, D and E, and back from E to A, will be found to characterize the analyses of levels of abstraction in mathematical logic in Chapter 9.

The Experimental Work and Discontinuity Theory

The chapters by Isaac and O'Connor in Part B describe the experimental work which was undertaken to explore two connected hypotheses about discontinuity in psychological development showing up in two different types of multi-modality.

The first hypothesis was that discontinuity in ability in problem-solving would manifest itself in the emergence with age of an increasing number of modes in the distribution of scores indicating level of performance – giving a series of discrete levels of ability, five in all.[2]

[2] It may be noted in Chapter 4 that the original hypothesis was that there would be six prime levels of abstraction. As the experimental work proceeded, however, this hypothesis was changed to five levels rather than six. There then emerged the more general conception of five fundamental levels, but reappearing as a coherent set in higher- and lower-level contexts as described on page 22.

The second hypothesis was that not only would there be a series of discontinuous levels, but that a different mode of work would emerge with each level. Each of the lower-level modes would reappear at each higher level, creating a number of different methods or styles of problem-solving at the higher levels. There would thus be one additional mode of problem-solving at each level; with the resulting pattern of fifteen components described in Chapters 8 and 9:

Level 5	A5	B5	C5	D5	E5
Level 4	A4	B4	C4	D4	
Level 3	A3	B3	C3		
Level 2	A2	B2			
Level 1	A1				

Both these hypotheses have been strongly supported by the experimental work. A point of great significance is that the problems were administered in a manner characteristic of real-life work, rather than like the artificial conditions of intelligence testing. There were two important features:

(a) the subject was given no practice sessions to familiarize him with the type of problem, but rather was required to discover for himself the nature of the problem as well as how to solve it;

(b) the available information did not remain constant; the problem required instead the accumulation of information and experience, the amount of information being well beyond what could possibly be consciously remembered.

In a brilliant experimental design, Isaac and O'Connor have vividly described in Chapter 4 how, when the problem-solving situations were administered under the usual intelligence test conditions of a familiar frame of reference, a uni-modal distribution of scores was obtained. It was only with the switch to the unfamiliarity which characterizes problem-solving in everyday life that multi-modality was revealed.

Confirmed by the experimental work described in Chapters 4, 5 and 6, a general theory of discontinuity in psychological development is described in Chapter 7. That chapter elaborates fifteen components, or modes of functioning. These fifteen components occur because each of the lower levels of abstraction reappears in a more complex context at each successively higher level of abstraction. There is thus one component at level one, two at level two, and so on up to five components at level five, giving fifteen components in all. The fifteen components are shown in later chapters to correspond to fifteen basic dualities in the analysis of mathematical logic (Chapter 8), and to fifteen styles of work-capacity (Chapter 17).

Conversion to Truth Tables and Logical Analysis

The experimental work and its derived discontinuity theory are converted for use in truth table analysis by the structure of bi-polar relationships and contrasts described in Chapter 8. The content of the fifteen modes of functioning is here further generalized, and by formulation in terms of relationships and contrasts lays the foundation for the relational statements and dualities of mathematical logic. The notion is introduced of interplay in movement back and forth between confusion and discrimination. This notion is later expressed in the interaction between T (discrimination) and F (confusion) in the truth table analysis.

The full system is then presented in Chapter 9, which sets out the creative analysis, carried out by Gibson and Isaac, of a structure of discontinuous levels inherent in mathematical logic as a complete system.

How this analysis was intuitively pursued is described by Gibson in Chapter 10. The succeeding chapters 11, 12 and 13 describe some general applications of the analysis to such diverse problems as the possible resolution of Fermat's last theorem, the humanizing of stimulus-response psychology, and a formulation of the two-culture issue. The question of Fermat's last theorem is resolved in the following sense:

All models of the levels-structure itself, that is all models or formulations of the authors' sociological perspective, necessarily mirror one another. Fermat's last theorem taken as a postulate, in the arithmetic model, corresponds to the parallel postulate in the geometry model. But the geometrical case is

generally regarded to have been established as postulational;
hence the impossibility of proving Fermat's last theorem.

Applications

The final chapters are included to illustrate the five-level conceptual scheme in practice. Chapter 15 (Jaques) describes the
general pattern of discontinuity in structure of levels of bureaucratic organization, and how this structure was discovered.
Chapter 16 by Rowbottom and Billis describes their formulation of the work content of the various levels of bureaucratic
organization.

The remaining chapters by Stamp, Macdonald and Jaques,
all have to do with human work-capacity. It is these papers
which serve to give psychological content to the more abstract
conceptions developed in the experimental work and logical
analysis.

Chapter 17, by Gillian Stamp, presents an extension of the
Isaac and O'Connor work into the assessment of work-capacity.
She gives the evidence for the existence of five levels of capacity.
At each succeeding level a new style or mode of working
emerges, alongside the preceding modes, all functioning at a
higher level as a result of being integrated within a more general
context. This research points to the same fifteen components
which appear in the experimental work and the logical analysis,
each of the fifteen modes suggesting a psychological meaning
for the fifteen components.

In Chapter 18, Ian Macdonald describes his work with
mentally handicapped individuals. The five levels he has developed for the assessment of their general capabilities were
quite independently derived from field work with nurses,
doctors and others concerned with the problem of how to make
such assessments. It was the striking similarity in feel between
those five levels and the five levels obtained from normal
populations and logical analysis, that led to the idea of the
possible existence of a range of more and more abstract contexts
within which the five levels of abstraction can be expressed (*see*
Chapter 2).

Chapter 19 (Jaques) outlines some of the original thinking
which gave rise to the hypothesis that the regular discontinuity
found in bureaucratic hierarchies is a straight reflection of the

existence of multi-modality in the distribution of work-capacity in human populations.

The Argument and its General Implications

Finally, a comment on Chapters 2 and 3. In these chapters I have tried to summarize the argument of the book, and to show the striking resemblances in results emerging independently from the experimental work, the logical 'analysis', and the applied field work. I have tried, further, to draw certain broad implications from the work: in particular with respect to the understanding of deductive and inductive logical processes, and the contextual theory of meaning. For the reader who is not too familiar with mathematical logic, it is hoped that these chapters will serve as a useful introduction to the logical 'analysis' which forms the core of the argument.

2

The System of Levels and Components

Elliott Jaques

This chapter presents an outline of the book. The purpose of the outline is to illustrate in advance the richness of the connections between, on the one hand, the conducted experimental work and the analysis of mathematical logic in the sense of facets of textbook logic taken and used to symbolize a sociological perspective, and, on the other hand, the research into organizations and human capacity conducted independently.

Intended as both an introduction and a summary, the chapter may be read at this stage or put off to the end.

First of all, a summary is given of the Isaac and Gibson 'analysis' of mathematical logic, for this provides the link between the quantitative experimental work and the more qualitative research into organization and human capacity. This analysis concludes with five levels of abstraction in logic generating five levels of extension of context. It is carried out in terms of dualities, a new duality emerging at each level, leading to fifteen dualities or components in all.

Second, the experimental work is summarized, showing the emergence of a five-level system with fifteen related components corresponding to the fifteen components of the logical 'analysis'.

Third, the evidence is summarized from the studies of organization and individual capacity, to support the existence of a five-level, fifteen-mode system.

Fourth, it is suggested that the five levels of abstraction, as systems of logical processes, may appear in higher or lower contexts. Three such contexts are described: one at so-called mental handicap level, concerned with concrete things; a second, within the usual range of human functioning, concerned with classes and sets; and a third, at higher level, concerned with classes of classes or infinite sets.

Levels and Dualities in Mathematical Logic

The Gibson–Isaac 'analysis' of mathematical logic arises out of their own logical intuitions, as described by Gibson in Chapter 10.

The movement along which the analysis proceeds is of great importance. It begins with the most primitive form of statement P – 'statement' in the sense of an actual response – and its 'negation' (NP). 'Negation' and 'affirmation' are associated with behavioural entities and are thus seen as unconventional language, language as direct action.

This starting point brings out a critical feature of the whole 'analysis' – a feature which may be of little interest to practising logicians, and may be emotionally disturbing, unpalatable, or even unacceptable to many of them. It may be felt as departing too far from the mathematician's heaven in which numbers, axioms, and deductive relations are seen as *a priori* games made in some sort of heaven (Russell himself professed a belief in some realm 'peopled by numbers'), rather than as the mere inventions of highly intelligent men living in a particular social context at a given stage in the development of the great construction which constitutes the sum of hard-won explications and formulations of human knowledge at any moment in time.

The argument here is that this *a priori* heaven may be a mathematician's delight, but it is a fantasy. Reality is much more mundane, but it at least leaves creativity and originality firmly in the grasp of men at work! All statements, even tightly formulated propositional statements deduced from internally consistent axiom sets and expressed in numbers and mathematical relations, take on meaning *only* in social use; that is to say, such symbolic hieroglyphics become statements in any meaningful sense, *if and only if* they are in social use, i.e. being thought over by a mathematician with his own personal motives and with communication with other mathematicians in mind; or being used in actual discourse between mathematicians.[3]

[3] Stephen Pepper argues precisely this point when he writes, 'The sentence

Gibson and Isaac introduce an unashamedly behavioural context into their logical 'analysis'. It is the context of the mathematician and logician himself at work, using and relying upon his social and cultural context, trying to give further meaning to what is already known, and so to extend knowledge. Hence their attempts to pursue their analysis in terms of behaviour based upon implicit, unconsciously motivated rational processes underlying explicit relations between propositions. The dynamic tension between explicit dualities and implicit duality becomes the key driving force in the emergence of the five levels of abstraction.

It is thus an integral part of the 'analysis' that at each of the levels described there is an implicit duality which underlies the explicit dualities which characterize that level. This implicit duality is implicit in the sense of being active behaviourally, intuitively, but as yet not accessible for use as a conscious, explicit, context. The qualitative shift, then, from one level to the next higher level, is one in which the implicit duality becomes explicit at the next higher level and thus joins the other processes at that level – while at the same time a new implicit duality emerges which gives the behavioural intuitive foundations of meaning at this higher level.

This process may be illustrated in the diagram on page 15 in general terms. This diagram shows five levels of abstraction. At each level (except the first) there are one or more *explicit* dualities, and one *implicit* duality, a new implicit duality emerging at each level. The dualities are between logical propositions $(1p)$.

The analysis then moves as follows. With each jump in level, the implicit duality becomes explicit, and a new implicit duality

---

"x is p" as it appears on a printed page is a set of symbols. These symbols acquire meaning only as they are interpreted by somebody reading or writing the sentence.' He states that the motivation of the person reading the sentence is usually considered irrelevant to its meaning, the meaning being taken as somehow derived from some detached 'truth reference'. He then goes on to argue the logical inconsistencies which are the consequence of any such approach to logic which is detached from the human motivation of the men using and making logical statements and furthering the instruction of logical systems. Pepper, S. (1970): *The sources of value*; University of California Press, pp. 23–6.

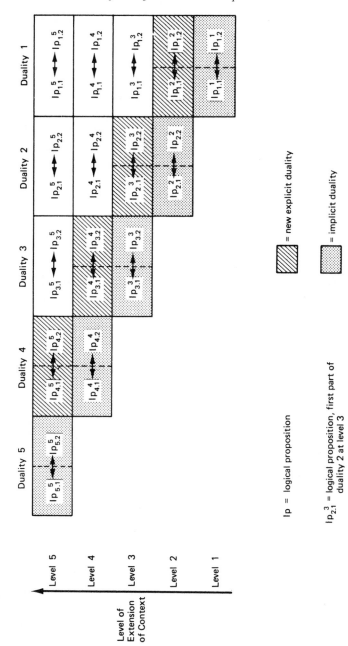

Level of Abstraction

Duality 1   Duality 2   Duality 3   Duality 4   Duality 5

$lp^5_{1,1} \leftrightarrow lp^5_{1,2}$ $lp^5_{2,1} \leftrightarrow lp^5_{2,2}$ $lp^5_{3,1} \leftrightarrow lp^5_{3,2}$ $lp^5_{4,1} \leftrightarrow lp^5_{4,2}$ $lp^5_{5,1} \leftrightarrow lp^5_{5,2}$

$lp^4_{1,1} \leftrightarrow lp^4_{1,2}$ $lp^4_{2,1} \leftrightarrow lp^4_{2,2}$ $lp^4_{3,1} \leftrightarrow lp^4_{3,2}$ $lp^4_{4,1} \leftrightarrow lp^4_{4,2}$

$lp^3_{1,1} \leftrightarrow lp^3_{1,2}$ $lp^3_{2,1} \leftrightarrow lp^3_{2,2}$ $lp^3_{3,1} \leftrightarrow lp^3_{3,2}$

$lp^2_{1,1} \leftrightarrow lp^2_{1,2}$ $lp^2_{2,1} \leftrightarrow lp^2_{2,2}$

$lp^1_{1,1} \leftrightarrow lp^1_{1,2}$

Level 5
Level 4
Level 3
Level 2
Level 1

Level of
Extension
of Context

▨ = new explicit duality

▦ = implicit duality

lp = logical proposition

$lp^3_{2,1}$ = logical proposition, first part of duality 2 at level 3 is introduced. The heart of the dynamic process which forwards logical discrimination and raises the total level of explicit understanding, is seen as occurring between the duality which has just become explicit and the new implicit duality; for example, at level 3, the live interaction is between duality 2 $(1p_2^3 \leftrightarrow 1p_{2.2}^3)$ (the explicit duality) and duality 3 $(1p_{3.1}^3 \leftrightarrow 1p_{3.2}^3)$ (the implicit duality).

The dynamic interaction between the two major dualities at each level can thus be seen to fall out into four-columnar analysis for each level:

$$
\begin{array}{c|c||c|c}
1 & 2 & 3 & 4 \\
1p_{m1}^n \;\longleftrightarrow\; 1p_{m2}^n & & 1p_{n1}^n \;\longleftrightarrow\; 1p_{n2}^n
\end{array}
$$

This four-columnar form will be found to be the central organizing feature of the Isaac–Gibson analysis, the four columns taking on an entirely new logical context at each level, each change representing a true jump. The four columns will be found to move diagonally up the right-hand side of the diagram.

At the same time, the dualities which have already become explicit at lower levels, remain explicit at the higher levels, maintaining their basic form but taking on a more extended meaning as a result of the more extended interaction with the other explicit dualities at that level, and the higher level of the logical intuitive foundation which has been introduced in the new implicit duality.

Summary of Content of the Levels and Dualities

The use of interacting pairs of dualities, the notion of underlying implicit dualities becoming explicit at the next level, the idea of using truth tables in the first place, to be followed by the use of the predicate calculus at higher levels, all these ideas and others are a creative construction of Gibson and Isaac, to be tested in practice.

It is because of the inherent interest of the process of construction of the analysis that Chapter 10 has been included, in which Gibson describes some of the elements, of which he is aware, that went into his own contribution to the analysis.

At *level one* T and F refer to unambiguous behavioural entities, T being used concretely in that it is strictly behavioural, that is associated with an object actually discriminated by a subject: if P (a 'statement' in the sense of an actual response) is T (accepted) then $\sim P$ is F (rejected) and vice versa. This sample behavioural acceptance–rejection (go–no go) pattern, however, is seen as expressing the mutual exclusion and exhaustive alternation in the ambiguity of the and/or connectives.

At *level two* the basic truth tables are introduced: the duality between the 'and ($\wedge$)' and 'or ($\vee$)' conjunctions is taken as having become explicit, and is joined by the at this level implicit duality between the 'if–then ($\rightarrow$)' and the 'if–and–only–if ($\leftrightarrow$)' conjunctions. Level 2 thus introduces explicit ambiguity.

At *level three* the truth tables are extended in the usual way, now making it possible to make a qualitative jump to the use of truth tables as such. The conjunctions or implicit duality arise out of relational statements between the items in the truth table columns. The ($\rightarrow$ and $\leftrightarrow$) duality is now shown to be explicit, but at a higher level of denotation and connotation in dealing with relations between truth table columns and not just with items from each column. The operations on the extended truth tables are shown to be irreversible, so that level 3 takes on the quality of a system of items occurring in unidirectional series from which extrapolations can now be made.

At *level four* the analysis shifts in quality. The new implicit duality arises out of the use of truth table columns as sets, and the relations are now between the truth table columns themselves. Individual T and F items are absorbed into these columnar sets. With the disappearance of individual items, generalized principle must now be intuitively employed, the implicit duality being that between the concept of relationship itself and the terms or poles of that relationship. Thus, at level 4, intuitive generalizations emerge, and behaviour becomes intuitively abstract in the innovative sense of detachment from specific items.

At *level five*, the analysis moves to the most general universe of discourse. The truth table analysis becomes that of relations between the columns combined into classes of columnar sets. The shift is now to a predicate calculus, the implicit duality introduced being that between the universal quantifier ($\forall$) and the existential quantifier ($\exists$), giving an underlying intuitive foundation of implicit theory – the relationship between the universal and the particular – in a specified domain. At level 5, the analysis thus returns to level 1 but in a general and encompassing form in that at level 1 T and F are implicitly or intuitively used, whereas level 5 states and defines in principle how T and F are to be used.

Comparison of the Logical Levels with the Experimental Work
The significant relationship between the logical analysis and the experimental work shows in the experimental demonstration of the two sets of multi-modality emerging from the developmental studies.

The first set points to a series of discrete levels emerging with age; and the second set points to a series of components at each level, each higher level containing one more component than the previous level.

The experimental work led to the confirmation of a theoretical formulation in terms of higher and higher level sets of relationships, the summary diagram for which matches precisely the summary diagram for the various levels and dualities. These two diagrams (one from page 16, and the other from page 114) are here presented side by side:

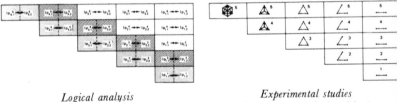

| Logical analysis | Experimental studies |
| (Levels and dualities) | (Levels and relationships) |

Chapter 6 describes the 'conversion' from (1) entities acquiring meaning through their context, to (2) context itself acquiring meaning through contrasted entities. In this respect the work radically differs from much of social science in which either (1) or (2) is simply negated, or they are confused.

Comparison of the Logical Levels with the Applied Research
The five applied research studies (Chapters 15 to 19) all provide supporting evidence for the existence of a general system of five fundamental levels of logical process, the system manifesting itself in a range of human activities illustrated here by social organizations and psychological behaviour. The evidence is qualitative and not quantitative (the quantitative component is in the experimental hypotheses and experimental research); that is to say, we are dealing here with the qualitative interaction between components D and E of the general structure described in Chapter 1.

The significance of the comparisons will lie in two features. First will be the general sense of connectedness and internal consistency and coherence which may – or may not – be intuitively felt to be contained in the various findings: this first feature may be tested in the descriptions to follow.

Second, and more substantial, will be the pragmatic evaluations in use of the applied studies. This testing has been pursued for some twenty years now in the most extended organizational studies.[4]

In the studies of psychological behaviour, testing is far more recent and tentative. It is being actively pursued, however, in studies, for example, of managerial and professional assessment in industry and in public services, and in the development of methods of assessment of the mentally handicapped, as described in Chapters 17 and 18.

With regard to the existence of five levels, the table at page 16 summarizes all five studies, as compared with the analysis of the logical levels. They are described in such a way as to heighten the common features which have impressed the investigators, and are therefore open to the criticism of biased distortion. Two factors may help to restore the balance: first, the fact that practical field testing is being pursued in the full spirit of Professor Popper's EE (error elimination) formula; and second, the fact that findings are presented in a manner allowing for independent testing by others.

From this table (for which additional summary columns from the research of other social scientists will be found in

---

[4] Jaques, E.: *A general theory of bureaucracy*: op. cit.

Chapter 17), the following generalizations about each of the five levels of abstraction and the levels of extension of context which they generate are suggested.

LEVEL ONE. Here the emphasis is upon concreteness, intuition, and uncertainty. The goals of activities are given in concretely prescribed form. Strict rules and procedures are either provided or assumed. The relationship with the object of activity is direct and concrete. Work is by the immediate process of operation upon the object, usually referred to as skill. This skill is based upon the 'touch and feel' of the situation, that is to say, it operates by intuition, by induction, within an externally given context. Based upon intuition, the situation is one of considerable uncertainty.

LEVEL TWO. Ambiguity enters into the situation in the form of incompletely specified goals or means. The ambiguity is handled by a flexible use of rules (deductive context) within which intuitive inductive process can be used to fill out the objectives and needs of each concrete situation. Each activity is handled in its own right. The flexible use of rules, and the elimination of complete dependence upon intuitive inductive processes, gives greater certainty than at level 1.

LEVEL THREE. The emphasis in all the data is now upon activities occurring seriatim. The work remains concrete in the sense that each task is specifically given, or in the use of the logical analysis each specific truth table item can still be used. But system is introduced, giving a feeling of maximum certainty and allowing for extrapolation from the trend of specific instances taken serially.

LEVEL FOUR. At this level there is a distinct and important change in the focus of activity. All the concrete items of activity can no longer be known. The individual is thrown back upon the use of inductive generalizations related only to particular examples of the concrete case. Recourse must be made to hypotheses about the unknown (identification of gaps), and the testing of hypotheses. The level of true abstraction and innovation has emerged, with increase in uncertainty as compared with level 3.

LEVEL FIVE. By this stage the emphasis changes to intuitive relationships with the universal – with theory construction or general rule-making – to be applied in relation to particular cases in a comprehensive domain. Uncertainty again dominates, as in level 1, because of the inductive intuitive relationship with the universal. This level completes the total system, for it exhausts the particular universe of discourse within which the five levels may be applied.

The Three Contexts

A problem in this analysis must, however, now be introduced. Organization studies suggest that there are more than five levels in, for example, the very large corporations. And surely it cannot be argued that the mentally handicapped are able to function at the same levels as the more normal range of members of the community?

The idea therefore suggested itself that the different levels of abstraction in the logical sense, may operate in a range of contexts of increasing generality. This idea first arose through the apparent inconsistency between the internally consistent and complete analysis in terms of five levels and five levels only, derived from the experimental work and from the analysis of logic, as compared with the seven or even eight levels which emerge from the analysis of bureaucratic hierarchies outlined in Chapter 15.

Moreover, examination of bureaucratic systems, as for example in the work described by Rowbottom and Billis in Chapter 16, suggests a dramatic shift between Stratum 5 and Stratum 6. At Stratum 5, buteaucratic systems seem to complete themselves as managerial systems. The move to the next level – Stratum 6 – is nearly always a move to a holding company or other type of strategic organization controlling a number of separate and independent Stratum-5 systems.

This change may be seen in military organization, where Stratum 5 is Divisional Command, the highest level of permanent organization. Divisions have a completeness and independence. Above that level comes Army Corps, made up by combining and recombining Divisions as required in particular circumstances. Armies equally may be reconstituted by the shifting of Corps and Divisions between them.

There is reason to argue, therefore, that the five levels described form a complete system, but that this complete system may begin again, but in a totally higher context at what would be organizational Stratum 6.

At the same time, the work described by Macdonald in Chapter 18 outlines the independently discovered system of five levels of functioning among a mentally handicapped population. As indicated in the foregoing table, these five levels have a remarkably similar feel to the other five-level systems summarized in the table. Thus, for example, there is increasing certainty of outlook from level 1 to level 3 – level 3 being the level of maximum certainty of functioning – indeed, certainty characterized by great obstinacy in behaviour. At levels 4 and 5 uncertainty enters once more, with greater flexibility in behaviour.

It is hypothesized, therefore, that the five logical levels are fundamental, but that they may repeat themselves within increasingly general overall contexts, analogously to the way in which the well-tempered musical scale repeats itself at higher and higher tonalities.

To make this hypothesis more explicit, it is suggested that the overriding context of the five mental handicap levels is that of relations and statements about individual things. The mentally handicapped individual finds it difficult to cope with categories of things: repeating situations must be dealt with afresh each time.

The overriding context for the five levels which constitute what might be described as the normal range of functioning, is that of sets rather than of individual things. That is why language can take on a plasticity as opposed to the concreteness of language among the mentally handicapped. It will be noted that the experimental work and logical analysis imply mental activity in terms of sets and categories.

The overriding content for the next higher context – that represented by Stratum 6 and above in bureaucratic hierarchies – is more difficult to define, because we have little concrete evidence. There is some experience of Stratum-6 holding groups, in which Stratum-5 subsidiaries are treated as units or entities; and of Stratum-7 corporations, in which the reorganization of Stratum-6 holdings groups (as for Corps in military organization) reflects some of the ambiguousness of level 2 in the next lower context. There is little experience of the organization of Stratum-8 super-corporations in these terms.

At a guess, therefore, with this incomplete experience, in this highest context entities would appear to be classes, socalled general strategy the issue, and the general context might be thought of in terms of classes of classes, or perhaps of infinite sets.

Schematically these three contexts may be summarized as follows:

Context	Entities
Mental Handicap	Concrete Things
Normal Range	Sets of things
High Range	Classes of Classes, or Infinite Sets

Components, Dualities, Modes of Work

Leaving levels of abstraction for a moment, we may now turn once again to the horizontal components and sets of dualities which appear in the experimental work and in the logical analysis. A striking relationship may be demonstrated with the different modes of working observed by Gillian Stamp in her managerial assessment research, and described in Chapter 17.

In her work, Stamp noted a multi-modal discontinuity at each work-capacity stratum. There appears to be an increasing number of modes of work at each level, with five modes at level 5 which can be summarized as follows:

MODE ONE: PROCEDURALISTS OR PRAGMATIC SPECIALISTS – competent, persistent and attentive to detail; frequently people with professional or technical qualifications who are competent in their specialist field but unlikely to succeed outside it; often used as back-up men to senior managers in the sense of providing essential specialist information, e.g. statistics, patent law.

MODE TWO: PRACTITIONERS OR PRAGMATIC GENERALISTS — pragmatic, good at organizing both their own work and that of others. Not particularly imaginative but successful at making the most of the current situation and at making quick decisions on the basis of information available.

MODE THREE: SYSTEM-SETTERS OR THEORETICAL GENERALISTS — good at gathering and organizing quantities of information, at using others constructively, at creating a context in which others can work; have a general ability which can operate across a wide field, and good planning ability.

MODE FOUR: STRUCTURALISTS OR THEORETICAL SPECIALISTS — intellectually very able, subtle, creative and very self-contained in their work towards which they take an essentially theoretical approach; described as excelling in research and staff or consultancy roles.

MODE FIVE: ORIGINATORS — the word most commonly used to describe people scoring in this mode is 'flair'; poor at routine work, usually taking an original approach to a problem even when this may not be appropriate.

The hypothesis, for which evidence is currently emerging, is that at level 1, only mode 1 is operative; modes 1 and 2 at level 2; and so on up to all five modes operating at level 5.

At any given level, one mode will be dominant for any particular individual, although he will function in that mode in the context of, and in integrative interactions with all the other modes operative at that same level.

Moreover, as described in Chapter 17, it is also assumed that an individual may move from his normally dominant mode to work in one of the other modes in relation to a particular problem, or perhaps to express a particular mood of the moment. Thus, for example, a person at level 4 who predominantly works as a system-setter (mode 3) may for a particular task adopt the very concrete and pragmatic specialist mode (mode 1), in the context of the other three modes functioning at this level.

This hypothesis would give the following psychological content to the full system of five levels and fifteen components derived from the experimental work and the logical analysis:

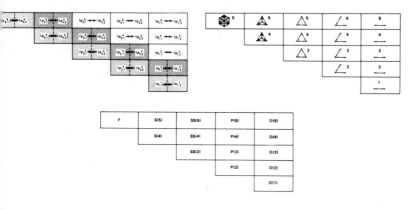

It would be tempting to speculate that the modalities in Gillian Stamp's construction were specifically comprehensible in psychological terms in relation to the contents of the dualities – both explicit deductive and implicit inductive – of the logical system. Further research is required, however, before any such neat connection might be established.

Summary Table

The total system of logical levels and dualities is summarized in the table printed at the end of the book. This table has been arranged so as to be available for ready reference at any point in the text.

3

Speculations on Deductive and Inductive Logic and Knowledge

Elliott Jaques

I wish here to present certain speculations about the possible consequences of the theory of discontinuity in the structure of logic and human action – with respect to an understanding of the nature of logical processes themselves, the theory of meaning and knowledge, and the temporal frame within which behaviour is organized.

First some possible implications of the analysis of logical dualities in relation to deductive and inductive logic are examined. The starting point is the fact that as each new duality emerges, it appears first as an implicit duality, becoming explicit only at the next higher level. It is suggested that these implicit dualities may point to the emergence of increasingly general inductive logical processes at each level, while at the same time the increasing range of explicit dualities at each higher level makes for greater generality of deductive logic as a setting for the inductive process. The various patterns of this counter-pointing of explicit and implicit dualities at each level may provide a basis for a systematic theory of deductive and inductive logical processes. It also gives a possible explanation for the various modes of work found at each level.

Second, it will be suggested that the postulated existence of discrete levels of abstraction, and of discrete modes at each level, may have implications for the theory of knowledge and a contextual theory of meaning in terms of fifteen specific contexts within which a person's relation with his world is mediated and within which his meaning of that world is generated. The connection between the levels of abstraction and feelings of certainty about meaning and knowledge is also discussed.

Finally, consideration is given to the possible relationship between the level of abstraction and its accompanying level of extension of context at which a person functions, and the scale of his space–time orientation and organization, with special emphasis upon the scale of his temporal frame.

Deductive and Inductive Logical Processes

The theory of inductive logic has always occupied a very uncertain position in general systems of logic. There is no rigorous systematic construction for inductive processes; and indeed many logicians would deny the very possibility of a true logic of induction. At the same time, in the approach to deductive logic, such matters as the mode of organization of the material, or which relations (conjunctions) are selected as being more or less central or important, depend to a large extent upon traditions or upon the taste and interest of individual logicians.

The present 'analysis' suggests that there might be a more fundamental and systematic basis for both deductive and inductive logic than has been previously envisaged. In this connection certain features of the logical analysis are worthy of note. First there is the pattern of two interacting pairs of dualities at each level of extension of context – one pair explicit and the other implicit. This interaction generates a new situation at the next higher level of extension of context. The implicit duality at one level moves up to become an explicit duality at the next level, where it is joined by a newly emerged implicit duality. There is thus derived a pattern of dualities, explicit and implicit, which is identical in form to the fifteen modes of functioning theoretically derived from the experimental work.

This general structure of dualities was outlined schematically as shown on page 16 of the previous chapter, in which the implicit dualities were shaded to differentiate them from the explicit dualities. Each newly emerging duality is at a higher level of abstraction, and thus gives the more abstract context for each higher level of extension of context.

If the meaning of explicit and implicit is considered, one possibility which it might be useful to examine is that we are here dealing with deductive and inductive processes. Implicit dualities would correspond to inductive processes; explicit dualities lend themselves to conscious deductive operation. From this point of view it may be noted that at each succeeding level of abstraction there are two important emergent features. First, it would mean that the conscious deductive logical process takes on an additional dimension: for example, level 2 has one explicit duality, whereas level 5 has four available explicit dualities. Second, and simultaneously, the nature of the inductive process would be seen as functioning at a discrete series of higher levels corresponding to the increasing level of complexity of the implicit dualities.

To be more specific, from the point of view being put forward, the explicit use of deductive logic would begin only at the second level of abstraction. At level 1, there is an implicit duality only, from which it might be concluded that the logical processes are inductive: the inductive logic available being limited to the logic of the 'and/or' conjunction. Induction at this level allows for the operation of concrete behavioural skills, the good enough being intuitively discriminable from the not good enough. By means of the 'and/or' inductive logic, a path can be traversed towards a goal, if the goal is sufficiently concretely specified.

At level 2, a more powerful logical weapon emerges. The individual now has available the interaction between an explicit and conscious 'and/or' deductive process, and an intuitive feeling for the more extensive relationship implied in the 'if-then' and the 'if-and-only-if' conjunctions as an implicit duality which could be interpreted as the mode of inductive logic at this level. It is the interaction between these logical 'deductive' and 'inductive' dualities which now makes it possible to handle ambiguity; that is to say, goals and means no longer need to be set in such completely concrete terms as at level 1.

Similarly at level 3, the individual would have two 'deductive' dualities interacting with a still higher 'inductive' duality available, allowing the development of systematic extrapolation, as described in the previous chapter.

This process of logical extension, and emergence of higher levels of inductive logic, at levels 4 and 5, similarly follow from our analysis. Thus, a person functioning at level 5 will use the four interactive explicit dualities, and the fifth implicit duality through which his intuitive mental processes will function. The higher-level explicit dualities remain grounded in the very concrete

$$\frac{P \mid \sim P}{T \mid F}$$

table of level 1 through the content of duality 1 at level 5. But at the same time the intuitive duality is at the very highest level – that of the interaction between the universal quantifier and the existential quantifier – the very general and the very specific. The individual can thus function at the level of intuitive 'inductive' theory formation – but within a context of four 'deductive' dualities which reach through to the first level of concrete reality.

Thus, a scheme of five discrete levels of qualitatively different deductive-inductive methods might be argued to exist – each successively higher level being more extensive, more abstract, more powerful. But, at the same time, each succeeding level contains within itself the more concrete and primitive dualities which existed at the lower levels. These more primitive dualities keep the higher-level dualities well grounded in the lower and more concrete levels of reality, while at the same time taking on the flexibility of meaning derived from functioning in the context of the more abstract dualities.

Here then is a possible means for extending the basis for deductive and inductive processes, a theory which in the case of inductive process could make the phrase 'inductive logic' meaningful. The hypothesis about deductive logic is that of a series of higher and more complex interactions of deductive methods arising from a series of more complex dualities. The hypothesis about inductive logic is that of the existence at each level of abstraction, not of the same implicit inductive process, but of a series of higher and more abstract inductive dualities emerging at each level. The higher-level dualities would provide for a hierarchical system of five levels of inductive logic.

A Contextual Theory of Meaning and Uncertainty in Psychology
There are two senses in which the experimental material, the analysis of logic, and the field work, may support a contextual

theory of meaning. The first sense, that of three general contexts, has already been described in Chapter 2. The second sense, which we shall now consider, is that there are five basic levels of meaning; statements and experiences at each level will take their meaning from the context of the logical processes and dualities which characterize that level.

To take the two extremes, the meaning of a concrete thing or piece of behaviour to a person functioning at level 1 would be seen as taking its meaning in terms of its being concretely true or false, good or bad, right or wrong. It would exist in its own right, with little relationship to other things or behaviours. It would be treated unambiguously, meaning what it means, and nothing more.

The same thing or piece of behaviour to a person functioning at level 5 would take on a quite different meaning. It is perceived and understood as an example of a much more general principle in the context of the most general level of abstraction, or component, at that level of extension of context. Or if it cannot be understood in terms of a known principle, it will become a problem, a specific instance of an unexplained occurrence – perhaps related to other occurrences as part of the creation of an explanatory principle. Or it may become part of a store of undigested experiences, to be worked over and connected with similar experiences in the future in the process of building up new generalizations, or revising and renewing old ones, so that the broad theoretical context within which life is lived and meanings are taken is kept constantly alive and maturing.

The contexts established by each of the levels could also be seen as setting the degree of certainty or uncertainty felt about the meaning of the world. At level 1, meaning is intuitively set and therefore leaves much more uncertainty in the sense that it is difficult to grasp in a conscious framework. At level 2, there is some increase in certainty because of the beginning of a system providing for judgment based upon explicit duality. This increase in certainty is, however, balanced to some extent by the appearance of ambiguity in the explicit 'and/or' duality, this ambiguity itself introducing the element of uncertainty.

At level 3, meaning tends to feel most certain. It is characterized by an explicit system, which has the serializing function of making for extrapolations. Working at level 3 has the greatest sense of security in knowing what is going on and what is likely to happen – within the limited future context, or course, allowed by the level-3 explicit and implicit dualities.

At level 4 the context of meaning broadens and generalizes into principles, rather than the system-bound extrapolations of level 3. Uncertainty therefore increases again. This lesser certainty can be seen in the incompleteness of itemization of sets in the logical analysis at level 4. It has become impossible to know all the relevant facts. Certainty is replaced by hypothesis and empirical testing – with uncertainty appearing as F in the truth tables and the hypotheses as T.

At level 5 meaning and knowledge take on their broadest and most extended character. The context is now the universe. Not only is it not possible to know all the items in sets of tables, but it is even impossible to establish hypotheses about all the members of a class. The most abstract classes at this level are classes of truth table columns. These columnar classes must be treated by statistics and by statements of probability; that is to say, by statements of uncertainty. Thus, probability becomes not just an experience but an explicit part of the content of level-5 meanings.

What emerges then is that an adequate theory of knowledge is a more complex matter than is commonly assumed in psychology. There is no single theory of knowledge, in the sense of a theory that applies to all men. There are different ways of knowing the world, depending upon the level of abstraction of the particular person engaged in constructing his particular picture of reality.

Before settling on such a conclusion, however, the two separate meanings of a theory of knowledge must be distinguished. The first is the propositional logic meaning, the encyclopaedia meaning, the collected statements, the historical accumulation of fact and theory, which together constitute man's third world in Popper's sense. This accumulation is explicitly formulated – or otherwise available in external form – as part of a socially shareable knowledge of the world, for those who share, always incompletely, the same language. It is in effect available to all men.

The second meaning is the more active one: it is that of the actively knowing man, in full interaction with his environment, perceiving, considering, subject to persuasive forces, ingesting and digesting information, giving out signs and signals, physically taking and replacing, acting and being acted upon, and 'knowing' always in a highly selective and limited sense.

It is in this second meaning that the schema of levels of abstraction and of fifteen components is relevant. It posits the obvious: namely, that men differ in their knowledge of the world not simply in terms of cultural differences, or in the amount they can know, but in the sense of knowing it within the context of very different organizing principles.

The world simply does not appear to be the same to a mentally handicapped person at level 3, say, and to a normal individual at level 4 operating predominantly as a theoretical specialist. In the one case the individual is having trouble just hanging on to contact with reality. He is struggling to maintain contact with a simple goal (such as making a cup of tea) which he has set for himself with some difficulty, and to keep in mind the awful complexities of the path he must traverse in order to get to that goal.

In the second case the individual's world is far more extended. He is firmly resting on an intuitive sense of gaps in knowledge – of new things, new ideas, unformed as yet but somehow called forth from within his mental being in relation to sensed needs to be fulfilled by as yet undeveloped means. This intuitive process, the product of constructive unconscious functioning, is settled in the context of an integrated triplet of conscious explicit dualities by which he can keep himself anchored in the reality of well-tested rules (duality 1), handle in a sensible manner any ambiguities in his immediate circumstances (duality 2), and use to the full extrapolations from past and current experience in explicit and systematic ways (duality 3); these three explicit dualities help to control the setting of consciously manipulated reality within which his innovative intuition (the fourth duality, which is implicit) may then have full play.

What I have here tried to illustrate is the constant interplay of explicitly logical processes and intuitively or unconscious rational processes – but at successively higher levels of complexity, of power for problem-solving, and of power of creating a more distant future. At each successive level, what was implicit and intuitive before becomes explicit and consciously usable, while a new and higher level of intuitive potential moves in.

Levels of Abstraction and Temporal Frame

In Chapter 17 a connection is presented between particular levels of abstraction and the resulting level of extension of context, and the distance into the future – his temporal frame – within which an individual can plan and execute specific and continual goal-directed activities. It is argued that the extent, or size, or quantity, or scale, of a person's work-capacity is decidedly time-related. The farther forward in time an individual is able not only to formulate goals but also to plan, progress, and carry them out to completion, the greater is his capacity. The work on bureaucratic organization structure[1] strongly suggests that there are strata with cut-off points at 3 months, 1 year, 2 years, 5 years and 10 years, these time-spans giving 5 bands. It is these bands which it is suggested correspond to the five levels of abstraction in human mental activity which have been described, and the higher levels of extension of context which they generate. In the case of the mentally handicapped context, the time-span brackets will be much shorter – up to one-day maximum. And the levels in the third or highest context begin at time-spans of 10 years and over.

It may well be, therefore, that the level of abstraction and its level of extension of context at which a person operates is objectively and uniquely correlated with the maximum temporal frame with which the individual can cope. Man has been described as a time-binding animal, and biologically as an animal with strong capacity for postponement of gratification so as to increase the temporal space within which he can function.

This relationship between level of abstraction and level of extension of context, and temporal space has in fact been implicit in the analysis of the various modes or components which appear at each level. It has been argued that at each level all the modes are used, but at any given time one mode

[1] Jaques, E.: *A general theory of bureaucracy:* op. cit.

will be dominant, and indeed will tend to be dominant for a particular peson. Some will tend to work with the more concrete modes, at their own level of extension of context.

What, however, should now be noted is that the more concrete modes are based more on past experience, and the more abstract modes are based more upon a view of future development. Thus, various modes give the interplay between organized experience and future context, the individual being able to move from dominance of one mode to that of another as he feels more need to rely directly upon concrete experience or future goals in solving a particular problem. It may also be noted that with each successive level of extension of context, the emergent explicit and implicit dualities have a longer reach into the future, so that the time-span of a person's work-capacity extends with each higher level. In effect, level of extension of context is operationally definable in terms of time-span as a measure of the space–time manifold.

A particularly important shift in time-scale occurs with the shift from the logical concreteness of level 3 to the logical abstractness or generality of level 4. This shift manifests itself in many forms. Even in role titles, the term 'general' appears at level 4 – 'Generals' in military terms, and 'General Managers' in commerce and industry. In terms of time, however, as Gillian Stamp shows in Chapter 17, it is a shift in which dualities concerned with the future enter into the work situation in explicit terms – hence the more explicit abstraction with the future deductively in the picture, as against the lower levels in which the future appears at most as a concrete extrapolation from the present.

The very ability which allows an individual to handle the higher levels of abstraction posited in this analysis, is thus the same ability which enables him to plan and work longer into the future, to take on and successfully to plan and progress longer projects; in short, to live and act within a more extended temporal frame.

The increasingly complex range of dualities described in the 'analysis' of logic, and the vastly wider range of sets of variables, which become available at higher levels may thus provide the basis of explanation for this increasing temporal frame with higher levels of abstraction.

Part A

Experimental Work on Discontinuity in Psychological Development

4

Experimental Treatment of Discontinuity Theory of Psychological Development

D. J. Isaac and B. M. O'Connor

The following describes an attempt to construct a discontinuity theory of the development of individuals from a statistical analysis of quantitative experimental work. With such a theory the individual would be considered to develop through distinct stages. These stages would be associated with qualitatively different modes of organizing the external world and with corresponding qualitatively different modes of interacting with it. The phrase 'qualitatively different' is used here and throughout to refer to difference in kind.

Organizing the world in qualitatively different ways suggests qualitatively different ways of behaving. Experimentation is directed towards testing whether this occurs. If such different modes of behaving actually take place, then experimental measurements of some parameter(s) expressing behaviour would give rise to multi-modal distributions. In contrast with uni-modal distributions a significant feature of the multi-modal distribution is inherent structure. There is thus the possibility that the structure inherent in a series of multi-modal distributions could be interpreted as directly expressing the developing structure of the individual. After describing the experimental work in this paper, a scheme is suggested regarding the development of the individual which realizes this possibility.

Levels of Abstraction
From a study of social organizations, Jaques[1] came to the

---

[1] Jaques, E. (1956): 'Preliminary sketch of a general structure of executive strata', *Glacier project papers*; London, Heinemann Educational Books; and see chapters 15 and 19 below.

conclusion that executive hierarchies are the most common form of social organization, but more significantly, that they are of the same form, regardless of time in history or of the socio-economic and political setting in which they occur. One outstanding feature of their organization is that they take on the same general pattern of managerial levels. Citing examples from modern industrial society, small firms are found to have two of three levels (including the shop and office floor), whereas the very large corporations have seven or eight levels.

In the article referred to above, Jaques has argued that the most likely explanation of this universal characteristic of executive hierarchies is that it reflects the existence of a hierarchy of discrete strata of capacity in any population. He has further suggested that the quality of capacity in each stratum is such as to enable persons whose capacity lies in a given stratum to manage persons whose capacity lies in the stratum below. He has suggested a series of steps in level of abstraction; each step coinciding with the nature at each executive level. Looked at in the manner described, a discontinuity theory of capacity could provide the basis for a general theory of executive organization.

The present work began from the general notion of levels of abstraction. From the point of view described above, and accepting that mathematics is man's most precise statement of his social relations, an examination was made of geometry and number theory. This examination suggested that in each case the material under consideration could be divided into six parts and the parts organized into a hierarchy expressing an ascending order of abstraction in thinking. Further examination indicated that one could suppose this order to be reflected, on the one hand, in the historical development of society, each part of this theoretical development being related to a particular phase of social growth, and on the other hand, in the way in which individuals in our present society meet the problems of the subject matter as it is organized in educational institutions.

This work led to the notion that men structure their experiences in at least six fundamentally different ways, and that these ways are expressed in the structure of social organizations and in the psychological growth of the individual.

From this point of view, the individual progresses continuously through a stage until the next stage is entered. Entering this next stage would involve the reorganization of existing mental content, with the emergence of a relatively new structure. Fundamental among the changes which might be expected would be a different level of abstraction in thinking, and an ability to tolerate uncertainty over a longer period. Thus, with respect to development of thinking, the individual is seen as progressing through a general order of levels of abstraction. This is not to suggest that an individual consistently operates in all problems at one level or that in any one area of his activities he consistently operates at the same level. Rather it would be expected that in different areas the levels achieved would differ and that in all areas all levels achieved would remain present as potential. The level at which he works in a problem situation would depend on his reaction to the situation. Furthermore, it would be expected that reiterated failure to cope with the problems of a particular area would lead to the emerging dominance of successive earlier levels, that is, the individual would regress.

The term 'levels of abstraction' has been used elsewhere to connote a series of plateaus in a continuous dimension. 'Our use of the term "stage" . . . refers to levels of cognitive functioning on what we assume to be a continuous dimension of concreteness-abstractness' (Harvey, Hunt and Schroder,[2] p. 24). In the present work the term 'levels of abstraction' is used to refer to separate stages in the development of the individual, not merely in the aspect of the development of purely cognitive functioning but also in the development of all other aspects. These stages are seen as separate in that they are not connnected in a dimensional continuum, but yet relate to a distinguishable order. At this juncture no further clarification of the term is possible: further clarification and an operational definition must await the completion of a series of experiments concerned with distinguishing this order.

The notion that men structure their experiences in up to six fundamentally different ways, operating at six corresponding levels of abstraction, leads to the proposition that men behave

[2] Harvey, O. J., Hunt, D. E. and Schroder, H. M. (1961): *Conceptual systems and personality organisation;* London, Wiley.

in up to six qualitatively different modes, or, restating the proposition, in a given situation an individual behaves in one of six qualitatively different ways.

At this stage in the progress of the work the foregoing ideas were regarded as no more than hypothetical. Since the above proposition is open to experimentation, it became immediately necessary to test experimentally the feasibility of the discontinuity idea as applied in this context. In addition it was hoped that experiments would provide the means of the further development of the ideas.

Experimentation

We are concerned in this work with the development of the individual in the fullest sense of the term. On the other hand, since we hope to obtain numerical data for the purpose of statistical analysis, we are forced into quantitative measurements relating to behaviour in specific experimental situations. Since we regard problem-solving as involving the whole person, and not merely some aspect of cognitive functioning, the two above requirements do not appear incompatible. We concur with Van De Geer's statements in his study of problem-solving:[3]

> Now psychology is beginning to emphasize the functional role of cognition in the whole of personality. Cognitive processes are conceived of as means by which a subject selects and assimilates information and comes to decisions and strategies on the basis of this information. All this is a really personal activity; a subject's personality make-up is revealed in it in the same way as in his choosing friends, writing stories, or interpreting ink blots. The cognitive theory should, therefore, leave 'degrees of freedom' for personal variants, not as distortions from the outside (from the emotional or motivational domain), but in the very way cognition proceeds (p. 198).

From this point of view it may be considered that experimental data from specific problem-solving situations may be used

[3] Van De Geer, J. P. (1957): *A psychological study of problem solving;* Haarlem, De Toorts.

in this particular investigation without necessarily losing generality.

The proposition that an individual behaves in problem situations in one of six qualitatively different ways could be investigated by confronting a number of subjects with the same problem situation and observing behaviour. From these observations qualitative differences in behaviour between individuals could be inferred in terms of the preconceptions upon which the experiment is based. The weakness of this mode of procedure is that the stated differences might be regarded by others as referring in essence only to the preconceptions of the investigator, or alternatively, accepting the differences, as referring only to differences in degree.

Regarding the six qualitative differences in behaviour suggested above, it is not expected that they can be so clearly discriminated as to give rise to a high degree of social agreement, as for example, in the discrimination of male and female among humans. These two sets are discriminated by direct observation of morphological difference. This morphological difference allows, in most cases, an individual to be assigned to either set. We may regard the morphological difference as the socially agreed distinguishing characteristic of the two sets. In the case of the six different behaviour patterns postulated it was not expected that an agreed distinguishing characteristic would appear from direct observation. Thus a major problem in the testing of the above proposition involved obtaining such a distinguishing characteristic.

Returning to the male and female example, if heights of adults males and females are measured and the data given to a statistician, qualifying each datum in terms of male or female origin, then he could show by statistical analysis (Blommers and Lindquist[4]) that the distribution consists of two normal distributions. He could then state that height is another distinguishing characteristic of the two sets. If only the height data were supplied to the statistician, then using a different statistical analysis (Warner[5]), he could show that the distribution was

[4] Blommers, P. and Lindquist, E. F. (1960): *Elementary statistical methods in psychology and education*; Ch. 8; London, University of London Press.

[5] Warner, B. T. (1953): 'Tests of heterogeneity based on taxonomically undifferentiated samples.' Unpublished Ph.D. thesis; University of London.

bimodal. He could then state that from the analysis he had discriminated two sets, the discriminating characteristic again being height. He could make no other statement of the two sets. Furthermore, he could not use the distinguishing characteristic to assign an individual to a set. With this mode of procedure, sets have been discriminated and a distinguishing characteristic obtained from purely numerical data. Further, the process is reproducible. This is the procedure we have adopted.

We are thus concerned in ascertaining whether multi-modal distributions arise from measurements made of the actions of individuals in solving problems. These multi-modal distributions would enable us to discriminate behaviour patterns and state the distinguishing characteristic in terms of a parameter or combination of parameters measured in the experiment. It must be emphasized that they would not enable us to make any other statement of these behaviours.

Much of the work of the experimental psychologist is concerned with the estimation of the variation of some attribute or factor through uni-modal distributions. In that the general purpose of the present work is the development of a theory relating to the developing structure of the individual, multi-modal distributions could conceivably be more useful. Because structure is inherent in the multi-modal distribution, it might be possible to suggest a scheme for the structure of the individual directly reflecting the structure in the distribution.

From the above discussion we may state that the experimental work is directed to testing the proposition that with a large number of persons involved in some problem situation, measurements made of each individual's performance in terms of a parameter or combination of parameters are distributed multi-modally. The parameters actually measured have been length of time taken and the number of operations required to solve the problem. These have been chosen only in that they appeared more relevant to performance in the situation than any other.

It has been stated that the distinguishing characteristic becomes recognizable as such only at the moment of discrimination of sets. Any attempt to discover the distinguishing characteristic before discrimination or any attempt to discriminate before recognition of the distinguishing characteristic is ruled out.

The only evidence that could be regarded as substantiating the proposition is the development of a multi-modal statistical distribution from an experiment using subjects not selected for the particular purpose of the experiment, and a problem situation not so structured that a multimodal pattern must arise.

The measurement of the variation of some factor often necessitates the use of refined experimental techniques and sophisticated statistical analyses. This arises from the necessity of excluding or stabilizing some factors or taking into account the effect of factors which could not be excluded or stabilized. Since we are concerned only with the discrimination of sets (and not with the measurement of variation), we are not confronted with these difficulties. On the contrary, our difficulty is that to obtain comparable quantitative data, individuals have to be presented with the same situations, and in the act of doing this, arbitrary constraints are imposed which may exclude relevant but unknown factors so that a multi-modal pattern does not emerge. Thus a complete contrast appears between the experimental procedure followed and that in more general use. We require as open a situation as possible, and have no interest in the various factors that might be considered to be operating in the situation. It follows that the only function of the statistical analysis used is to enable a judgment to be made regarding whether a distribution is multi-modal or not.

It will be necessary to run more than one experiment to obtain adequate information for judgment of the hypothesis, but since it is assumed that an individual may enter different situations at different levels of abstraction, it must be anticipated that multi-modal statistical distributions obtained will not be stable in the sense that subjects fall into corresponding modes in distributions arising from different experiments. This instability and the form of the experimental procedure mean that the expected multi-modal pattern cannot be construed as referring to the measurement of some particular personal factor, e.g. ability, personality trait, etc.

Experimental Work

Three experiments have been completed. The first involved a

card-sorting problem. In the second, a machine which presented a problem involving the recognition of a time sequence was used. In the third experiment, a machine again was used, the problem being designed in terms of spatial and numerical structures. A second purpose of this experiment was to relate the multi-modal distributions to the uni-modal distributions generally attributed to measurements of performance on problems. To effect this, the problem was designed so that the structure imposed on the display by the designer and the structure developed by the subject in solving the problem could interact in such a way that multi-modal and uni-modal distributions of scores could be expected at various distinct stages readily recognizable, during the process, to both subject and observer.

CARD-SORTING EXPERIMENT. In this experiment, designed and conducted by M. Featherstone, subjects were given a pack of 96 cards – 3 of each of 32 patterns – to sort into 3 piles, two of which were marked with a display card. The first 40 cards in this pack were arranged in a pre-set order and the remainder shuffled, as was the whole pack if another run-through was required. The prearranged order was based on the preliminary investigation of the appropriate difficulty level of the problem.

The patterns on the cards in the pack could differ from each other in one or more of five ways:

> Colour – yellow and red
> Shape – round and square
> Size – large and small
> Number – one and two
> Content – filled and unfilled

The two display cards did, in fact, differ in all five of these respects:

> Display card A – Two large red filled circles
> Display card B – One small yellow unfilled square

Thus the display confronting a subject as he approached the problem illustrated all the variables to be considered in solving it and the total variation within the pack itself.

The problem was simply to continue to sort cards from this pack into the three piles until they were all being placed 'correctly', i.e. sorted according to a particular principle selected by the experimenter prior to the test. Each time a card was placed, the subject was told 'right' or 'wrong', which provided a guide to recognizing the principle. The criterion of success was 20 successive cards placed without error. The total number of cards placed by the subject was counted. The score used for statistical purposes was obtained by subtracting 20 from the total. The sorting principle used was 'Colour and Shape', or at a more specific level 'all red circles under display card A and all yellow squares under B (red squares and yellow circles go into the third pile)'. When, after solving the problem, subjects were asked to verbalize the principle by which they had been sorting, not all of them could do so, even when expressing it in more concrete statements than those given above.

Results. About 500 subjects attempted the problem. Of these 50 failed to solve. A few subjects provided very large scores giving some very scattered results which were not of consequence for the type of statistical analysis used. The histogram of the distribution of scores is shown in Figure 4.1.

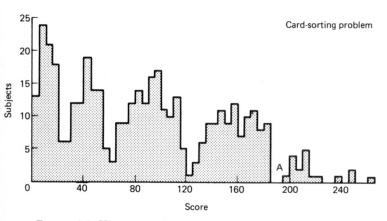

FIGURE 4.1. Histogram of scores for card-sorting problem

TIME SEQUENCE EXPERIMENT. In this experiment the Problem-solving and Information Apparatus of John[6] was used. The

[6] John, E. R. (1957): 'Contributions to the study of the problem solving process', *Psych. Mono. 71*, 447.

apparatus appeared to the subject as a circular array of nine
lights with a press button for each, and a tenth light with no
press button at the centre. A card indicating the connections
between the lights was placed over the array (Figure 4.2). The
apparatus functions as follows. When a button is pressed, the
associated light is illuminated immediately and stays alight for
three seconds. At the end of the three-second period, the light
goes out and the next light in the sequence goes on, and so on
until the sequence is complete. Pressing a button anywhere in
the sequence puts on the associated light, and, in turn, all successive ones.

Sequences

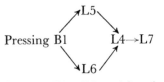

Pressing B2→L9 and break connection
                between L8 and L10
Pressing B3→L8
Pressing B7 and B8 coincidently   L10

Problem. To light centre light L10 five times successively using
B1, B2, B3. (Initially any button may be used to find out how
to solve the problem.)
Solution. L10 comes alight after L7 and L8 are coincidently
alight. To obtain this, press B1, wait until L4 comes alight, then
press B3. L3 and L4 will then be alight coincidently, followed
by L7 and L8 coincidently, followed by L10. Pressing B2 is
avoided, because in time L9 comes alight, during which time
L10 is prevented from lighting.

In this experiment, the time taken to solve the problem was
measured and also the total number of button pressings
counted. Neither of these parameters alone gives rise to a distribution with a well-defined structure. A scatter diagram was
plotted with time along one axis and number of button pressings along the other (Figure 4.3), each point representing a
subject's performance. It was noted that the points do not
appear randomly distributed, but grouped in well-defined

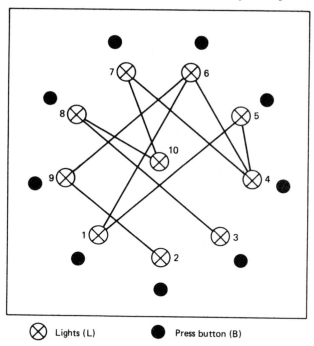

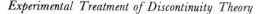

Lights (L)   Press button (B)

FIGURE 4.2. Display for time sequence problem

clusters. It was also noted that the gaps between clusters appear to lie roughly on arcs of circles of differing radii but with a common centre (at the origin). This suggested that a means of combining the two parameters into one (for statistical purposes) would be simply to measure the distance of each point from the origin. This was done. Expressed numerically this distance is $(\alpha^2 T^2 + \beta^2 N^2)^{1/2}$, where N is the number of operations, T the time, and α and β constants. There can be no *a priori* justification for combining the parameters in this way. Justification for making particular measurements and the manipulation of the measurements depends on the extent to which these operations serve man's purposes. In the particular case, the combination gives rise to a distribution with a clearly defined structure, and furthermore this structure is very similar to that of the card-sorting problem.

Results. 350 subjects attempted the problem. About 50 failed to solve the problem. A few subjects solved the problem using

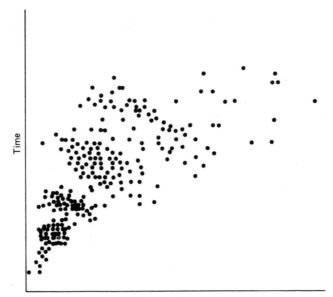

Number of presses

FIGURE 4.3. Scatter diagram of scores for time sequence experiment

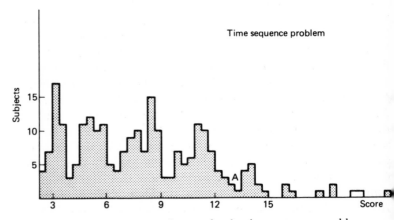

FIGURE 4.4. Histogram of scores for the time sequence problem

a large number of operations and giving a few scattered results. The histogram illustrating the distribution of scores is shown in Figure 4.4.

SPACE AND NUMBER EXPERIMENT. The display panel, as it appears to the subject, consists of 448 press buttons arranged in a rectangle (Figure 4.5). Around two sides are 67 electric

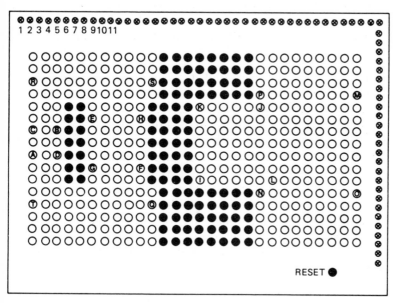

FIGURE 4.5. Display panel for space-number problem

bulbs, which can be illuminated by pressing particular press buttons in a sequence described below.
Problem as stated to the subject. 'The aim is to get bulb No. 11 alight. In order to do so, you have to get on other lights beforehand, which come on and go out in sequence. Your problem is to use the press buttons to find out how you can get these lights to come on so that you end with bulb No. 11 on. If you have lights on, and wish to start again, press the RESET button. This puts the lights out and enables you to make a fresh start. You are free to use the RESET button whenever you wish.'
Solution. There are 20 operative press buttons, indicated in

Figure 5 as A, B, C,..., T, which if pressed in alphabetical order result in the lights coming on as follows:

Pressing button A, bulb No. 1 comes on.

Pressing button B, bulb No. 1 goes out, and two bulbs nearest the bottom right-hand corner come on.

Pressing button C puts out the two bulbs and bulb No. 2 comes on.

Pressing button D puts out bulb No. 2, and the next three bulbs on the right-hand side come on.

And so on, until finally pressing button T puts on bulb No. 11.

The operative buttons A, B, C, ... lie at the corners of five squares of increasing size: 3, 5, 7, 9, 11. The gap between consecutive squares also increases: 2, 4, 6, 8. The sequence of operations required to complete the squares is consistent, except that with alternate squares the operations are laterally inverted. The operative buttons have been lettered in the illustration to show the spatial relations which have to be structured to solve the problem. To assist the subject, a black and white pattern was imposed on the buttons. In addition, the operative buttons A, C. E were coloured green, buttons B, D, F coloured red.

All press buttons were connected to a counter. The time and number of pressings were recorded from the commencement of operations to the stage when:

(1) button A was pressed;
(2) button D was pressed, i.e. at the completion of the 1st square;
(3) button H was pressed, i.e. at the completion of the 2nd square;
(4) button L was pressed, i.e. at the completion of the 3rd square;
(5) button P was pressed, i.e. at the completion of the 4th square;
(6) button T was pressed, i.e. at the completion of the 5th square.

Each time measurement and the corresponding number of operations were reduced to a single score in the manner described in the time sequence problem. Since little or no meaningful information was available to the subject before button A was pressed, the scores used for statistical purposes were obtained from times and numbers of operations from the stage when button A was pressed to the stage when the 2nd, 3rd, 4th and 5th squares respectively were completed. As a consequence of experience with the card and time sequence problems, it was expected that scores to the completion of the 2nd square would be distributed multi-modally.

Regarding the 3rd square, the following general assumptions relate to the expected distribution:

(a) The multi-modal distribution obtained from a problem-solving process is related to the scheme of differing levels of abstraction in that corresponding to each level of abstraction there is a particular mode of organizing information from what to the subject is a new problem situation.

(b) Problems requiring the further exploitation of a general structure already acquired, or the detailed explication of a situation already structured, give rise to uni-modal distributions.

From these assumptions and the assumption that completion of the 3rd square requires exploiting the general structure obtained in completing the 2nd square, it was expected that the distribution of scores to the completion of the 3rd square would be uni-modal.

The 4th square has a new structural feature. Compared with the 3rd square, the sequence of operations required to complete the 4th square is inverted both laterally and longitudinally. Reorganization is thus required, and consequently it was expected that scores to the completion of the 4th square would be distributed multi-modally. To complete the 5th square, no further structuring was needed, and thus it was expected that the corresponding scores would be distributed uni-modally.

In contrast with the two previous problems, the goal of the present one could be reached by randomly pressing buttons either in a haphazard manner or systematically row by row. Subjects operating this way developed no idea of structure. In this context their behaviour was classed as random. For the purposes of statistical analysis, scores resulting from these modes of operation were disregarded. In any case, all such scores could not have been used for the type of analysis applied on the grounds of being too large.

Results. Over 500 subjects attempted the problem, of which 328 provided a useful score by completing the 2nd square. The others provided either too large a score, behaved randomly, or failed to complete the 2nd square. Two hundred and forty subjects provided useful scores by completing the 3rd square. The large difference in the number of subjects providing scores in completing the 2nd square and the 3rd square is because, initially, only scores to the completion of the 2nd square were taken. This was done so as to decide quickly whether to proceed with the experiment. Also, some subjects did not wish to proceed with the problem. Two hundred and thirty-four and 191 subjects respectively completed squares 4 and 5.

Mention must be made at this stage of an experiment involving a similar problem on the same machine but having a very simple structure. Over 600 useful scores were obtained, which gave rise to uni-modal distributions at every stage for all tried values of α and β (thus indicating that a multi-modal distribution does not necessarily follow from the mode of combining). Of the subjects who attempted this problem, about 100 also attempted the problem discussed in this paper.

The histogram of scores to the completion of the 2nd square is shown in Figure 4.6, that of the 3rd square in Figure 4.7,

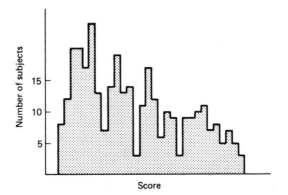

FIGURE 4.6. Histogram of scores to the completion of 2nd square of space-number experiment

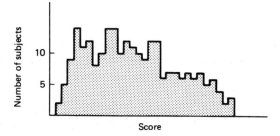

FIGURE 4.7. Histogram of scores to the completion of 3rd square of space-number experiment

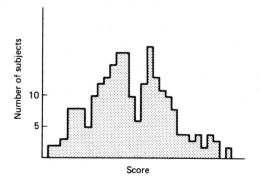

FIGURE 4.8. Histogram of scores to the completion of 4th square of space-number experiment

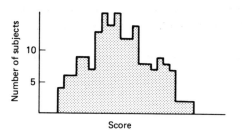

FIGURE 4.9. Histogram of scores to the completion of 5th square of space-number experiment

that of the 4th square in Figure 4.8, and that of the 5th square is shown in Figure 4.9.

Statistical Analysis[7]

The object is first of all to fit a linear combination of normal curves to a given histogram of discontinuous appearance. The best fit is obtained by the principle of maximum likelihood. Then a χ^2 goodness of fit test, with a 5 per cent level of significance, provides a *criterion* of multi-modality.

For this purpose the method of Rao,[8] for dealing with grouped data, was used, at first.

Suppose

$$f_1, f_2, \ldots, f_k$$

are observed frequencies in k classes with probabilities

$$P_1, P_2, \ldots, P_k$$

which are defined as functions of $3r-1$ parameters

$$p_1, p_2, \ldots, p_{r-1}; \quad \mu_1, \mu_2, \ldots, \mu_r; \quad \sigma_1, \sigma_2, \ldots, \sigma_r \qquad (1)$$

The total frequency is n, that is, $\Sigma f_i = n$, and the functions P_i are actually defined as

$$\sum_{j=1}^{r} \frac{P_j}{\sigma_j} \int_{a_i}^{a_{i+1}} Z\left\{\frac{x-\mu_j}{\sigma_j}\right\} dx$$

where $p_r = 1 - p_1 - p_2 \ldots - p_{r-1}$, a_i and a_{i+1} are the boundaries of the group with frequency f_i' and

$$Z\{x\} \equiv \frac{1}{\sqrt{2\pi}} e^{-(1/2)x^2}$$

That is to say, the parameters (1) are weightings, means, and standard deviations of a linear combination of normal distributions.

Maximizing the function

$$\sum_{i=1}^{k} f_i \log P_i$$

---

[7] By R. O. Gibson.

[8] Rao, C. R. (1948): 'The utilisation of multiple measurements in problems of biological classification', *J. R. statist. soc. B*, *10*, 159.

leads, by means of a generalized Newtonian iterative procedure, to a set of $3r-1$ equations of the form

$$n \sum_{u=1}^{3r-1} \Delta\theta_u \sum_{i=1}^{k} \frac{1}{P_i}\left(\frac{\partial P_i}{\partial \theta_t}\right)\left(\frac{\partial P_i}{\partial \theta_u}\right) = \sum_{i=1}^{k} \frac{f_i}{P_i}\frac{\partial P_i}{\partial \theta_t}$$

$$(t = 1, 2, \ldots, 3r-1) \qquad (2)$$

where, for the sake of uniformity, the parameters (1) are rewritten as $\theta_1, \theta_2, \ldots, \theta_{3r-1}$.

The main problem is to solve the set of equations (2) for the differences $\Delta\theta_u$, after substituting provisional values of the $3r-1$ parameters, together with the data, consisting of the f_i and the a_i $(i=1, 2, \ldots, k)$.

The quantities such as $\partial P_i/\partial \theta_t$ in equations (2) are, of course, obtained by substituting the provisional values in the derivatives of P_i.

Provisional estimates of the parameters were found by an *ad hoc* method of breaking up a given histogram into separate parts and fitting a normal curve to each part in turn, thence fitting combinations of two curves, and so on. However, in general it is very difficult to solve the equations (2), given provisional estimates.

A complex computer programme was devised, but so much time was absorbed by the process of ironing out programming errors and considering possible difficulties of convergence, that it was decided to use, instead of the analysis due to Rao (1948), a method which is approximate in the sense that it treats a normal curve as a number of thin rectangles, a method due to Hasselblad.[9]

If the σ_j's are relatively large compared to the lengths of the intervals (which, without loss of generality, are taken as unity), then the probability of an observation from the jth population following in the ith interval can be approximated by the integrand evaluated at the mid-point:

$$q_{ij} = \frac{1}{\sqrt{2\pi\sigma_j^2}} e^{-(x_i - \mu_j)^2/2\sigma_j^2}$$

---

[9] Hasselblad, V. (1966): 'Estimation of parameters for a mixture of normal distributions', *Technometrics*, *8*, 3.

$$\text{Let } Q_i = \sum_{j=1}^{r} q_{ij} p_j,$$

so that the logarithm of the likelihood function is approximately

$$L = \sum_{i=1}^{k} f_i \log Q_i$$

The maximum likelihood estimates are those values of the parameter which satisfy the equations:

$$0 = \frac{\partial L}{\partial \mu_j} = \sum_{i=1}^{k} \frac{f_i}{Q_i} p_j q_{ij} (x_i - \mu_j)/\sigma_j^2, \qquad j = 1, 2, \dots, r$$

$$0 = \frac{\partial L}{\partial \sigma_j} = \sum_{i=1}^{k} \frac{f_i}{Q_i} p_j q_{ij} \left\{ \frac{(x_i - \mu_j)^2}{\sigma_j^3} - \frac{1}{\sigma_j} \right\}, \quad j = 1, 2, \dots, r$$

$$0 = \frac{\partial L}{\partial p_j} = \sum_{i=1}^{k} \frac{f_i}{Q_i} (q_{ij} - q_{ir}), \quad j = 1, 2, \dots, r-1$$

A simple iterative scheme is derived (Rao[8]) enabling the solution of these equations, and thence the calculation of χ^2.

In the case of the card experiment ($r=4$, $k=38$), it was found that $\chi^2 = 27.39$. Combination of theoretical class frequencies less than 5 reduced the number of classes to 35, giving $35 - 11 - 1 = 23$ degrees of freedom. From the tables, for 23 degrees of freedom the 95 per cent point is 35.17. Thus the results obtained are consistent with the hypothesis of multi-modality. In the case of the time sequence experiment ($r=4$, $k=31$), it was found that $\chi^2 = 13.74$. Combination of theoretical class frequencies less than 5 reduced the number of classes to 24, giving $24 - 11 - 1 = 12$ degrees of freedom. From the tables, for 12 degrees of freedom the 95 per cent point is 21.03. Thus again, the results obtained are consistent with the hypothesis of multi-modality.

For the space and number experiment to the end of the 2nd square ($r=4$, $k=31$), $\chi = 28.16$, the number of degrees of freedom being 18. From the tables for 18 degrees of freedom the 95 per cent point is 28.87. These results are consistent with the hypothesis of multi-modality. For the same experiment to the end of the 4th square ($r=3$, $k=29$), it was found that $\chi^2 = 26.71$, the number of degrees of freedom being 20. The corresponding 95 per cent point of the χ^2 distribution is 31.41. Again the results obtained are consistent with the hypothesis of multi-modality.

For the histograms treated above, the σ_j are only moderately large compared with the class intervals, the results thus being very approximate. On the other hand, the goodness of fit approach gives a stringent criterion of multi-modality. It would have been preferable to use a test enabling a decision between uni-modality and multi-modality applicable to histograms not so strongly suggestive of either uni-modality or multi-modality. However, such a test appears not yet to have been devised. Further, it should be noted that although the goodness of fit approach uses a combination of normal curves, the normality condition is not vital to our purpose, which is to establish multi-modality.

With respect to the histogram relating to completion of the 3rd square in the space and number experiment (Figure 4.7), the pattern is so ill-defined that the above statistical analysis could not be applied. Concerning the histogram relating to scores to the completion of the 5th square, the appearance strongly suggests that the distribution is uni-modal.

Discussion of Results

Accepting that the distributions analysed statistically are multi-modal, the series of experiments substantiates the proposition regarding the multi-modal distribution of scores. Four sets have been discriminated, the score combination being the distinguishing characteristic.

The 100 subjects who had previously used the machine of the space and number experiment behaved differently from the other subjects in that the first button pressed was usually the 1st operative button (A) in the sequence. However, the scores they produced were distributed in the four modes as for the other subjects. It seems that the distribution of scores arises not from the subjects coping with a novel situation *per se*, but from the problem of structuring the particular display.

A large number of subjects participated in at least two of the experiments. On examining the results, no consistent relation emerged from the comparison of the particular mode in which the score of an individual fell for one problem and the mode in which the score of the same individual fell for the other problem, which is as expected. Thus, as previously stated, the distributions cannot be interpeted as relating to the measurement of some consistent factor.

The four mode patterns were obtained from three diverse problems, involving: (a) recognition of shape, colour, size, number and filled/unfilled, (b) recognition of time sequence, (c) recognition of space-number relations. The conditions of the problem giving rise to these distributions were similar. Despite the diversity referred to above, and the differing difficulty levels, the general structure of the distributions are similar. The ratio of distances between minima are almost the same. For the two problems in which time and number of operations were measured, these ratios are the same. To demonstrate the similarity between the three histograms, they have been superimposed on one another to give Figure 4.10. It is apparent that the composite picture is essentially similar in structure to any one. Thus it may be concluded that the form of these distributions is dependent, not on the forms of the particular problems from which they arose, but on the psychological structures of the subjects who solve the problems.

In judging whether these distributions are multi-modal or not, their similarity of structure may be regarded as more significant than the statistical analysis.

The four distributions arising in the space-number experiment are sufficiently close to the expected to justify the assumption that one source of uni-modal distribution of scores in problems is that the subjects are required only to exploit a general structure previously acquired or explicate in detail a situation already structured.

With these experiments a consistent structure was obtained to which the levels-of-abstraction scheme could be directly related. Other interpretations of the experimental work are, of course, possible, but the evident consistency rules out interpretations which explain the separate multi-modal patterns in terms of the particular problem structures. Any interpretation must be sufficiently general to subsume all problems giving rise to the same multi-modal distribution. Furthermore, the discontinuities evident in the distributions indicate that such a general interpretation must involve a discontinuity idea, as exemplified in the levels-of-abstraction proposition.

Interpretation of Distributions

The three experiments were conducted only as tests of the hypothesis regarding the multi-modality of the distribution of performance scores. They have been described and discussed only in this context. Nevertheless it was anticipated that if the experiments were successful, interpretation of the multi-modal distributions obtained would lead to the construction of a discontinuity theory of the development of the individual, this being the general purpose of the project.

When putting forward the ideas of levels of abstraction it was stated that all levels attained would be retained. This suggests that the psychological structure may be regarded as made up of a limited number of discrete components. Each component would correspond to a particular level of abstraction and thus the number of components would correspond to the number of levels of abstraction attained. To demonstrate this suggested composite psychological structure directly with rigour, by the separate investigation of individuals, would be impossible.

In the discussion of levels of abstraction, it was also stated that an individual might enter a situation at any one of the levels attained. From the point of view expressed above, this means that any one of the components could become operative in a particular situation. Now consider a large number of individuals all of whom have reached the same level of abstraction,

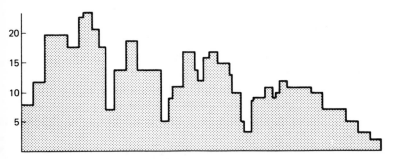

FIGURE 4.10. Composite picture of three superimposed histograms

say the *n*th. With each individual there would be associated *n* components. Since each individual could enter a situation with any of these *n* components operative, it would be expected that if such a population were confronted with some problem situation, *n* components could operate in the solution of the problem. The resulting statistical distribution of performance scores would then be multi-modal, the number of modes being *n*. Thus the discrete structure of the individual solving the problem would be reflected in the discrete structure of the resulting distribution pattern. From these considerations the experiments can be regarded as demonstrating rigorously through the investigation of a population a discretion in the psychological structure of the individual which could not be demonstrated rigorously through the investigation of separate individuals.

On these grounds the multi-modal pattern obtained from the experiments can be seen as demonstrating the presence of four components in the students entering university. The mode involving the highest scores, the least efficient, is associated with the level 1 component, the next more efficient mode with the level 2 component, the next with the level 3 component, the most efficient mode being associated with the level 4 component. It is of interest but of no significance at this stage in theory construction that after many hundreds of hours of discussion with these students, the majority have been judged as having attained level 4, a few level 5 and a larger number level 3.

Experimental Test of this Interpretation
Attempts were made to work with children below the ages 16–17 years, employing the three problems used in the experiments described above. Such a small percentage of these subjects solved the problem that the attempts were abandoned. They appeared unable to structure from the situation the problem to be solved. These experiences suggested that a discontinuity in development occurs at this age range for a large proportion of the general population. On the interpretation discussed above, the majority of students entering university at the age of 18 years have attained level 4. With a discontinuity occurring at 16–17 years, the majority of children immediately below this

ige would have attained level 3. If a problem of the right difficulty level were presented to these children, a three-mode distribution would be expected. The three modes would correspond to the three components of the level 3 person. Furthermore, it should be possible to identify them as such using the ratios between the minima of the four mode histograms. It is assumed that these ratios refer to some fundamental aspect of mans' organization and thus are of general applicability. It would be expected that the three modes in the three-mode histogram would be identical with the three least efficient modes in the level 4 histogram. The three modes of the three-mode histogram would thus be shown to reflect the level 1, the level-2, and the level-3 components of the level 3 person. An experiment was conducted to test this.

Experiment.[10] The apparatus used was adapted from a Multiple Choice Apparatus constructed by R. M. Yerkes (1924). The display confronting the subject consisted of two rows of lamps, twelve in each row, and a corresponding row of press button switches (Figure 4.11). Each press button is linked with the lamp directly above it in the lower row. The lamps in the top row are operated only by the experimenter using a row of switches at the back. Any combination of the twelve lamps can be illuminated. Employing a second row of switches at the back, the experimenter can determine which lamps in the lower row can be illuminated by the subject using the press button switches. For example, Figure 4.11 illustrates a combination of five lamps illuminated in the top row, with only one lamp in the bottom row, the one under the centre lamp of the five, coming alight when the corresponding button is pressed.

In use, the experimenter illuminates a series of combinations of lamps in the top row, and having chosen a particular relation between these combinations and the lamps in the bottom row, he uses the switches associated with the bottom row so that for each combination only the lamp which expresses the chosen relation comes alight when the appropriate button is pressed. The problem confronting the subject is to find the chosen relation using the press button switches.

[10] Designed by M. Featherstone and P. Critten.

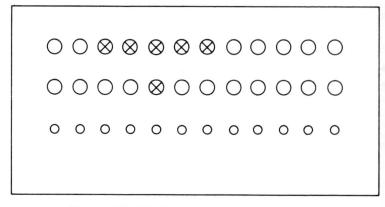

FIGURE 4.11. Display panel for level 3 experiment

Instructions to subjects. 'You have a number of buttons in front of you, twelve altogether. Each button, if you push it, puts on a light immediately above it in the bottom row (Demonstration). Now for each light in the bottom row which you can work, there is a light in the top row which I can work. Each time I am going to put a different set of lights on in the top row. Although the number of lights I will put on will change, every time I shall pick out one particular light which will remain in the same place all the time. What you have to do is to find out which light it is. To help you find it you use the buttons.'

The experiment was conducted in two parts. In the first part the subjects familiarized themselves with the nature of the problems. There were three separate examples to be worked out, all comparatively easy. The relevant lamp was the third in from the right of any set. The second example was used for scoring. In this case, the relevant lamp was located immediately to the right of the centre. The subject was presented at random with a set of three, five, seven, nine or eleven lamps. The criterion of success was that the subject should be able to find the correct button in one operation only for all five sets of lights. The number of operations used was counted and the time taken measured.

Results. Two hundred and sixty-four subjects aged between 12 and 17 attempted the final example. One hundred and ifty-three subjects solved the problem; of these, 10 gave very large scattered results. The number of operations and time taken were used as in the previous experiments to give the histogram shown in Figure 4.12. The statistical analysis applied was the same as in the previous cases. For this histogram, taking three modes, it was found that $\chi^2 = 19.31$. The number of degrees of freedom was 12. The corresponding 95 per cent point

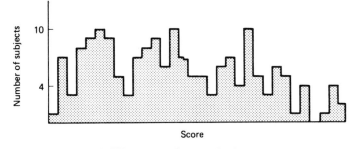

FIGURE 4.12. Histogram of scores for level 3 problem

on the χ^2 distribution is 21.03. Thus the results are consistent with the hypothesis of multi-modality. When the same problem was presented to university students a right skew distribution was obtained.

Discussion

The experiment gave rise to a three-mode statistical distribution, and furthermore, the structure of the distribution is such that the histogram illustrating it fits the last three modes of the four-mode histograms. It may be concluded that the three modes correspond to the three least efficient modes of the four-mode histograms. Thus the three-mode histogram can be regarded as portraying the three components of the level 3 person.

The experimental work has proceeded sufficiently to enable one to propose for the psychological development of the individual the scheme illustrated in Figure 4.13. The five histograms displayed refer to five discrete stages of development. At some early age the level 1 component emerges. It is illustrated by the imaginary uni-modal histogram at the

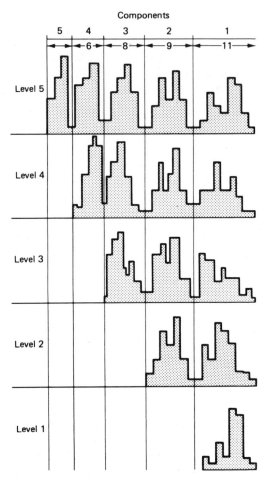

FIGURE 4.13. Proposed scheme for the development of personality

bottom. At some later age the level 2 component develops – illustrated by the bimodal histogram. Level 1 and level 2 components then develop continuously until level 3 component emerges – the three-mode histogram. The three components then develop continuously until the level 4 component emerges and so on until the level 5 component develops. It is not to be expected that all persons pass through all stages. A large number develop to level 3 and no further. A number develop only to level 4. Only a small fraction of the general population would reach level 5.

To test the general scheme, two further experiments were performed to obtain two level 2 histograms. With regard to the level 1 diagram, since it depicts a uni-modal distribution, experimental work along the lines described above is not possible. A uni-modal distribution can be obtained under a variety of conditions at all ages. Any experimental work of the form above could proceed only in a negative fashion, i.e. an attempt could be made to show that in working with children under a particular age only uni-modal distributions are obtained. This is hardly a practical proposition, and even if such uni-modal distributions were obtained, they would be meaningless since they could not be related to other distributions. An important feature of the scheme outlined is that all the modes and components from level 2 to level 6 have meaning only in that they are related to other modes and components. The only apparent means of operationally defining a level 1 population and of giving meaning to the histogram arising from work with such a population would be to resolve the components of a level 2 population with a problem so simple that it could be solved by level 1 persons. If the scores obtained with these supposed level 1 persons corresponded to the scores in the less efficient mode of the level 2 histogram, the unimodal distribution obtained, in that it is related to another distribution, becomes meaningful and could operationally define a level 1 population. All the experimental work done suggested that this was not possible in that a problem which resolves at one level is impossible to solve at a lower one. Nevertheless, while proceeding with the level 2 experiments, an attempt was made to define operationally a level 1 population along the lines suggested above.

LEVEL 2 EXPERIMENT (A). The display consists of 15 lights and 15 press buttons arranged in two equilateral triangles placed opposite one another, apex to apex (Figure 4.14). Each press button was connected via a transistor to a single light. The press button operation was such that successive pressings of a particular button resulted in the corresponding light going alternately on and off. The connecting structure was one of

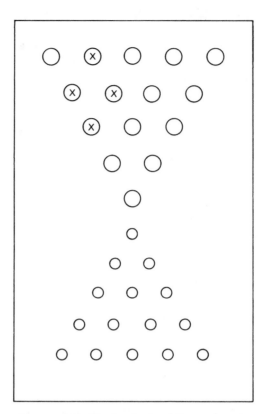

FIGURE 4.14. Display for level-2 experiment

lateral inversion; that is, for example, to operate the light at the right-hand corner of the triangle of lights required the button at the left-hand corner to be pressed. In addition, all lights could be switched off remotely by the experimenter. The lights were coloured red except for a group of four (marked 'X' in the figure) which were white. The machine was placed with the triangle of press buttons near the subject. At the start of each test, all lights were off.

Problem as stated to subject. 'These are lights (pointing to the triangle of lights), and these are press-buttons (pointing to the triangle of press buttons). What I would like you to do is to try and get the white lights alight, but not the red ones, using the press buttons. Remember, the white ones alight, not the red ones.'

The solution requires the recognition of the button operation and the spatial relations of buttons and lights. Solution of the problem was taken when the subject lit the four white lights three times in succession without error. Time and number of pressings to solve the problem were recorded, and later reduced to a single score in the same way as for the other experiments.

LEVEL 2 EXPERIMENT (B). For this experiment, the same apparatus was used as for the level 3 experiment, but the problem was simpler in that the combinations of lights in the top row presented to the subject were 3, 5, 7, 9, 11 adjacent lights, and the relevant light in the bottom row corresponded to the middle light of the combination. No attempt was made to familiarize the subjects with the nature of the problem as was the case for the level 3 experiment, but in all other respects the mode of procedure was the same.

Results. For Experiment A, over 200 subjects attempted the problem, of which 184 solved the problem. The histogram of scores is shown in Figure 4.15 (Level 2 'A'). For Experiment B, over 200 subjects attempted the problem, of which 157 solved the problem. The histogram of scores is shown in Figure 4.15 (Level 2 'B'). The age range of subjects for both experiments was 6 to 10 years, most subjects attempting both problems. The same statistical analysis was applied to the two sets of results as for the other experiments. For the histogram of Experiment A, taking two modes, it was found that $\chi^2 = 9.81$. The number of degrees of freedom was 12. The corresponding 95 per cent point on the χ^2 distribution is 21.03. For the histogram of Experiment B, taking two modes, it was found that $\chi^2 = 14.44$. The number of degrees of freedom was 12. The corresponding 95 per cent point on the χ distribution is 21.03. Thus the results of both experiments are consistent with the hypothesis of multimodality.

From observations of children operating in Experiment B, and also subsequent questioning of the children, it appeared that some had grasped the principle involved (i.e. middle light), but were unable to put it into effect without error for the series of combinations of 3, 5, 7, 9, 11 lights. The combinations of lights of larger number required counting from the edge, and this dependence on counting introduced an additional difficulty for those children, specially the younger ones, who were relatively unskilled in counting, resulting in deterioration of performance. This variable factor probably accounts for the large scores outside the bimodal distribution, and the large number who did not solve the problem. However, the effect was not sufficient to alter the general conclusions of the experiment.

The same problem of Experiment A was presented to a further 25 subjects aged 5 years (a school grade lower than the lowest used in Experiment A). Only two succeeded in solving the problem. This was consistent with the other experimental work in showing that a problem which resolves a population at one level cannot be solved by a population at a lower one. The attempt to define operationally a population by the means outlined above was consequently abandoned.

In addition, both experiments were tried with subjects older than 12 years, yielding results which in both cases gave rise to right skew distributions.

Figure 4.15 presents the structure for relating the histograms obtained. It consists of the level 4 histogram obtained from the time sequence experiment, the histogram from the level 3 experiment, and the two level two histograms. (The difference in structural detail of the level 4 histogram in Figure 4.15 and that of Figure 4.4 is because a slightly smaller class size was chosen for the former histogram compared with the latter). The three level 4 histograms obtained have been shown to have essentially the same structure (Figure 4.10). In Figure 4.15 one' of the level 4 histograms is related to the level 3 and level 2 histograms, and thus all histograms have been interrelated, and the whole can be related to the proposed scheme for the psychological development of the individual.

Conclusion
The experimental work has proceeded to the extent that a system of interrelating histograms has been constructed which can be directly related to the theoretical levels-of-abstraction scheme outlined above. It is proposed to complete the relevant experimental work by conducting at least two level 5 experi-

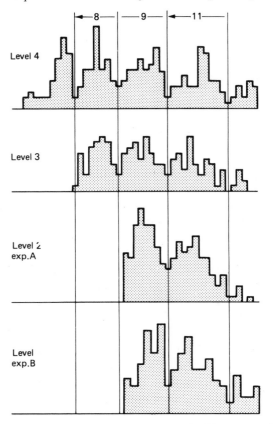

FIGURE 4.15. Structure relating level 2, 3 and 4 histograms obtained

ments and a further level 3 experiment. It is expected that the level 5 experiments will be considerably more laborious and time-consuming to carry to completion by virtue of the large number of subjects required, and also that it seems unlikely that level 5 subjects are congregated within institutions in large numbers as is the case with university students and schoolchildren. From the present viewpoint, a level 6 experiment would be even more difficult to carry out, again for the reasons suggested above, but in addition because it is believed that the proportion of level 6 persons within the general population is very small.

5

Use of Loss of Skill under Stress to Test a Theory of Psychological Development

D. J. Isaac and B. M. O'Connor

This paper describes two experiments involving loss of skill under conditions of increasing stress, imposed by excessive rates of information input. The purpose of these experiments was further to test a stage theory of psychological development, as outlined in Chapter 2. The experiments described below (as well as those of the earlier paper) were directed towards making manifest developmentally related psychological structures.

Experiments were conducted with subjects ranging in age from 5 years to 24 years. The scores obtained provided a series of multi-modal distributions: two-mode histograms for subjects from 5 to 11 years, three-mode histograms for 11 to 17 years, and four-mode histograms for the range 18 to 24 years. The structure inherent in this series of multi-modal distributions was interpreted as directly expressing the developing structure of individuals.

Scheme for the Developing Structure of the Individual

The general scheme for the psychological development of the individual which emerged was as follows. For the approximate age range 0 to 5 years, one component is present. Between approximately 5 and 10 years, a second component emerges, after which both components develop continuously. Between approximately 10 and 16 years, a third component emerges, after which the three components develop continuously, and so on until six components are present. In that any one stage subsumes the lower, and comprises one more component, the scheme refers to an ascending order of organizational complexity. Not all persons are expected to develop to the higher stages. Further, for an individual in any situation, any one of the components associated with the stage of development reached could become operative.

The essential feature of the approach adopted in the earlier paper to the problem of psychological development was the use of multi-modal distributions resulting from investigations of populations to make inferences about individual psychological development. The notion of psychological development proceeding through stages has, of course, been put forward by many authors (Piaget;[1] Werner;[2] Jacques;[3] Harvey *et al.*[4]). However, the general approach referred to above which provides a rigorous statistical treatment of the problem, has not hitherto been adopted. This paper describes a further test of the theory which uses the same general approach.

Ideas Underlying the Experiments
The scheme was derived from problem-solving experiments. The same process could be repeated to test and provide additional support for the scheme, but a more demanding test would be to use experiments based on a different process.

The loss of an acquired skill, or more generally, the collapse of ordered behaviour, through the imposition of excessive levels of information input, is a well-known phenomenon. Under certain circumstances this breakdown occurs suddenly. Regarding the effect of information input overload on behaviour, Miller[5] states that there is a maximum rate of information input beyond which the output falls drastically; the operator is overloaded and can no longer operate effectively. The experiments described below were based on this phenomenon.

[1] Piaget, J. (1050): *The psychology of intelligence*; London, Routledge. Piaget, J. (1954): *The construction of reality in the child*, New York, Basic Books.

[2] Werner, H. (1948): *Comparative psychology of mental development*; New York, International Universities Press. Werner, H. (1957): *The concept of development from a comparative and organismic point of view*; Minneapolis, University of Minnesota Press.

[3] Jaques, E. (1956): 'Preliminary sketch of a general structure of executive strata. *Glacier Project Papers*; London, Heinemann Educational Books.

[4] Harvey, O. J., Hunt, D. E. and Schroder, H. M. (1961): *Conceptual systems and personality organization*; London, Wiley.

[5] Miller, J. G. (1960): 'Input overload and psychopathology', *Amer. J. Psychiat. 116*, 695.

A conclusion of the earlier experimental work was that the multi-modal distributions obtained were dependent both upon the problem used and on the particular age range from which subjects were selected. This association of problem solved and age range through the multi-modal distribution obtained, and also the relating of these multi-modal distributions into the scheme outlined above, enabled the problems used to be classified in terms of the associated stages. Thus, for instance, a problem which gave rise to a three-mode histogram could be termed a 'stage-three' problem. The higher-stage problems differed from the lower-stage ones in respect of total information content, having a greater amount of information and/or greater degree of abstractness. It was found that subjects at a lower stage could not solve the higher-stage problem; they appeared unable to form a problem from the situation. The person at the higher stage is able to organize the information and perform successfully in a situation containing information in excess of the organizing abilities of the person at the lower stage. Thus it would appear that a characteristic difference between subjects at different stages lies in their abilities to organize information. Assuming that this difference would show up in situations where the total information content remains constant but where the rate of presentation is varied, it could be expected that if some measurement could be made of the maximum rate of information input tolerable in a particular situation without breakdown in performance, the distribution of scores provided by a large number of subjects within an age range presumed to include two stages would be bimodal.

This proposition concerning bimodality of performance scores can be reached from a different point of view, that is, from an accepted association of stages of development with tolerance of stress. For instance, discussing the transition from a lower to a higher stage, Harvey, Hunt and Schroder[4] (p. 108) state: 'The subject not only develops autonomous skills and informational standards for problem solution but also a high degree of tolerance of anxiety and resistance to stress.' This proposition suggests that individuals who have reached a higher stage of development may continue to function effectively under greater stress than those who have reached only a lower stage. Furthermore, on the basis of the scheme put forward, it would be expected that comparison of the degree of stress the higher-stage individual could tolerate in contrast with those at the lower stage would reflect the distinct organizational complexities of the two stages. Considering that one means of imposing stress is to increase the rate of information input, one arrives at the proposition stated in the previous paragraph. The purpose of the experiments described below was to test this proposition.

Experimental Procedure

It was decided that the general mode of procedure should be one in which subjects were first taught a simple skill which they were then required to repeat. With each repetition, the speed of the operations was increased, thereby increasing the rate of information input. The experimental problem was to design a skill which was readily acquired, and which with repetition at progressively faster speeds might be improved, but which would at some point produce a demonstrable collapse of performance.

It is conceivable that a bimodal distribution arising from an experiment could be derived from a particular choice of subjects or from the structure of the situation. Obviously these two sources of bimodality must be avoided. For instance, a bimodal distribution obtained by using subjects selected from two groups widely separated in age would merely reflect the age difference. Similarly, a bimodal distribution achieved by selecting two groups of subjects according to some preconceived psychological criterion would be a test only of that criterion. It follows that the only selection procedure which could give a rigorous test of the theory put forward is one which provides equal representation of all ages over an extended age range, regardless of all other differences.

To avoid the possibility of a bimodal distribution arising from structure within the situation, the machines used in the experiments were so designed that no sudden changes would occur in machine functioning which would of themselves lead to a bimodal distribution of scores.

EXPERIMENT 1. An electronic machine was constructed which

presented a display of lamps and press button switches to the subject. The display (Figure 5.1) consists of a rectangular grid array of press buttons, a row of lamps at the top of the display, and a single green lamp in the space between the buttons and the row of lamps. In the bottom right-hand corner were nine electric lamps.

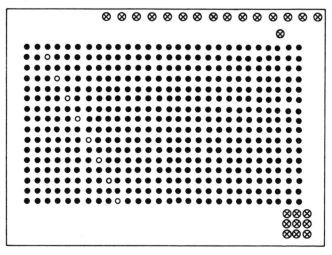

FIGURE 5.1

The skill which the subject was required to learn, and then repeat, involved pressing a sequence of sixteen buttoms arranged in a particular spatial pattern, each press to coincide with flashes from a pair of lamps. The first button in the sequence was the lowest in the row of white buttons; the next was the black one second on the right; the next was the second white one going up; the next was the second black one on the left, and so on.

In addition to pressing the buttons in the right sequence, the skill required pressing all but the first button to coincide with two flashing red lamps of the group of nine. These nine lamps were connected electrically in four groups. Two of these groups (of red and white lamps) flshed at a constant frequency. The other two groups of lamps, one of which consisted of two red lamps (Group A), and the other two white and one red (Group B) also flashed on and off alternately, but at a frequency controlled by the experimenter by means of multi-pole switches which enabled a total gradation of 36 equal time increments. The electronic arrangement was such that the Group A lamps were alight for a fixed period, whereas the time the Group B lamps were alight was variable. Pressing the first button in the sequence brought on the green lamp and started the nine lamps flashing. All subsequent buttons of the sequence had to be pressed only when Group A lamps were alight. Thus to light a particular lamp, the subject must press the corresponding button when the red Group A lamps flash, and thus has to abstract the appropriate lamps from the matrix of flashing lamps. Each successful pressing of the buttons in the sequence brought on a lamp at the top of the panel. If any button other than the correct one in the sequence was pressed, or if the right one was pressed at a time when the lamps of Group A were not on, all lamps went out and the subject had to start again.

After the subject had learnt the skill at the slowest speed, the speed was increased and the subject required to repeat the sequence. After each successful sequence operation, the speed was increased by a fixed amount, and the sequence operation repeated until four consecutive errors at one speed were made, when it was taken that loss of skill had occurred.[6] The switch position at which this occurred was a measure of the speed at which loss of skill took place. This provided a score for each subject. In addition, the age of each subject was recorded. From the work described in the earlier paper, it was inferred that the age range 11 to 23 years would be associated with stages three and four. It was decided to work within this age range.

Accepting that subjects pass from one stage to the next at different ages, it was expected that some subjects at a particular age would be associated with one mode, some with the other. Of interest was the variation of relative frequency (i.e. the proportion of scores in one mode compared with the total number of scores) with age, in that it would show the increasing proportion of subjects in the higher stage. Efforts were made to

---

[6] It was observed while designing the experiment that it was very rare for subjects to be successful after making four consecutive errors.

have the same number of subjects in each age group. Subjects were taken from secondary schools and a university.

Results. Justification of the way scores were obtained in the experiment was provided by the dramatic change in behaviour shown by subjects when loss of skill occurred. Most subjects operated efficiently a number of times, and then suddenly the behaviour changed. The hands wandered over the panel, or the finger would go to the right button but would not press at the appropriate time, or would not press at all. Some subjects were so disconcerted that they insisted that the last movement of the timing switch altered the functioning of the machine in a radical way. Before loss of skill occurred, indications of increasing anxiety were often observed, such as finger tremor, wiping the forehead, giggling, etc.

The number of subjects was 378, approximately 35 per year. The sexes were equally represented up to the age of 19, thereafter there was a predominance of males.

The histogram of scores is shown in Figure 5.2. The statistical analysis used in the previous paper was applied.[7] This is a goodness of fit test, in which the hypothesis under test is that the distribution is bimodal. The value of χ^2 from the analysis was 20.6; the corresponding 95 per cent point of the χ^2 distribution was 23.7. The hypothesis of bimodality is thus supported.

The proportion of subjects falling into the faster mode was calculated for each age. These values are plotted on a graph shown in Figure 5.3. Since the faster mode is associated with the higher stage, the curve in the figure can be interpreted as showing the age range over which the change from stage three to stage four occurs. For each age there was no significant difference in relative frequency for male and female subjects.

EXPERIMENT 2. A similar experiment was performed over the age range 7 to 15 years using the same machine but employing a simpler skill. This simplification was necessary because

---

[7] In this analysis the initial step was to fit a linear combination of normal curves to a given histogram of discontinuous appearance, the best fit being obtained by the principle of maximum likelihood. A χ^2 goodness of fit test, with a 5 per cent level of significance, then provided a criterion of multimodality.

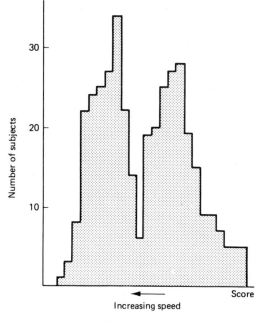

FIGURE 5.2

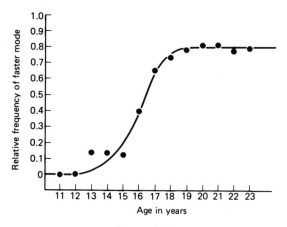

FIGURE 5.3

most children under 11 years of age could not learn the skill used in the previous experiment. The total information content was beyond their organizing ability. To obtain a skill which could be used over the required age range, the amount and abstractness of information was reduced as follows:

1. The spatial pattern: The same left–right movement was kept, but the general movement across the matrix was altered from a diagonal shift to a shift at right angles to the line of switches. The number of switches to be pressed in the sequence was reduced from 16 to 12.

2. The signal lamps: The matrix of flashing lamps was removed. The duration of the flash of the two remaining stimulus lamps was increased from 0.60 seconds to 0.85 seconds.

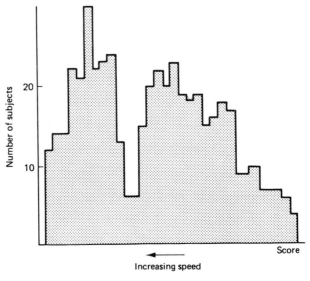

FIGURE 5.4

Results. The number of subjects was 488, roughly half male, half female, and approximately 50 per year, all from primary and secondary schools. The histogram of scores is shown in Figure 5.4. Using the same statistical analysis as in the first experiment, we calculated a χ^2 value of 34.7; the corresponding 95 per cent point of the χ^2 distribution was 36.4. The hypothesis of bimodality is thus supported.

As in Experiment 1, the proportion of subjects falling into the faster mode was calculated for each age. These values are

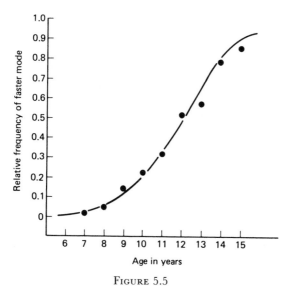

FIGURE 5.5

plotted on the graph shown in Figure 5.5. Since the faster mode is associated with the higher stage, the curve in the figure indicates the age range over which the change from stage two to stage three occurs. Again, for each age there was no significant difference in relative frequency for male and female subjects.

Conclusion

The purpose of the experiments was to test the proposition that a bimodal distribution of scores would be obtained from subjects in the age range 11 to 23 years in the one case, and from subjects in the age range 7 to 15 years in the second, in situations of increasing stress. Bimodal distributions were obtained and the proposition statistically confirmed. Validation of the proposition under test, derived from the general scheme regarding psychological development of individuals, lends further support for the scheme. Furthermore, it appears that this type of experiment could be used to identify the highest stage reached by a particular individual. This, of course, requires further investigation. Having discriminated two populations from a given age range, it now becomes possible to consider further experimental work aimed at investigating the distinguishing characteristics of the psychological processes involved.

A third experiment, similar to those described above but involving stages four and five, is being conducted. Although not yet completed, a bimodal histogram is appearing. Thus, up to the present, nine experiments using over 5,000 subjects have been carried out, which (1) provide a statistical test of the general notion of discontinuity in psychological development, (2) led to the development of the scheme for the composite psychological structure of individuals referred to above, (3) provide a rigorous test of this scheme. The multi-modal distributions obtained interrelate to form a coherent system. To complete the system, further experimental work is necessary, with problem-solving experiments used to obtain five-mode and six-mode histograms, and also loss-of-skill experiments relating to stages one/two and stages five/six.

6

Separation of Two Adult Populations Identified with Two Levels of Psychological Development

D. J. Isaac and B. M. O'Connor

Abstract

Results are presented of the third experiment of a series designed to test a discontinuity theory of psychological development. Use is made of the phenomenon of loss of skill under conditions of increasing rate of change of perceptual field. The scores provided by a population mixture of university undergraduates and graduates separate out clearly into two groups which are identified with levels 4 and 5 of the theory. The series provides a compound indirect test of the theory and also substantiates earlier problem-solving experiments. A secondary analysis of the results provides indications of the proportions of schoolchildren (and university undergraduates) corresponding to the different levels of psychological development. Much wider differences in development are revealed than are suggested from conventional psychological and educational research.

In this chapter we present the results of an experiment designed to test a theory of psychological development which makes use of the phenomenon of eventual loss of skill under conditions of increasing rate of change of perceptual field. A position is reached finally where two populations are clearly discriminated, and identified with two consecutive stages of psychological development.

A comprehensive account of the theory is given in Isaac and O'Connor (Chapters 4 and 7). Briefly, this theory was constructed from an elementary dynamic structure, which is an abstract model for the interaction of the self and associated perceptual field. Using this model, a series of related structures of increasing complexity was systematically built up. These increasingly complex structures formed a system of levels for psychological development, expressed in terms of increasingly abstract modes of functioning.

In testing the theory, the experimental work has proceeded on the supposition that individuals would, as they grow up normally in industrialized society, proceed through successive stages of development corresponding to the levels of the theory, these stages being manifest in fundamentally different modes of behaving. In common with the concept of psychological development generally accepted, it is assumed that not all individuals develop to some common upper limit, but that in proceeding through stages the final stage reached by an individual and the age range corresponding to the different stages of his development depend on situational and dispositional factors, and that considerable variation between individuals is therefore to be expected. Allowing for extreme variations, it is assumed that large numbers of individuals from a population conform in their essential functioning so that they may be grouped together and associated with a particular stage of development, the ages of the individuals comprising the group corresponding with a specific age range.

Earlier experimental work involving a series of problem-solving experiments (Isaac and O'Connor, Chapter 4) related stages of development, levels of the theory, and age range of the group corresponding to a stage. Level 1 was associated with the age range 0 to 5 years, level 2 with 5 to 11 years, level 3 with 11 to 17 years, and level 4 with 18 to 22 years. The present series of experiments makes use of this correspondence between stage of development and age range.

The series of experiments of which the experiment described in this chapter is the latest all rely on the principle that for individuals in a situation in which the perceptual field is changing at increasing rates, a point is reached at which the existing order can no longer be maintained. If the changing perceptual field is directly associated with the performance of a skill (commensurate with an individual's stage of development), then increasing the rate of change of perceptual field beyond the limit at which the existing order could be maintained would manifest itself in loss of skill. The experiments of the series were designed in such a way that an individual was required to perform a skill at gradually increasing rates made dependent on visual perception. Further, the rates at which the skill was executed could be measured, and thus the point at which loss of skill occurred provided a measure of the maximum rate of change of field which could be maintained by that individual in that situation. The design of the experiments also makes use of the idea that individuals corresponding to a higher level could maintain order at significantly greater rates of change (i.e. could perform the skill at greater rates) than could individuals corresponding to a lower level. With this idea in mind, and having regard for the usual variation in measures provided by homogeneous populations, it was sufficient for the purposes of the experiments that the measures provided by subjects from a population mixture (i.e. a mixture in respect of different levels of psychological development) separate out into identifiable clusters, corresponding in number to the number of different levels previously attributed to the mixture. More particularly, the purpose of the present series of experiments was to see whether from the scores provided by subjects in a given loss-of-skill experiment, the subjects being uniformly selected from age ranges previously associated with two successive levels, a separation of scores into two clusters would be obtained, or, if the scores were presented as a frequency distribution, a bimodal distribution would be presented. Obtaining a bimodal distribution was taken as a successful indirect test of the general theory, and a further substantiation of the earlier experimental work.

The first experiment of the series used subjects age range 11 to 23 years, corresponding to levels 3 and 4. A bimodal distribution was obtained. The skill used in this experiment could not be used with subjects below the age of 11 years. Too few could learn it. A simpler skill was designed and used with subjects age range 7 to 15 years, corresponding to levels 2 and 3. A bimodal distribution was obtained. These two experiments are described in Isaac and O'Connor (Chapter 5). The present experiment is aimed at the separation of populations corresponding to levels 4 and 5, again by seeking a bimodal distribution of scores from a loss-of-skill experiment. The skill required to be learnt would be significantly more difficult than that of the level 3/4 experiment.

Experiment

An electronic machine was constructed which presented a display of lamps and press button switches to the subject. The display (Figure 6.1) consists of a square grid array of press buttons (8 × 8), and four groups of four red lamps at each corner of the rectangular display panel, the four in each group forming a square.

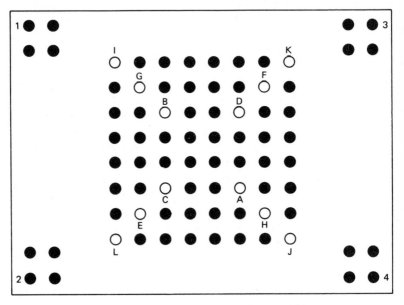

FIGURE 6.1. Display panel presented to subjects

The skill which the subject was required to learn, and then repeat, involved pressing a sequence of twelve buttons arranged in a particular spatial pattern, each press to coincide with a flash from one significant lamp from a particular group of lamps. The sequence of buttons to be pressed is depicted in the figure using the sequence of letters A to L (such lettering being absent in the actual experiment, the operative buttons being plain white, the non-operative ones black).

Apart from the first of the sequence, each button had to be pressed during the time a particular lamp was alight. There were four significant lamps, one in each group of four lamps.

The four significant lamps flashed in regular sequence, indicated in the diagram by the number sequence 1, 2, 3, 4 (such numeration being absent in the actual experiment). The duration each of the significant lamps was alight remained fixed throughout the experiment. The remaining three lamps of each group flashed on and off in an apparently random fashion during the whole of the skill sequence, the mode of flashing being similar to that of the significant lamps. The purpose of these additional lamps was to make it necessary for the subject not only to learn the lamp sequence, but also correctly to anticipate each significant lamp in the sequence.

Essentially, executing the skill required having in mind two sequential/spatial patterns which had to be correctly related for each step in the action sequence (button pressing) for the skill to be successful. The associated electronics was designed to detect 'correct' action and 'incorrect' action. Correct action required prompt pressing of the right button at the right time, the subject being informed that his particular action was correct by a soft tone from a loudspeaker within the box. Incorrect action resulted in a harsh tone, all the lights going out, the sequence coming to an end. To restart the time sequence, the subject was required to press the first of the button sequence. The rate at which the skill had to be executed was determined by the periodicity governing the lighting sequence of the four significant lamps, which was maintained constant during a given skill sequence. This rate, which was under the control of the experimenter, could be accurately and finely varied by means of decade switches, permitting a range of periodicity between successive moves from 6 seconds down to 1 second with a minimum gradation of 0·05 seconds.

After the subject had learnt the skill at the slowest rate, the rate was increased and the subject required to repeat the sequence. With each sequence operation completed, the rate was increased by a fixed amount. This was repeated until the subject made four consecutive errors, this being taken as a criterion of loss of skill. The numbered switch position at which this occurred provided a measure of the rate at which loss of skill took place. In addition to this measure, the age of each subject was recorded.

In judging whether the results of the experiment provide a

rigorous test of the general theory, the specification of the population from which subjects were taken for the experiment is critical. The successful test of the theory involves obtaining a bimodal distribution of scores, the histogram being related to the other histograms already obtained through the specification of the populations used, and hence to the general theory. For the experiment to be a rigorous test of the theory also requires the population used to be such that there could be no association of clustering of scores with the selection procedure employed. This requirement was satisfied in the first two experiments of the series by specifying the population in terms of a continuous variable (age) and ensuring that the subjects were selected uniformly from the entire age range; the frequency distribution of ages of subjects used would thus ideally be rectangular: the selection procedure sought to approach this ideal.

Relating the bimodal distributions obtained follows immediately from the fact that the associated population mixtures share in part a common age range: that is, the respective frequency distributions of ages overlap by approximately one half. Thus to relate the expected level 4/5 histogram to the level 3/4 histogram required specifying the population to be used in seeking the former such that the lower part of the age range was the same as the higher part of the age range used to obtain the level 3/4 histogram. The university undergraduate population fulfils this requirement.

However, unlike the two previous experiments of the series, it was not possible to specify the population to be used in the present experiment completely in terms of a continuous age range. While the comparatively small age range of a university undergraduate population would be used in the same way as in the previous experiments, that part of the population mixture presumed to correspond broadly with level 5 could not be prescribed in terms of a continuous age range simply because there was no practical way of ensuring uniform selection. However, with regard to the main purpose of the experiment, this presented no difficulty. To establish continuity with the undergraduate population it was judged sufficient to specify the individuals making up the population to be associated with level 5 as 'university graduates'. It was therefore assumed that university undergraduates and graduates would provide a population mixture corresponding largely to levels 4 and 5. Individuals within that broad definition were used as subjects in the experiment. A bimodal distribution of scores was expected.

RESULTS. The number of subjects providing scores was 210. The histogram of scores is shown in Figure 6.2. The statistical analysis used in the previous experiments (and described in

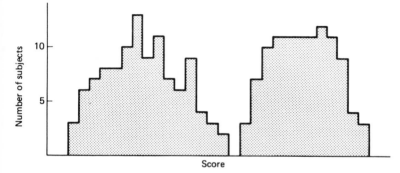

FIGURE 6.2. Histogram of scores showing separation into two groups

Isaac and O'Connor, 1969) was applied.[1] This is a goodness of fit test, in which the hypothesis under test is that the distribution is bimodal. The value of χ^2 from the analysis was 11.3; the corresponding 95 per cent point of the χ^2 distribution is 25.0. The hypothesis of bimodality is thus confirmed.

A population mixture of university undergraduates and graduates provided a bimodal distribution of scores, which, from the specification of the populations used, was related to the earlier bimodal distributions obtained. Through such relating the modes of the histogram were identified with levels 4 and 5 of the theory.

[1] In this analysis the initial step was to fit a linear combination of normal curves to a given histogram of discontinuous appearance, the best fit being obtained by the principle of maximum likelihood. A χ^2 goodness of fit test, with a 5 per cent level of significance, then provided a criterion of multi-modality. This involved an iterative process for which a computer program was constructed.

In contrast with the two earlier experiments, a graph showing the variation with age of the proportion of subjects corresponding to levels 4 and 5 is not presented. Firstly, the number of subjects involved was much less than in previous experiments, the values obtained consequently showing greater variation; secondly, in selecting subjects for the present experiment, age *per se* was not used as a criterion. Further, in defining the population used in terms of individuals who had proceeded to a university education, the values for the relative frequencies corresponding to the two levels applied only to that specific population and were thus not strictly comparable with the earlier results.

Bearing in mind the above qualifications, our results indicate that about 25 per cent of 18- and 19-year-old university students have reached level 5, 44 per cent of 20- and 21-year-old students, and 47 per cent of 22- and 23-year-old students.

Conclusion

The general purpose of the series of experiments of which this chapter describes the latest was to see whether a population mixture could be separated into two groups, the population mixture being defined in terms of results of the earlier problem-solving experiments so that it was presumed to be composed of individuals corresponding to two consecutive stages of psychological development. Successful separation of the groups permits the groups (and the individuals comprising them) to be related to a levels theory of psychological development. More particularly, the two earlier experiments were directed towards testing the proposition that a bimodal distribution of scores would be obtained from subjects in the age range 11 to 23 years (corresponding to levels 3 and 4) in the first experiment, and in the second experiment from subjects in the age range 7 to 15 years (corresponding to levels 2 and 3), the scores obtained being measures of the maximum rate of change of perceptual field which could be tolerated without breakdown of skill. The present experiment was concerned with using the same procedure to obtain a separation of two populations from a mixture of undergraduates and graduates (corresponding to levels 4 and 5). Bimodal distributions were obtained for all three experiments. Taken together, the experiments provide a successful compound test of the general theory, and also substantiate the earlier problem-solving experiments.

Further corroboration of the results of the present experiment is provided by a problem-solving experiment nearly completed, aimed at obtaining a five-mode histogram from a university population made up of graduates and older undergraduates. Although the statistical analysis has yet to be carried out, it is clear that a five-mode histogram has been obtained.

Taking a synoptic view of the work, we can now state that a position has been reached where the problem-solving experiments, the loss-of-skill experiments, and the theory, are systematically interrelated to a degree that the mutual support of the parts thus provided lends general confirmation to the work as a whole. To complete the system, a bimodal histogram corresponding to levels 1 and 2 is required. However, at this stage we are uncertain whether an experiment of the same kind as that of the present series would be appropriate for use with very young children.

A co-ordinated and integrated experimental-theoretical system having been established, future work will be directed towards developing the experimental and theoretical implications of the system. It is envisaged that this will involve further interpretations of the structures and ideas comprising the theory, and also the creation of new experiments which will serve the purpose of testing the developing theoretical ideas further and of establishing new ways of interpreting, organizing and predicting human behaviour.

Finally, it is worth recording some results emerging from a secondary analysis of the present experimental work. By relating the relative frequencies of children at different ages corresponding to different stages of psychological development, one can obtain estimates of the proportion of children corresponding to the stages over a range of ages. Graphs showing this variation are shown in Figure 6.3. It should be noted that these results are incomplete: the resolution of the proportions corresponding to levels 1 and 2 is clearly necessary. Nevertheless, sufficient information has been obtained to illustrate two features of the general school population which emerge from the analysis: firstly, the wide age range corresponding to a particular level, and secondly, the presence at any particular age of at least two and usually three levels of psychological development. For instance, at age 9 years, 10 per cent of school-children appear to have reached level 3, whereas at age 15 years, 10 per cent are still at level 2. Or, again, at age 15 years, 10 per cent of children appear to have developed to level 2, about 73 per cent to level 3, and 16 per cent to level 4. While

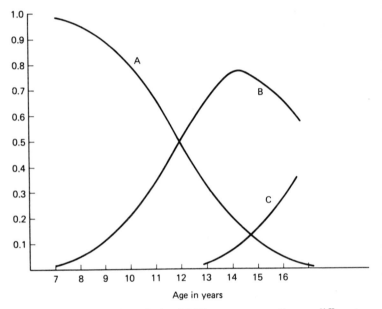

FIGURE 6.3. Proportion of schoolchildren corresponding to different levels of psychological development:

Graph A: Level 2 (and 1)
Graph B: Level 3
Graph C: Level 4

not attaching, for the present, any significance to the accuracy of the numbers obtained, these results clearly indicate that for significant proportions of children at a particular age, individuals may correspond to any one of three levels of psychological development.

We observe that this analysis reveals much more pronounced differences in the development of children than typically emerge from conventional psychological and educational research. A fuller realization of the implications of this feature could be of considerable importance for education and also in remedial work.

We would like to suggest, in conclusion, that with the validation and acceptance of the theory and its associated experimental work, there emerges the means of establishing a mapping of the school population (and the adult population as well) in terms of levels of psychological development. Such a mapping could be of functional value to educationists and in the selection of personnel for employment.

Part B

Abstract Relations Structure

7

A Discontinuity Theory of Psychological Development

D. J. Isaac and B. M. O'Connor

A discontinuity theory of psychological development is designed such that the associated experimental work relies on quantitative variates of behaviour to discriminate stages. Using a dynamic element, expressed abstractly in terms of 'poles' and 'relations', a series of structures relating to developmental stages is constructed. The element operates in either of two ways: in a discriminating mode or confusing mode. Operating in the discriminating mode, poles and relations become more defined; operating in the confusing mode leads to loss of discrimination of poles and relation. The element is applied to an imaginary situation of baby with mother. In the course of applying the element, a resolution of the situation into two components is introduced, which leads finally to a unity which comprises a self-structure and two classes of objects, things and persons. The essential structure of this unity, expressed in terms of a self-pole related to an object-pole serves as the level 1 structure of the series. In moving from one level to the next, a transformation of self and objects of the preceding level takes place, elements of the preceding level becoming integrated and serving as poles for the succeeding level. Finally, five levels of psychological development are constructed, comprising fifteen fundamentally different modes of functioning. The quantitative statements arising from the theory opened possibilities for rigorous experimental testing. Problem-solving experiments and experiments involving loss of skill under increasing stress have been designed to test the theory, the results of which support the theory.

The theoretical system for psychological development presented below was constructed about 1962. Subsequently, a series of experiments was carried out to test the system. With the successful outcome of these experiments (Isaac and

O'Connor, Chapters 4–6), it is now appropriate to communicate the theory.

The theory is based on the idea that psychological development proceeds discontinuously; that is, individuals develop through a sequence of clearly discriminated stages or levels, the term 'clearly discriminated' here implying a lack of intermediate forms between an earlier and later stage. The term 'psychological' is used here as a general non-specific reference: the theoretical structures put forward are not presumed to refer to specific aspects of mental functioning, as would, for instance, be denoted by the association of such terms as 'cognitive' or 'intellectual' to development.

The idea that development proceeds discontinuously is, of course, central to other theories. Where the present work differs from other treatments is in the direct use of quantitative variates to discriminate stages of development; other treatments invariably rely on qualitative variates of behaviour to discriminate stages.

As an introduction to the present work, it may be useful to indicate, by way of contrast, the mode of procedure of this alternative approach and some of the difficulties ensuing from its application. The work of Piaget and his collaborators is used to exemplify this approach.

In general, Piaget has proceeded from detailed observation and description of behaviour to the construction of systems of abstract ideas and models believed to represent the basic cognitive structures inherent in the organism and underlying its behaviour. While it is generally agreed that the procedure Piaget has followed has yielded a wealth of qualitative material and also a comprehensive conceptual scheme for intellectual development, it has not provided the degree of rigorous testing of his ideas which some feel as necessary for the general acceptance of his conclusions. As Hunt[1] states; '[Piaget] has been singularly unconcerned with ... testing experimentally the implications of his interpretations, even though his interpretations clearly require validating.'

---

[1] Hunt, J. McV. (1961): 'The impact and limitations of the giant of developmental psychology'. In Elkind, D. and Flavell, J. H. (Eds.): *Studies in cognitive development;* London, Oxford University Press.

Concerning the concept of 'stage', Piaget[2] lists different 'attributes' which, for him, condition the use of the term in the study of mental development. These 'criteria' include hierarchization, integration, consolidation, structuring, and equilibration. A problem for the worker wishing to test Piaget's notions lies in translating the above general terms into specific behavioural acts directly observable such that judgments can be made. If, on the other hand, behavioural criteria are specified, then judgments can be made only in respect of these, and not of Piaget's list of criteria. Either way, Piaget's use of the word 'criterion' in this context and the particular criteria he lists can have little significance in behavioural terms for the developmentalist intending to test Piaget's stage heories. Pinard and Laurendeau[3] make a corresponding observation when they write, 'It seems that the more rigorous the criterion, the more it becomes surrounded with ambiguities and misunderstandings, perhaps because the difficulty of the problems becomes more and more apparent and because empirical verifications decrease in frequency as the criterion increases in rigor.'

It is also stated of Piaget's work that it is 'devoid of statistical methods and systematic design'.[4] In an attempt to meet this criticism, Elkind[5] attempt a direct statistical proof of Piaget's stage theory. Essentially, this work involved determining the proportion of subjects for each of three Piagetian stage/age-related groups who, in a particular test situation, satisfied a specified criterion of behaviour. The results showed that the older the group the greater the proportion of subjects providing the specified criterion of behaviour, in agreement with Piaget's observations. (The use of attribute statistics, as for instance by Elkind, although giving rise to numerical statements, must not

---

[2] Piaget, J. (1960): 'The general problems of the psychobiological development of the child'. In Tanner, J. M. and Inhelder, B. (Eds.): *Discussion on child development. Volume IV;* London, Tavistock Publications.

[3] Pinard, A. and Laurendeau, M. (1969): '"Stage" in Piaget's cognitive-developmental theory: Exegesis of a concept'. In Elkind, D. and Flavell, J. H. (Eds.): *Studies in cognitive development;* London, Oxford University Press.

[4] Lerner, H. (1948): *Comparative psychology of mental development;* New York, International Universities Press.

[5] Elkind, D. (1961): 'The development of quantitative thinking – A systematic replication of Piaget's studies'. *Journal of General Psychology,* 1961, *98,* 37.

be confused with the use of statistics directed to the analysis of quantitative variates.) In our view, such work does no more than corroborate Piaget's observations; it adds in no way to the acceptance of his interpretations. Engelmann[6] similarly distinguishes between acceptance of observations and acceptance of interpretations when he writes, 'The main point of confusion associated with Piagetian theory has to do with the relationship between the observations of what children normally do and the theoretical principles that account for these observations. It is quite possible for one to acknowledge that the Piagetian observations are generally quite accurate and for one to totally reject the theory.'

Furthermore, modes of procedure which rely on qualitative variates of behaviour are characterized by the close association of the empirical work and the subsequent interpretative theories to the extent that the objective and subjective aspects of the work often appear confused. Piaget himself has recently expressed uncertainty in this regard: 'The existence of these overall structures raises a problem: do they in fact really exist in the mind of the subject being studied, or are they merely an invention of the psychologist who studies children or adults? If we are to be convinced of the existence of these structures, we should be able to formalize them in logical terms. We then try to adapt this formalization to what we are able to observe in the child. But we can never be sure whether we have invented the formalization or whether it really is an expression of what is to be found in the mind of the child'.[7]

From considerations such as the foregoing one is led to the conclusion that theories which derive purely from the observation of qualitative aspects of behaviour, and are consequently no more than abstract accounts of that behaviour and/or associated psychological functioning, cannot be satisfactorily tested when the means of testing them depends on further

---

[6] Engelmann, S. E. 'Does the Piagetian approach imply instruction?' In Green, D. R., Ford, M. P. and Flamer, G. B. (Eds.): *Measurement and Piaget;* New York, McGraw-Hill.

[7] Piaget, J. (1971): 'The theory of stages in cognitive development'. In Green, D. R., Ford, M. P. and Flamer, G. B. (Eds.): *Measurement and Piaget;* New York, McGraw-Hill.

observation of qualitative variates. Beilin[8] appears to make the same point when he states, '... the empirical criterion of emergence (of developmental stages) is defined by qualitative differences in behaviour between two time periods... the empirical identification of qualitative differences alone will not provide an adequate basis for establishing that the qualitative differences are in fact emergents'.

A contrasting approach to the problem of psychological development is one in which the empirical work is directed exclusively towards quantitative variates. With this approach, discrimination of a series of stages can proceed only from numerical data. This presents the problem of designing experiments and organizing the data obtained such as to lead to the possible emergence of structures. These structures then become the means whereby stages are discriminated. Such experiments cannot be devised in the absence of an adequate theory for psychological development. Thus the initial problem with this approach is that of theory construction. To be judged adequate, the work must satisfy the following requirements:

1. The theory must comprise a system of structures relating to a sequence of developmental stages.

2. The system of structures must provide quantitative statements. The theory must also provide ideas suggesting the general form of experimental procedure. The experiments designed to test the quantitative statements provided by the theory must be such that the data obtained would be immediate, quantitative expressions of behaviour, such as, for example, the length of time required by a subject to complete a task, of which the commencement and completion are unambiguously specified and readily recognized. This would exclude the use of verbal reports, questionnaires, qualitative analysis of behaviour, etc.

3. To permit a demanding test of the theory, it must be sufficiently abstract for the experiments designed to test it to be in no way related to the sources of the theory. From this it follows that the theoretical work would be completed before experimental work commenced. Thus the confusions between

[8] Beilin, H. (1971): 'Developmental stages and developmental processes'. In Green, D. R., Ford, M. P. and Flamer, G. B. (Eds.): *Measurement and Piaget;* New York, McGraw-Hill.

theoretical and empirical work referred to above would be avoided.

4. For the theory to be judged of value, the distributions of the statistical data must provide structures which clearly conform to the structures comprising the theoretical system.

Theory Construction

GENERAL VIEWPOINT. The general viewpoint adopted in the present work is similar to that which has been expressed by Werner.[9] Speaking very generally, he states, 'This human process of becoming familiar with one's milieu is not simply a mirroring of an external prefabricated "reality", but it involves a formation of the world of objects by the human being in terms of his equipment and biopsychological "goals". The human world, then, cannot claim to reflect an independent "reality per se"; it is rather a coherent, man-specific umwelt, a representation of "what there is" by means available to the human being.'

This implies that the objects of a man's world are brought into being through creative acts. These objects include things, images, ideas, persons, etc. The totality of a man's objects constitutes his *umwelt*. The components of the *umwelt* are not to be seen as the consequences of free unconstrained creation. Assuming that man is born with immanent needs, the objects of the *umwelt* and the related self are seen as coming into being out of the satisfaction of these needs. These needs may be seen as comprising two aspects, the needed and the needing. In acting to satisfy these needs, that which is needed becomes the realized characteristics of the objects, and that which is needing becomes the realized self.

From this point of view, self and *umwelt* are inevitably mutually involved, and consequently psychological development can be seen only as the development of this interrelatedness. Development is regarded on the one hand as the continuous growth of the structure expressing this interrelatedness at one stage, and on the other hand, as the movement from

---

[9] Werner, H. (1967): 'The concept of development from a comparative and organismic point of view'. In Harris, D. B. (Ed.): *The concept of development;* Minneapolis, University of Minnesota Press.

one stage to the next, in which the general structure of the interrelatedness is transformed, the previous structures being still present and integrally basic to the new.

These ideas, while basic to the present work, are essentially pre-theoretical.

THEORY CONSTRUCTION. The aim of the theory which follows was to express these ideas in such a precise form that quantitative experimental work became possible. The initial problem became the devising of a dynamic element to be used in building up a series of structures relating to developmental stages such that the stages and the differences between them could be expressed quantitatively.

THE ELEMENT. The element is expressed abstractly in terms of 'poles' and 'relations' (association between the poles). Priority is given to the relation in that the poles emerge from it. This is in contrast to the view which gives priority to the poles, the relation emerging from them. Giving priority to the relation becomes necessary following the acceptance of the view stated earlier that the world of objects is formed by the human being in terms of his needs.

The formal statement of the element is:

> Relation discriminates pole;
> Discrimination of pole leads to discrimination of relation;
> Discriminated relation discriminates other pole;
> Discrimination of this pole further discriminates relation;
> and so on.

The continuously operating element constitutes an oscillation from pole to pole through the relation; the poles and relation become successively more clearly defined as operating proceeds. The term 'discriminate'[10] will be used to refer to this mode of operating. The two poles are in dynamic equilibrium. The degree of discrimination of one pole is dependent upon the degree of discrimination of the other. The mode of operating can reverse. Loss of discrimination of one pole leads to loss of discrimination of the relation and hence to loss of discrimination of the other pole. The process continues to disintegration

[10] Discriminate to set up and distinguish.

of poles and relation. The term 'confuse'[11] will be used to refer to this mode of operating.

Operating continuously, the element is always either discriminating or confusing. No static position is allowable. Any entities may be postulated as poles and any association as the relation. This unity is symbolized by

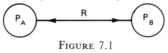

FIGURE 7.1

where P_A refers to the one pole, P_B refers to the other pole and R the relation.

USE OF ELEMENT TO ESTABLISH FIRST STRUCTURE OF SERIES. The element is now applied in the context of psychological development. Starting with the newly born baby, we imagine the initial state to be one of chaos, nothingness. For this baby there is no self and no object, but immanent needs are attributed to it. These needs are satisfied and not satisfied. With satisfaction of needs the element operates in the discriminating mode; discrimination of poles and relations begins.

Taking the situation of the hungry baby sucking at its mother's breast as a specific instance in which the element is initially applied, we imagine a unity of tastes, smells, and pleasant feelings being discriminated out of the initial chaos. With the element continuing to discriminate, 'self', 'need', and 'mother' gradually emerge. If 'need' is subsequently not satisfied, the element moves into the confusing mode of operation, and 'self', 'need' and 'mother' fade. With further successful sucking, the element moves again into the discriminating mode, 'self', 'need' and 'mother' re-emerging. With the element continuing to operate in this mode, 'self', 'need' and 'mother' become more and more clearly defined. 'Self', 'need' and 'mother' become increasingly differentiated, but always together within an interrelated unity. The unity is symbolized by

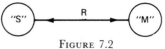

FIGURE 7.2

---

[11] Confuse: to throw into disorder.

where '*S*' refers to 'self', '*M*' refers to 'mother' and *R* refers to that activity necessary for need satisfaction.

With the use of this element, the picture which emerges is that of 'self' and 'mother' growing out of each other through the satisfying and dissatisfaction of needs.

In order that the *umwelt* should comprise a number of fundamental types of object, it is necessary at this stage of theory construction to introduce a resolution of the initial situation. The situation of baby and mother is resolved into baby acting on breast and baby reacting to the maternal matrix within which baby's action is embedded.

Applying this resolution to the unity above, the need is resolved into a need to maintain sensual contact with the breast and a need to maintain the matrix. Correspondingly, the 'self' is resolved into 'breast-self' and 'matrix-self', and 'mother' is resolved into breast and matrix. Out of action with it, the breast becomes eventually a thing. Out of reacting to it, the matrix eventually becomes a person, in the particular case, mother.

The resolved 'breast-self'/thing unity and 'matrix-self'/person unity is symbolized by:

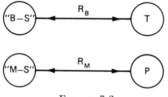

FIGURE 7.3

where R_B refers to actions necessary to maintain sensual contact with the thing, and R_M refers to the reactions of '*M-S*' necessary to secure the approval of *P* regarding the action of '*B-S*' with respect to the thing.

With the introduction of another element which relates '*M-S*' to *T*, the thing, *T* acquires personal characteristics. Similarly, with the introduction of a further element which relates '*B-S*' to *P*, the person, *P* acquires thinglike characteristics. Thus on the one hand, the original resolution permits the permanent establishment of two general types of object in the *umwelt*, thing, and person; on the other hand, with the introduction of two further elements, an object of one type acquires (in certain circumstances) the characteristics of the other type. The foregoing is summarized in the following diagram.

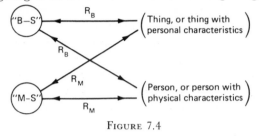

FIGURE 7.4

It will be noted that '*B-S*' is related to '*M-S*' only through an object in the *umwelt*.

The element, as designed, is such that it operates either in the discriminating mode or the confusing mode. In applying it, as above, it is seen that the self/*umwelt* unity must either develop or regress. With the element alone, movement in either direction is equally probable. In order to make development the more likely, it is necessary to attribute to the self-structure a drive which is directed towards maintaining the element in the discriminating mode. All discriminated needs can then be regarded as the overt expression of this drive to maintain the self-structure in being.

With the drive to maintain itself in being, the resolved self-structure acts through the operation of the associated elements in the discriminating mode to bring other objects into being. Through being related to many things, 'breast-self' becomes the more general 'thing-self', and through being related to many persons, 'matrix-self' becomes the more general 'person-self'.

The first self/*umwelt* unity of the series mentioned earlier can now be symbolized by

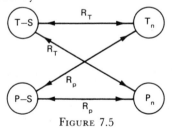

FIGURE 7.5

where, depending upon the elements operating, T_n refers to things or things with personal characteristics, and P_n refers to persons or persons with physical characteristics.

In what follows, we are concerned only with the essential structure constituting the above self/*umwelt* unity which is symbolized by

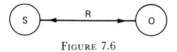

FIGURE 7.6

where S refers to the self-structure 'T-S' and 'P-S' related by objects O in the *umwelt*.

Finally, the general picture presented is that with the element discriminating, self and *umwelt* grow out of each other. The movement is to increasing order. With the element confusing, self and *umwelt* disintegrate. The movement is now to increasing disorder. Thus two types of experiment can be envisaged: the one involves movement to order, the other movement to disorder.

System of Levels of Extension of Structure and Associated Modes of Functioning

Commencing with the first self/*umwelt* unity above, a series of increasingly complex structures is built up to serve as the basis of a stage/level system for psychological development. Each of these structures expresses a discrete extension of the preceding structure. This discrete extension occurs through the introduction of one or more relations. With this discrete extension of structure a transformation of the self and the objects of the preceding structure takes place.

The structures are analysed to explicate the associated modes of functioning, which are expressed abstractly in terms of self-object interrelationships. From this analysis two modes of functioning are associated with the level 2 structure, three with level 3, four with level 4 and five with the level 5 structure.

Level 1 structure

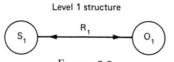

FIGURE 7.7

where S_1 refers to the level 1 self, and O_1 to the level 1 'objects'.

Each object-pole in the *umwelt* or object field is related directly to the self-pole. With only one relation in the structure, at level 1 there is only one basic mode of functioning.

Level 2 structure.

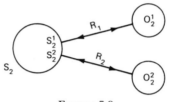

FIGURE 7.8

To the level 1 structure is added a more abstract self-pole S_2^2 and a correspondingly more abstract object-pole O_2^2, these being related by R_2. With this extension of structure, a transformation of the self and object of the preceding level takes place, S_1 transforming to S_2 and O_1 to O_2^1. O_2^1 is related to S_2^1 through R_1, this element being symbolized by

$$S_2^1 \xleftrightarrow{R_1} O_2^1.$$

This unity integrated, and symbolized by

$$\left(S_2^1 \xleftrightarrow{R_1} O_2^1 \right),$$

serves as a self-pole for the relation R_2 This self-pole is symbolized by S_2^2. Being of this form, S_2^2 is more abstract than S_2^1 and S_1 of the previous level. Thus the level 2 self, S_2, constitutes a composite structure of which S_2^1 and S_2^2 are the components. In the following, S_2^1 is referred to as the level 1 component of the level 2 self, S_2^2 as the level 2 component.

Modes of functioning. Accepting that either of the two components may operate, the level 2 self functions in either of two basically different ways. Either S_2^1 functions through R_1 in the satisfaction of its associated need, or S_2^2 functions through R_2 in the satisfaction of its associated need. The two modes of functioning are symbolized as follows:

1. S_2^1 operating: $S_2^1 \xleftrightarrow{R_1} O_2^1$

2. S_2^2 operating: $S_2^2 \xleftrightarrow{R_2} O_2^2$ or $\left(S_2^2 \xleftrightarrow{R_1} O_2^1\right) \xleftrightarrow{R_2} O_2^2$

since S_2^2 is the integrated unity

$$\left(S_2^1 \xleftrightarrow{R_1} O_2^1\right).$$

The first mode of functioning is similar to that of level 1, but not identical since a transformation of the self and objects has taken place. For simplicity, the first mode is symbolized by 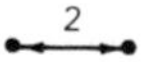 the second by

Level 3 structure

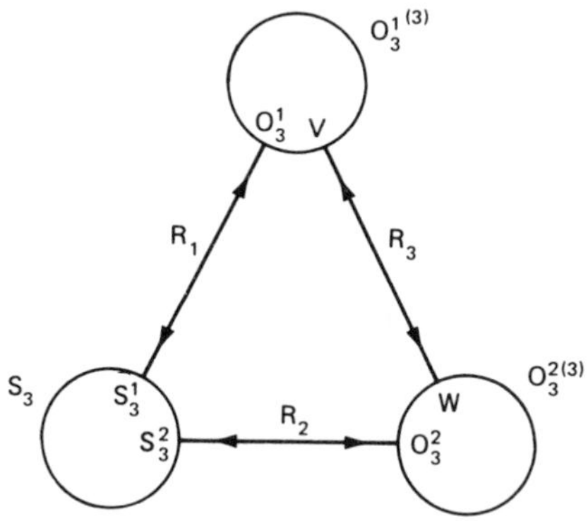

$$V \text{ is} \left(S_3^1 \xleftrightarrow{R_1} O_3^1\right)$$

$$W \text{ is} \left(S_3^2 \xleftrightarrow{R_2} O_3^2\right)$$

FIGURE 7.9

To each object of the level 2 structure is added a more abstract pole, these poles being related by R_3. With extension of structure, a transformation of the self and objects of the preceding level takes place, S_2 transforming to S_3, O_2^1 to $O_3^{1(3)}$, and O_2^2 to $O_3^{2(3)}$. $O_3^{1(3)}$ comprises the two poles O_3^1 and the integrated unity

$$\left(S_3^1 \xleftrightarrow{R_1} O_3^1\right);$$

$O_3^{2(3)}$ comprises the two poles O_3^2 and the integrated unity

$$\left(S_3^2 \xleftrightarrow{R_2} O_3^2\right).$$

S_3^1 is related to O_3^1 through R_1, symbolized by the unity $S_3^1 \xleftrightarrow{R_1} O_3^1$, which when integrated becomes

$$\left(S_3^1 \xleftrightarrow{R_1} O_3^1\right),$$

and serves as one of the more abstract poles for R_3. S_3^2 is related to O_3^2 through R_2, symbolized by the unity

$$S_3^2 \xleftrightarrow{R_2} O_3^2$$

which, when integrated, becomes

$$\left(S_3^2 \xleftrightarrow{R_2} O_3^2\right)$$

and serves as the other more abstract pole for R_3.

With the level 3 structure comprising three forms of the element, S_3 is composed of three components, S_3^1, S_3^2 and S_3^3, associated respectively with relations R_1, R_2 and R_3. Through R_3, S_3^3 is identified with

$$\left(S_3^1 \xleftrightarrow{R_1} O_3^1\right)$$

and

$$\left(S_3^2 \xleftrightarrow{R_2} O_3^2\right)$$

conjointly.

Modes of functioning. With the level 3 self comprising 3 components, any one of three different ways of functioning can operate in the satisfaction of the three associated needs. These three basically different ways are symbolized by R_1, R_2 and R_3. The modes of functioning are as follows:

1. S_3^1 operating: $S_3^1 \xleftrightarrow{R_1} O_3^1$

2. S_3^2 operating: $\left(S_3^1 \xleftrightarrow{R_1} O_3^1\right) \xleftrightarrow{R_2} O_3^2$

3. S_3^3 operating: $\left(S_3^1 \xleftrightarrow{R_1} O_3^1\right) \xleftrightarrow{R_3} \left(S_3^2 \xleftrightarrow{R_2} O_3^2\right)$

The first two modes of functioning are similar to those of level

2, but not identical since a transformation of the self and objects of level 2 has taken place.

For simplicity, the first mode is symbolized by •——³—• the second by $\overset{\bullet}{\diagdown}_3$. and the third by $\triangle_3$.

Level 4 Structure

The diagram is seen as a tetrahedron:

X is the integrated unity $\left(S_4^1 \overset{R_1}{\longleftrightarrow} O_4^1\right)$

Y is the integrated unity $\left(S_4^2 \overset{R_2^A}{\longleftrightarrow} O_4^{2A}\right)$

Z is the integrated unity $\left(S_4^2 \overset{R_2^B}{\longleftrightarrow} O_4^{2B}\right)$

O_4^{4A} is the integrated unity

$$\left[\left(S_4^1 \overset{R_1}{\longleftrightarrow} O_4^1\right) \overset{R_3^A}{\longleftrightarrow} \left(S_4^2 \overset{R_2^A}{\longleftrightarrow} O_4^{2A}\right)\right]$$

O_4^{4B} is the integrated unity

$$\left[\left(S_4^1 \overset{R_1}{\longleftrightarrow} O_4^1\right) \overset{R_3^B}{\longleftrightarrow} \left(S_4^2 \overset{R_2^B}{\longleftrightarrow} O_4^{2B}\right)\right]$$

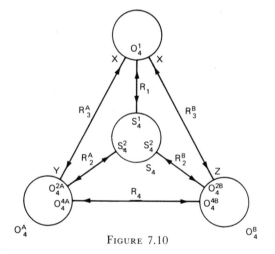

FIGURE 7.10

With the extension of structure, a transformation of self and objects takes place, S_3 transforming to S_4, $O_3^{1(3)}$ to O_4, and $O_3^{2(3)}$ transforming into two objects O_4^A and O_4^B. To each of these is added a third more abstract pole, these poles being related by

R_4. Thus O_4^A and O_4^B each comprise three poles. For O_4^A, the first of these poles is O_4^{2A}, related through R_2^A to S_4^2, symbolized by the unity $S_4^2 \xleftrightarrow{R_2^A} O_4^{2A}$,

which when integrated becomes $\left(S_4^2 \xleftrightarrow{R_2^A} O_4^{2A} \right)$.

This is the second pole of O_4^A, labelled Y in the diagram, and which is related through R_3^A to the pole $\left(S_4^1 \xleftrightarrow{R_1} O_4^1 \right)$

of O_4. This element is symbolized by the unity

$$\left(S_4^1 \xleftrightarrow{R_1} O_4^1 \right) \xleftrightarrow{R_3^A} \left(S_4^2 \xleftrightarrow{R_2^A} O_4^{2A} \right).$$

which when integrated becomes

$$\left[\left(S_4^1 \xleftrightarrow{R_1} O_4^1 \right) \xleftrightarrow{R_3^A} \left(S_4^2 \xleftrightarrow{R_2^A} O_4^{2A} \right) \right]$$

This is O_4^{4A} in the diagram, the third more abstract pole of O_4^A, which serves as one of the poles of R_4.

Similarly, the integrated unity

$$\left[\left(S_4^1 \xleftrightarrow{R_1} O_4^1 \right) \xleftrightarrow{R_3^B} \left(S_4^2 \xleftrightarrow{R_2^B} O_4^{2B} \right) \right]$$

which is O_4^{4B} in the diagram, is the third more abstract pole of O_4^B, and serves as the other pole of R_4.

With the level 4 structure comprising four kinds of element, S_4 is composed of four components, S_4^1, S_4^2, S_4^3 and S_4^4, associated respectively with relations R_1, R_2, R_3 and R_4.

Modes of functioning. With one of four components operating, the level 4 self functions in any one of four basically different ways:

1. S_4^1 operating: $\qquad\qquad\qquad\qquad S_4^1 \xleftrightarrow{R_1} O_4^1$

2. S_4^2 operating: $\qquad\qquad \left(S_4^1 \xleftrightarrow{R_1} O_4^1 \right) \xleftrightarrow{R_2} O_4^2$

3. S_4^3 operating: $\quad \left(S_4^1 \xleftrightarrow{R_1} O_4^1 \right) \xleftrightarrow{R_3} \left(S_4^2 \xleftrightarrow{R_2} O_4^2 \right)$

4. S_4^4 operating:

$$\left[\left(S_4^1 \xleftrightarrow{R_1} O_4^1 \right) \xleftrightarrow{R_3^A} \left(S_4^2 \xleftrightarrow{R_2^A} O_4^{2A} \right) \right] \xleftrightarrow{R_4}$$

$$\left[\left(S_4^1 \xleftrightarrow{R_1} O_4^1 \right) \xleftrightarrow{R_3^B} \left(S_4^2 \xleftrightarrow{R_2^B} O_4^{2B} \right) \right]$$

The first three modes of functioning are similar to those of level 3, but not identical, since a transformation of self and object has taken place.

For simplicity, the first mode is symbolised by ●—→● , the second by △₄ , the third by △₄ , and the fourth by △₄ .

Level 5 Structure

This is composed of an indefinite number of tetrahedra joined to one another through shared faces and all sharing a common apex. With a sufficiently large number of tetrahedra, the outer surface corresponds to the surface of a polyhedron, the common apex lying at the centre, and all triangles on the surface being identical. The diagram illustrates four such joined tetrahedra, the self lying at the common apex. It is impossible to illustrate more without confusion.

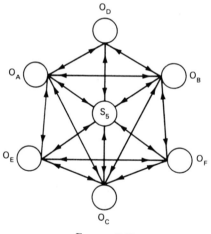

FIGURE 7.11

With extension of structure, a transformation of the self and objects of the preceding level takes place, S_4 transforming to S_5, and level 4 objects transforming to a multiplicity of level 5 objects. With the conjoining of the multiplicity of tetrahedra, all objects become equally abstract, being constituted of the same number and type of poles. These objects are more abstract than those of the preceding level through the addition of a more abstract pole and corresponding relation R_5. This, in principle, permits the relating through R_5 of any object with any other object. As in the preceding levels, S_5 has a composite structure. This comprises five components, S_1, S_2, S_3, S_4 and S_5, corresponding respectively to the relations R_1, R_2, R_3, R_4 and R_5.

Modes of functioning. Referring to the general structure, all objects and associated relations lie on the surface, S_5 being at the centre. To specify the basic modes of functioning requires consideration of only two joined tetrahedra. This involves four objects, referred to as O_A, O_B, O_C and O_D in the diagram, which illustrates the two corresponding triangles in the surface.

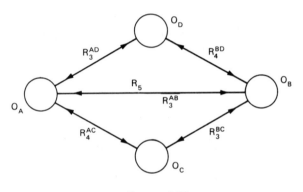

FIGURE 7.12

The line joining the objects O_A and O_B signifies two relations: R_5, relating the level 5 poles of O_A and O_B in terms of the joined tetrahedra, and R_3^{AB}, relating the level 3 poles of O_A and O_B in terms of the tetrahedra taken separately for the purpose of stating the less abstract modes of functioning.

The five modes of functioning are as follows:

1. S_5^1 operating: $S_5^1 \xleftrightarrow{R_1} O_5^1$

2. S_5^2 operating: $\left(S_5^1 \xleftrightarrow{R_1} O_5^1 \right) \xrightarrow{R_2} O_5^2$

3. S_5^3 operating: $\left(S_5^1 \xleftrightarrow{R_1} O_5^1 \right) \xleftrightarrow{R_3} \left(S_5^2 \xleftrightarrow{R_2} O_5^2 \right)$

4. S_5^4 operating:

$$\left[\left(S_5^1 \xleftrightarrow{R_1} O_5^{1A}\right) \xleftrightarrow{R_3^{AB}} \left(S_5^2 \xleftrightarrow{R_2} O_5^{2B}\right)\right] \xrightarrow{R_4^{BD}}$$
$$\left[\left(S_5^1 \xleftrightarrow{R_1} O_5^{1A}\right) \xrightarrow{R_3^{AD}} \left(S_5^2 \xleftrightarrow{R_2} O_5^{2D}\right)\right]$$

5. S_5^5 operating: $M \xleftrightarrow{R_5} N$ where M is

$$\left\{\left[\left(S_5^1 \xleftrightarrow{R_1} O_5^{1A}\right) \xleftrightarrow{R_3^{AB}} \left(S_5^2 \xleftrightarrow{R_2} O_5^{2B}\right)\right] \xrightarrow{R_4^{BD}}\right.$$
$$\left.\left[\left(S_5^1 \xleftrightarrow{R_1} O_5^{1A}\right) \xrightarrow{R_3^{AD}} \left(S_5^2 \xleftrightarrow{R_2} O_5^{2D}\right)\right]\right\}$$

and N is

$$\left\{\left[\left(S_5^1 \xleftrightarrow{R_1} O_5^{1B}\right) \xleftrightarrow{R_3^{AB}} \left(S_5^2 \xleftrightarrow{R_2} O_5^{2A}\right)\right] \xrightarrow{R_4^{AC}}\right.$$
$$\left.\left[\left(S_5^1 \xleftrightarrow{R_1} O_5^{1B}\right) \xrightarrow{R_3^{CB}} \left(S_5^2 \xleftrightarrow{R_2} O_5^{2C}\right)\right]\right\}$$

For simplicity, the first mode is symbolized by $\overset{5}{\bullet\!\!-\!\!\!-\!\!\bullet}$, the second by $\triangle_5$, the third by $\triangle_5$, the fourth by $\triangle^5$ and the fifth by ⬡.

General Comments

The above analysis derived from a series of levels of extension of structure, each structure incorporating the preceding structure. The analysis of these structures gave rise to expressions for the modes of functioning for each level. From an examination of the expressions for a particular level, it will be seen that the most abstract mode of functioning incorporates the less abstract modes of functioning. Further, if the expressions for the modes of functioning of two successive levels are compared, it will be seen that the most abstract mode of the higher level incorporates, with transformation of self and objects, the modes of functioning of the lower level. Thus, with respect to modes of functioning, the whole system may be regarded as a complex expression of the well-known idea of 'levels of abstraction'.

The purpose of the foregoing was to provide a basis for a stage/level system for psychological development. Figure 7.13 illustrates the 15 modes of functioning corresponding to the 15 components of the five levels, and may be seen as providing a scheme for psychological development.

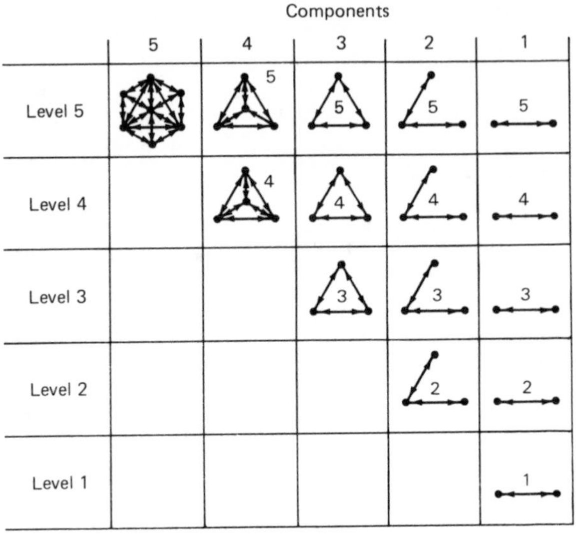

Components

	5	4	3	2	1
Level 5	⬡	△5	△5	∠5	5 •—•
Level 4		△4	△4	∠4	4 •—•
Level 3			△3	∠3	3 •—•
Level 2				∠2	2 •—•
Level 1					1 •—•

FIGURE 7.13. Diagram illustrating theoretical systems of modes of functioning associated with the five levels

Experimental Work

The 15 modes of psychological functioning stated in the theory above refer to 15 essential modes of interaction between self and object field. The experimental work designed to test the theory was initiated on the assumption that these 15 modes of interaction would be manifested in 15 basic modes of behaving, namely, five modes associated with an individual who had reached level 5, four with an individual who had reached level 4, three with level 3, two with level 2 and one with level 1. These definite quantitative statements led to the possibility of the whole theory being subjected to rigorous quantitative testing.

The experimental work in the first instance was designed to test the proposition regarding number sequence above. Secondly, the experimental work was directed towards relating the sequence of numbers obtained to the chronological age of subjects. With these aims realized, the scheme for psychological development put forward above would be substantiated.

Earlier it was stated that two general types of experiment could be envisaged, the one involving movement from order to disorder, and the other movement from disorder to order. Problem-solving can be regarded as representative of the former, loss of skill as representative of the latter. The theoretical work was completed in 1962, and since then a number of experiments of the above two general types have been carried out. These are described in the two papers mentioned earlier (Isaac and O'Connor, Chapters 4 and 5). The results of the experimental work are now given.

PROBLEM-SOLVING EXPERIMENTS. From the above it would be expected that if a number of subjects who had developed to level 5 were confronted with a suitable problem, five basically different modes of behaving could operate in the solution of the problem. Four, three and two modes would operate with subjects who had reached levels 4, 3 and 2, respectively, when confronted with problems suitable to the particular level. The purpose of the experimental work was to discriminate these different modes and relate them.

Assuming the measure of a subject's performance in a problem-solving situation is dependent upon the basic mode of functioning employed, it would be expected that the scores obtained from a large number of subjects solving the problem would be grouped in clusters, five clusters for level 5, four for level 4, three for level 3 and two for level 2. Expressing these scores in a frequency distribution would give rise to multi-modal distributions. Such multi-modal distributions would provide the means of discriminating the basic modes of functioning.

Three experiments were conducted with subjects aged 17 to 21 years. Each experiment gave rise to a multi-modal distribution containing four modes. Although the problems were dissimilar, the structures of the distributions were almost identical. From this it was clear that the structure of the distributions was related to the subjects solving the problems, but independent of the structure of the particular problems.

The problems giving rise to the four-mode distributions with subjects aged 17 to 21 years could not be used with subjects under 17 years; very few could solve them. A simpler problem was designed and used with subjects aged 12 to 17 years. A three-mode distribution was obtained. The three modes fitted the least efficient three modes of the four-mode distributions. This problem could not be used with subjects aged 6 to 12 years. Two simpler problems were designed and used with subjects aged 6 to 12 years. Two two-mode distributions were obtained. These two modes fitted the least efficient two modes of the other distributions. These problems could not be used with subjects under 6 years. No attempt was made to design a problem to work with subjects under 6 years of age, since a uni-modal distribution would be expected and so experimental work would be pointless. Incidentally, it was found that when the problem which gave rise to a three-mode histogram was presented to the older subjects who had solved the problem giving rise to a four-mode histogram, they solved it with ease, the distribution of scores being right skewed. The results of the experiments are illustrated in Figure 7.14. For completeness, the expected distributions for levels 5 and 1 are also included.

Considering the histograms in relation to the age of subjects whose scores make up the histograms, a direct correspondence appears between the numerical order of the histograms (2, 3, 4) and the rank order of age ranges (6–11 years, 12–16 years, 17–22 years). This feature, together with the fact that subjects within an age range generally cannot solve the problems associated with the higher age range, but can solve those associated with a lower age range, permits the series of histograms to be seen as indicating discrete stages of psychological development.

Considering the performance of particular individuals in these experiments, it was found that where an individual solved more than one of the problems corresponding to a particular level, there was no consistency regarding the mode in which the scores fell. For one problem the subject might provide a score corresponding to one mode, for another, a score corresponding to a different mode. Thus, while the histograms are stable with respect to populations, the scores provided by individuals are unstable.

LOSS-OF-SKILL EXPERIMENTS. With increase in the rate of change of the object field, a rate of change must be reached at which the self is no longer able to maintain order. In the performance of a skill which is made dependent on a changing object field, maintaining the skill would depend on maintaining the order associated with the changing field. Therefore, if the rate of change of the field was increased to a point of breakdown of order, this would manifest itself in loss of skill. Thus loss of skill could provide an indication of the maximum rate of change of field at which order can be maintained. In comparing individuals who had developed to different levels, it would be expected that the more organized higher-level individuals could maintain order at greater rates of change than could the lower. It would thus be expected that the distribution of measures of the maximum rate of change which could be tolerated without loss of skill provided by a large number of subjects from an age range corresponding to two successive levels would reflect the differing organizational complexities of the two levels; that is, it would be bimodal. Three experiments to test this proposition have been carried out.

The first experiment used subjects age range 11 to 23 years. The results of the problem-solving experiments indicated that this age range would include level 3 and level 4 subjects. A bimodal distribution was obtained. The skill used in this experiment could not be used with subjects below the age of 11 years. Too few could learn it. A simpler skill was designed and used with subjects age range 7 to 15 years, corresponding to levels 2 and 3. A bimodal distribution was obtained. A third experiment has been carried out using a more complex skill with subjects age range 17 to 26 years. A bimodal distribution was obtained. It is believed that this distribution relates to levels 4 and 5. The bimodal distributions obtained for levels 2 and 3, 3 and 4, and 4 and 5, together with the expected bimodal distributions for levels 1 and 2, are illustrated in Figure 7.14.

Conclusion

Comparing the general structure of the series of histograms with that of the theoretical system, it can be seen that they are identical, and thus the modes of the histograms can be directly associated with the corresponding components of the theoretical system. To complete testing the system, it is necessary to carry out further problem-solving experiments aimed at obtaining the five-mode histogram anticipated for level 5, and a loss-of-skill experiment relating levels 1 and 2.

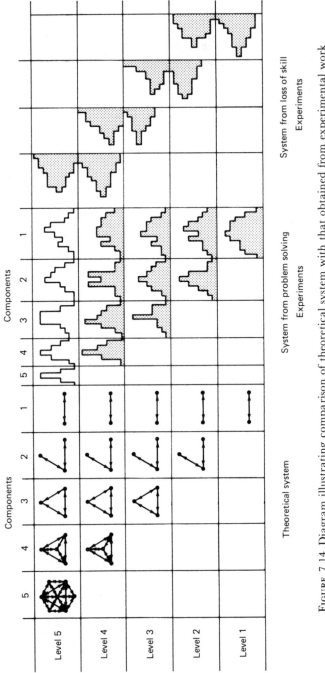

FIGURE 7.14 Diagram illustrating comparison of theoretical system with that obtained from experimental work

The fact that a problem may be solved by any component of a level but not by any of the components of a lower level is the expression, in the experimental work, of the theoretical idea of transformation of self and objects with extension of structure.

The general scheme for psychological development which emerges from the theoretical and experimental work is as follows. For the approximate age range 0–5 years, one component is present. Between approximately 5 and 11 years a second component emerges, with a corresponding transformation of the other component, after which both components develop continuously. Between approximately 12 and 16 years a third component emerges, with a corresponding transformation of the other two components, after which the three components are present. In that any one stage subsumes the lower, and comprises one more component, the scheme refers to an ascending order of organizational complexity.

Regarding the application of the theory in assessing an individual's stage of development, the work has not yet proceeded sufficiently to permit reliable statements to be made of individuals. This is because the problems used were designed to be very general, in order to ensure that subjects had no previous experience of the type of problems presented. It was considered that only such problems would permit any one of the possible components to function. The instability of an individual's scores, referred to earlier, is believed to be the consequence of the general nature of the problems used.

If, on the other hand, a number of problems confined to a particular area in which subjects had experience were used, it is conceivable that the scores provided by individuals would be consistent – consistent in the sense that the scores of an individual would fall into the same mode for each problem. This is to suggest that in a particular area the same component consistently operates. Working with problems from a variety of areas would enable an individual's characteristic modes of functioning in these different areas to be determined.

Since the theory did not originate from systematic observation of behaviour, and since the experiments were designed strictly for the purpose of obtaining measures of quantitative variates, it is not possible at this stage to give a descriptive account of the 15 modes of functioning. The theory having been substantiated, it now becomes reasonable to design experiments aimed at characterizing the modes of functioning in terms of described behaviour. Thus, whereas the psychologist usually proceeds from observation of behaviour to theory, the present work is peculiar in that it proceeds from theory to experimental measures and ultimately to descriptive accounts of behaviour.

Part C

Conversion to System of Truth Tables

8

Conversion from the Relational to the Contrast System

R. O. Gibson and D. J. Isaac

Initially it is necessary to examine in detail the distinction made in the introduction between the basic viewpoints of the two systems, viz. in the original system entities, defined by general conditions underlying their contexts, acquire meaning only in the contexts; whereas in the new system behavioural entities, defined by normative distinctions, are expressed as interpretations of systems. In the very examination of this distinction the two systems are linked.

The diagram below illustrates the movement from system to system.

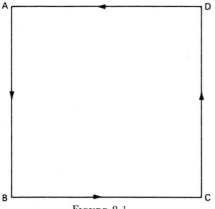

FIGURE 8.1

An undefined term *A* is brought into being by a condition *B* which in doing so defines it. *B* refers to the elemental relations used in the relational structure. Through the conditions underlying the context in which the defined term is used *A* acquires meaning in undefined action *C*. This context refers to the relational structure associated with the first stage of psychological development. Thus B underlies C in the sense that C emerges from further conditions upon B. These are the general premises upon which the relational system is based.

The undefined action becomes a significant act in the satisfying of some need, i.e. undefined action becomes definite only in an actual normative distinction, D. The possibility of a normative distinction emerging rests upon the initial undefined term's having become defined. In this sense the normative distinction overlies the undefined term A. With no normative distinction emerging the hitherto defined term loses definition. These are the general premises upon which the contrast system is based.

In the conversion, with the defining role of D, i.e. the imposing of normative distinction on C, there is a switch in the role of C. As a consequence of the imposition, on C, of normative distinction, the role of C is now not the relating but the distinguishing of entities. The possibility of this switch in the role of C is grounded in the inseparability of 'object for an individual' from 'the individual as a member of society'. In the previous chapter the passage 'Correspondingly, the "self" is resolved into "breast-self" and "matrix-self"; and "mother" is resolved into breast and matrix. Out of action with it the breast eventually becomes a thing. Out of reacting to it the matrix eventually becomes a person, in the particular case, "mother"' led to the formulation of the relational structure associated with the first stage of psychological development. The change of role of C refers to the change of view of the relational structure necessary for the conversion, a change illustrated diagrammatically later.

With the imposition of the new form of C upon B, B which formerly was only the condition defining A now becomes a behavioural system. A, which acquired meaning through C in its first role, now through the second role of C, determined by D, becomes an interpretation of the behavioural system B.

The switch in the role of C linking together the relational and contract systems is intimately bound up with the distinction between (a) analysis of the structure of the relational system as stated in the previous chapter and (b) analysis of the movement from structure to structure. The detailed treatment of (a)

and (*b*) is the conversion from the relational theory to the use of truth tables.

Figure 8.2, reproduced from the previous chapter, illustrates the structure of the relational theory.

The horizontal aspect depicts the structures themselves, the meaning of the poles at any one level of extension of context remains invariant in the transformation associated with a level of abstraction.

The vertical aspect depicts the succession of structures, the extension of which metamorphoses the poles to give successive interpretations of systems (referred to in the previous chapter as transformation of entity with extension of context).

The change of aspect from the horizontal to the vertical reflects the switch in the role of *C* in the above analysis.

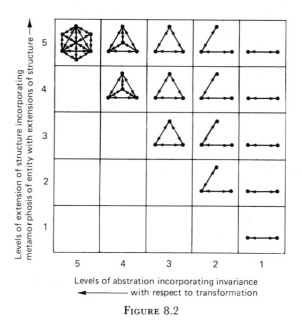

Levels of abstration incorporating invariance
◄――――― with respect to transformation

FIGURE 8.2

Detailed Treatment of (*a*) *and* (*b*)
Considering the horizontal aspect:

I. POSITING OF UNDEFINED TERMS. A pole at (1) is posited by a relation. A new pole at (2) is posited by a second relation upon the first. This new pole may be regarded as posited by the characteristic (of pole *qua* pole) that two new poles are together equivalent to one new pole (*see* 'integrated unity', Ch. 7 cit.). The characteristic of the level (3) pole has the same form as that of level (2) but is essentially relative to the level (2) pole and so on. (*See* 'Through R_3, S_3^3 is identified with

$$\left(S_3^1 \xleftarrow{R_1} O_3^1\right)$$

and

$$\left(S_3^2 \xleftarrow{R_2} O_3^2\right)$$

conjointly.', loc. cit.).

II. INVARIANCE WITH RESPECT TO TRANSFORMATION. A pole at (1) as posited by a relation is invariant with respect to transformation, i.e. it is preserved in a positing by a new relation at (2) Similarly the pole (•——•) of level (2) is an invariant with respect to transformation from (2) to (3) and so on (*see* modes of functioning, loc. cit.).

Considering the vertical aspect:

III. TRANSITION FROM LEVEL TO LEVEL. Here it is important to distinguish the difference between the *steps* from level to level, i.e. the *acts* of imposition of successive conditions, illustrated in the vertical aspect of the diagram, from the conditions of characterizing the successive levels, a condition being regarded as *at* a level, illustrated in the horizontal aspect of the diagram.

In the transition from level to level, a pole having been posited by the level (1) relation •——• . this relation then becomes a structure in its incorporation in the level (2) relation

∠—• . Thus, in the movement, the posited pole posits the level (2) relation ∠—• in that it permits the very incorporating of the level (1) structure •——• in the level (2) relation ∠—•

Considering the terms 'relation' and 'structure', 'structure' includes 'pole' and/or 'relation' and in the movement from level to level the structure at the one level becomes the pole in positing the relation at the next level; this relation in turn posits the structure *at* this next level. This alternation expresses the switching in the role of *C* referred to earlier. In the same way, in the movement from (2) to (3) the level (1) structure ●—● becomes a pole positing the level (3) relation △ in that it permits the incorporation in the level (3) relation △ of the level (2) structure ∠

The level (2) relation in that it involves a pole which has already been posited may be said to denote − *T*, whereas the level (1) relation in that it only posits does not − *F*. In this denoting or not by a relation, *T* and *F* are completely independent. *See* rudimentary truth tables and the remark that *F* and *T* do not yet refer to contrasting behavioural entities (Chapter 9).

IV. INTERPRETATIONS OF SYSTEMS. In the incorporation of the level (1) relation ●—● in the level (2) relation ∠ the former is actually subjected to a condition. Under this subjection the level (1) relation becomes organized as a system. Since this condition is posited by the pole posited by the level (1) relation, this pole ●— is an interpretation, I_1, of the level (1) system ●—●. Similarly, in that △ is posited by a pole of ∠ , this pole (●—●) is an interpretation, I_2 of the system ∠ . Moreover, as this pole involves the pole ●—, interpretation I_1, there is duality in the interpretation I_2. Interpretation I_1 lies within interpretation I_2. This duality is the source of the explicit duality of the truth tables for 'or' and 'and' brought out later.

Pole Unity and Pole Multiplicity
The concepts 'pole unity' and 'pole multiplicity' are inherent in the concept of a pole of a relation as used in the modes of functioning of the previous paper. Considering the original element

$$P_A \xleftarrow{\quad R \quad} P_B,$$

P_A and P_B are the same as poles *qua* pole. Similarly, in

$$P_B \xleftrightarrow{R} P_C,$$

P_B and P_C are the same as poles *qua* pole. This sameness as poles can be regarded as expressing pole unity, each pole being a unit pole.

In $\qquad P_A \xleftrightarrow{R} P_B \xleftrightarrow{R} P_C,$

P_A, P_B and P_C are the same as poles and this pole repetition can be continued indefinitely. This pole repetition can be regarded as expressing pole multiplicity, any multiple pole forming a unity. Thus

$$(P_A \xleftrightarrow{\hspace{1cm}} P_B)$$

may be regarded as a double pole, and

$$(P_A \xleftrightarrow{R} P_B \xleftrightarrow{R} P_C)$$

as a triple pole.

In their sameness as poles *qua* pole, P_A, P_B, P_C etc., cannot denote. In the above, emphasis has been placed on the sameness of P_A, P_B, P_C etc., as poles, yet, if

$$P_A \xleftrightarrow{R} P_B, \; P_B \xleftrightarrow{R} P_C$$

are not to express mere trivialities P_A, P_B, and P_C must be different. Out of this difference between P_A, P_B, P_C, etc., when involved in multiple poles, multiple poles denote.

Returning to IV where poles are treated as interpretations of systems, from the above it will be seen that the unit pole $\bullet\!\!-\!\!-$, interpretation I_1, cannot denote and consequently is associated with F; the double pole ($\bullet\!\!-\!\!-\!\!-\!\!\bullet$), interpretation I_2, denotes and is associated with T. Thus since I_1 lies within I_2, F now underlies T. They are now mutually involved as in the truth tables for 'or' etc. Thus while F and T are independent when considering successive positing relations, they are not so when considering successive interpretations.

Pole and its Transformation by Relations treated as Alternatives to arrive at Negation and Assignment
The imposition of the level (2) relation is itself posited by the pole of the level (1) relation. This pole, as posited by the level

(1) relation, is an absolute invariant in that it remains fixed during the step of imposing the level (2) relation. The imposition of the level (3) relation is itself posited by the pole of the level (2) relation. In that one relation is imposed upon another the level (2) pole is not an absolute but a relative invariant; i.e. we now have an invariance which is relative to the previous invariance seen as absolute.

The imposition of the level (4) relation is itself posited by the pole of the level (3) positing relation.

In that a further relation is imposed upon the first two, the level (3) pole is a relative, relative, invariant. We now have a relative, relative, invariance, one which is connected with the distinction between absolute and relative invariance, i.e. brings together the absolute and relative invariances as mutually exclusive. Since these invariances are associated with poles as posited by relations and so correspond to the successive positing relations (1) and (2), not both terms in this mutual exclusion denote (*see* iii), briefly 'not both *T*' (or 'not both *F*'). Thus the terms are marked off from each other in the way in which *T* and *F* are marked off in the table for negation.

The imposition of the level (5) relation is posited by the pole of the level (4) positing relation. Now we have a set of three relative invariants with respect to successive transformations, i.e. relative, relative, relative invariance. The third *relative* invariance is posited by the other two relative invariances, i.e. 'pole posits relation', although formally the transformations associated with the imposition of the level (5) positing relation is still 'relation posits pole'.

Throughout the whole movement the emphasis has been upon 'relation posits pole' yet in the element pole also posits relation. Thus the consistent development of one aspect of the element forces the return of the other. No further development is possible of 'relation posits pole' and so the alternatives, 'not both *T*' or 'not both *F*', referred to after the imposition of the level (4) relation, are also exhaustive; this is the way in which assignment is defined.

It should be noted that with the return of the 'other', pole-positing relation, there is the admission of value and hence psychological meaning, as indicated earlier in the section headed 'Change of view of relational structure'.

Movement to Truth Tables

As shown above single pole and double pole are fundamental
to the duality in the interpretation of the system corresponding to the level (2) positing relation. Two analyses of the
duality are possible, the one concerned with maintenance of
pole *qua* pole, i.e. pole unity, within the new posited pole; the
other is concerned with the maintenance of pole multiplicity
within the new relation, i.e. the incorporation of the original
relation in a new one. With respect to the first analysis the
essential function of the level (2) pole, as NEW pole is the
keeping of pole unity, in which at least one pole has to be
taken as single pole. Thus the 'equivalent to' of *I* becomes,
stating all the alternatives implied in 'at least', the following
conditions (*a*), (*b*), (*c*) and (*d*) taken together as necessary and
sufficient.

(*a*) Two double poles equivalent to one double pole.
(*b*) One double and one single pole equivalent to a single
pole.
(*c*) One single and one double pole equivalent to a single
pole.
(*d*) Two single poles equivalent to one single pole.

Comparing (*a*), (*b*), (*c*) and (*d*) with the rows of truth table
for ∧ and remembering that double pole and single pole are
associated with *T* and *F* (*F* and *T* no longer independent),
this analysis of the duality is formally characterized by the
truth table for ∧.

With respect to the second analysis the essential function of
the level (2) positing relation as NEW relation is the carrying
on of pole multiplicity, for which at least one pole has to be
taken as double pole. Thus the 'equivalent to' of *I* becomes,
stating all the alternatives implied in 'at least', the following
conditions (*a*), (*b*), (*c*) and (*d*) taken together as necessary and
sufficient.

(*a*) Two double poles equivalent to one double pole.
(*b*) One double pole and one single pole equivalent to a
double pole.
(*c*) One single and one double pole equivalent to a double
pole.
(*d*) Two single poles equivalent to one single pole.

So this analysis is formally characterized by the truth table for $\vee$.

The truth tables for $\rightarrow$ and $\leftrightarrow$ can be reduced to those for $\sim$, $\vee$ and $\wedge$. Also it is shown in the section on 'dualities of tables and modes of functioning' in Chapter 9 that the tables for $\rightarrow$ and $\leftrightarrow$ express the duality of the tables for $\vee$ and $\wedge$. The tables for negation, assignment, $\vee$ and $\wedge$ having been dealt with, we regard the truth tables for $\rightarrow$ and $\leftrightarrow$ as formally expressing two further analyses of duality in interpretation.

The successive metamorphoses of entity with extensions of content are equivalent to the successive interpretations of systems. These interpretations are constituted by a succession of dualities originating in '*F* underlies *T*' (*see* section on dualities and modes of functioning – Chapter 9).

9

Truth Tables as a Formal Device in the Analysis of Human Actions

R. O. Gibson and D. J. Isaac

Abstract

This chapter provides a systematic qualitative version of a quantitative theory put forward in Chapter 7, 'A Discontinuity Theory of Psychological Development'. In this theory a series of structures, based upon an elemental relation with four conditions obtaining in its operation, was designed such that the associated experimental work relied on quantitative variates of behaviour to discriminate stages of psychological development. The series consisted of five structures with which were associated five stages of psychological development. Analysis of the structures suggested fifteen fundamentally different modes of functioning related to each other hierarchically. However, the modes of functioning are expressed so abstractly that direct interpretation in terms of human experience is not possible. In this paper, using the four conditions appertaining to the operation of the elemental relation, a conversion is made from the hierarchical relational structure to a hierarchy expressed in the logical symbolism of the statement or sentential calculus. For the general purpose truth tables of this calculus are organized into a certain hierarchy of five 'levels'. The dualities inherent at each level are traced. Fifteen dualities emerge, again organized hierarchically, the form of the organization corresponding to that of the fifteen modes of functioning; and each duality is similar in form to the corresponding mode of functioning. The dualities are seen as expressing abstractly the conflicts of decision-making, the truth tables being a formal device organized for elucidating the complexities of decision-making. Finally the hierarchy of dualities is characterized in conventional psychological terms.

Introduction

A theory of psychological development which has been successfully tested by experiment has been published (Isaac and O'Connor, Chapter 7). This theory is composed of successively extended relational structures, the entities involved having meaning only through their functioning as poles in the relations. Relations posit poles in the sense of bringing them into being. This is the fundamental concept of Chapter 7, the understanding of which is essential to following the argument of this chapter. Thus the general characteristic of the theory is that entities are given *meanings* only by their contexts, that is in their use. But it is to be noted that the entities, as such, acquire meaning only if they have already acquired *definition*. They are defined only through their satisfying general conditions underlying their contexts; that is undefined terms are defined by the way in which they are used, meanings being acquired from the use to which they are put. The distinction between 'way' and use is the distinction between conditions underlying the context and the context itself. Otherwise stated the distinction is between the contraction of meaning (through 'way') and expansion of meaning (through 'use').

The general form of the theory is such that it could be tested by experimental work involving only quantitative data such as number of buttons pressed or number of cards laid down by a subject seeking to realize a goal. Furthermore these data could be organized using only direct quantitative analysis (Isaac and O'Connor, Chapters 4 and 5). This form of theory and experiment is generally similar to that of modern work in the physical sciences. The published work thus appears 'scientific' and rigorous; the experimental data are 'hard', the theory does not arise immediately from and is not dependent upon qualitative observations. Nevertheless it is to be noted that the *form* of the work is akin only to that of physical science, since the only acts counted are those which appear to the observer to be relevant to the subjects' intentions. Thus the observer is always inevitably involved in the situation.

In the following 'behaviour' is not used to refer merely to bodily actions, but to refer to responses to situations as interpretations of actual systems.[1] In proceeding to the completely

[1] We are not concerned with 'behaviour' in the sense of an observable

operational it follows that rigour has been achieved at the expense of psychological meaning. The bodily actions counted by the observer in an experiment are meaningful to the subject since he judges them with respect to a desired goal. To the observer, concerned only with the total number of buttons pressed or cards laid down, and apparently ignoring the fact that he is related to the subject through the objects of action, all individual acts and series of acts are psychologically meaningless. The theory, based upon an abstract element in which entities acquire meaning only through functioning as poles of a relation, is itself only functional in an abstract sense. It leads to statements regarding modes of behaving expressed in terms of the basic element but these statements cannot be directly interpreted in terms of subjects' courses of action. These statements can be used only to make predictions regarding specific numbers of modes of behaving, albeit predictions which can be tested by experiment. Thus the theory, like the experimental work, lacks psychological meaning.

The purpose of this paper is to give psychological meaning to the theory. As stated above this cannot be achieved through the direct intepretation of the particular statements of which the theory is composed. The purpose can be realized only by treating the theory as a whole. This necessitates a conversion of the theory. The hierarchical system of relations in which entities acquire meaning through functioning in a context is to be converted to a hierarchical system of contrasts, through which context itself acquires interpretation. In the original system entities, defined by general conditions underlying their contexts, acquire meaning only in the contexts; whereas in the

---

object. As writers of this chapter we analyse. Any analysis of a total neural–glandular–motor bodily process, whether only in principle or by experiment, constitutes reference to objects external to the observed, behaving individual. Through these objects about which they necessarily communicate, the psychological observer and his subjects are socially related. In placing emphasis on the social aspect of the relation between psychologist and subject we are focusing attention on mind rather than on brain.

Whereas, in the experimental work referred to in the previous chapter, attention was focused on the object seen as actually discriminated by the subject as his response object, we are concerned in this chapter with the subject's response as integrated by the psychologist, something inseparable from the 'experience' of the psychologist when perceiving and acting with respect to the common object.

new system behavioural entities, defined by normative distinctions, are expressed as interpretations of systems. A 'normative distinction' is that between a thing as a mere object-of-*action*, defining action in general, and a thing such as a tool or one's hand, which is an instrument defining an act. We do not refer here to an individual's making a value judgment (interpretation of system) but to the fact that the distinction between (1) a mere action object and (2) a thing as an instrument, is impossible without the distinction between an individual and his being related to another individual through an object, i.e. something strictly objective.

The conversion of the initial system does not commit us to any particular philosophic view of 'judgment', but merely to the fact that individuals, including philosophers, classify behaviour or statements by actual distinctions. In all we do choice-making is expressed in the very singling out of an object of action rather than an object of an alternative kind. G. A. Miller has written (*Psychology, the science of mental life*, 1962): 'Along with every name and every skill a child learns he also absorbs an evaluation.' ... 'These evaluations are different in every society and a person who does not know them cannot function in a manner acceptable to the members of that society.' ... 'Within any single realm it may be possible to develop a consistent system of values, but the demands from separate areas may conflict in ways that seem impossible to reconcile.' ... 'Why do we have to learn these value systems? What purpose do they serve? The answer springs directly from the fact that we are constantly being put into situations where we must express a preference, must make a choice between two or more courses of action.' ... 'The act of choice is often embedded in great conflict and uncertainty.' ... 'In these and thousands of similar conflicts, what we must do is to decide which values are greater, which more important. And to facilitate the constantly recurring processes of choice we try to organize our values into a coherent usually hierarchical system.'

Miller, while referring to the possibility of organizing values into a coherent hierarchical system, does not go further to explicate such a system. This paper is intended to provide an explication of such a system using the original relational system as a basis.

Thus a relational system is substantiated by experiments which may be loosely regarded as scientific and given meaning by a hierarchical system of values. In this way a psychological theory is completed.

Recapitulation of the Relational System
The element used in the construction of the successively extended systems of relational structures is symbolized by

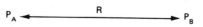

$$P_A \xleftarrow{\hspace{1cm} R \hspace{1cm}} P_B$$

in which the relation R discriminates a pole. Discrimination of this pole leads to discrimination of the relation. Discriminated relation then discriminates the other pole. Discrimination of this pole leads to further discrimination of the relation and so on. The term 'discriminate' is used to refer to this mode of operation. The mode of operation can reverse. Loss of discrimination of one pole leads to loss of discrimination of the relation, and hence to a loss of discrimination of the other pole. This continues to the disintegration of poles and relation. The term 'confuse' is used to refer to this mode of operating. Operating continuously the element is always discriminating or confusing. No static position is allowable. Any entities may be postulated as poles and any associations as the relation.

In Chapter 7 the element was used as a continuously operating mechanism to construct a relational structure associated with a first stage of psychological development. This stage was symbolized by

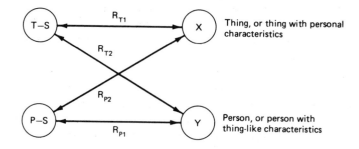

where 'T-S' refers to thing-self, 'P-S' person-self, and R_{T1}, R_{T2}, R_{P1}, R_{P2} to activities necessary to need satisfaction. This is the structure of which all subsequent structures of the relational system are composed and thus the element is basic to the whole system. Since the problem in Chapter 7 was to produce a relational system as a prerequisite for a particular type of experimental work it was possible to reduce the above structure to

$$S_1 \xleftarrow{\quad R \quad} O_1$$

where S_1 refers to the self structure composed of '*T-S*' and '*P-S*' as related through objects in the *umwelt*. The problem dealt with in the present chapter will necessitate considering the detailed structure.

Alternative View of Element required to construct a Contrast System
It is necessary for the purpose of this paper to emphasize those features of the element which express *distinctions* at the expense of the relational feature as used in the above.

It will be noted that in the symbolizing of the element,

$$P_A \xleftarrow{\quad R \quad} P_B$$

it is necessary to introduce a distinction as expressed in P_A and P_B. With identical poles the element would express only a triviality. Thus with a change of emphasis the element may be viewed as expressing a distinction rather than a continuously operating mechanism involving a relation and the structure above may be viewed as expressing contrasts between the entities *B-S* and *X*, the entities *B-S* and *Y*, the entities *P-S* and *X* and the entities *P-S* and *Y*.

Not concerned in this chapter with actually using the element as a mechanism for constructing a series of self/*umwelt* structures we now place emphasis on the conditions obtaining in its use.

These are:

1. It may operate in the confusing mode.
2. It may operate in the discriminating mode.
3. It is always operating in the confusing mode or the discriminating mode, i.e. if not operating in the confusing mode it is operating in the discriminating mode and vice versa.
4. No static position is allowable, meaning that no particular degree of definition of poles is attained and maintained.

These conditions provide the basis for the conversion from the relational to the contrast system.

The possibility of conversion rests completely upon the clearcut distinction between the element operating in the confusing mode (movement to disorder) and the element operating in the discriminating mode (movement to order).

Change of view of the Relational Structure necessary for the Conversion
In Chapter 7 the element was used to bring different entities into being, these entities acquiring meaning from the relation which served as context. In the construction of the successive relational structures emphasis was placed on the developing entities, this development occurring through successive extensions of context. The relation, referring very generally to actions necessary to the satisfaction of need, remained unchanged. Since we are now concerned with the development of behaviour we place the emphasis on the actions necessary to need-satisfaction. This necessitates a change of view of the relational structures. Referring to the level one structure, the four poles of the relations, the entities T-S, P-S, X and Y are now to be regarded as the context within which action occurs, and correspondingly the relations become the entities, behavioural entities in the sense of courses of action evaluated with respect to a desired goal. In the contrast of these entities the context as actual system acquires interpretation, that is in comparing the different consequences of different courses of action, the context within which action is to take place becomes meaningful. For example, G. A. Miller in the publication referred to above writes of the child wanting his pennies but wanting his sweets too. To the child, contrasting the consequences of the two possible courses of action and realizing that he must fix upon one of them, the context (self, pennies, sweets) becomes particularly meaningful.

As stated above, in the development of the relational system the emphasis was on the entities as transformed through successive extensions of context. Again, in the development of the contrast system emphasis will be on the entities but now contrasting behavioural entities transformed in the development of the system through the admission of further contrasts of behavioural entities.

Conversion to the Contrasts Hierarchy
To arrive at a system expressing a hierarchical organization
of values it is necessary to make recourse to a system which
lends itself to precise formulation of a hierarchy of contrasts.
The organization of truth tables is such a system. In what
follows the hierarchy of formal relational structures, given in
the previous chapter, is converted to a hierarchy based on truth
tables. This organization is then used as the instrument for the
elucidation of the complexity of decision-making, as referred to
by Miller.

Understanding a statement to be a sentence which can be
classified as either true (T) or false (F) but not both, truth
tables are used in the classical statement calculus to display the
truth value assignments to composite sentences for all possible
assignments of truth values to the constituent sentences, out of
which a sentence is composed by means of connectives such as
'or' $(\lor)$, 'and' $(\land)$ 'if ... then' $(\rightarrow)$, 'if and only if' $(\leftrightarrow)$. A
fundamental role is played by the table for negation, not-p
symbolized by $\sim$.

p	$\sim p$
T	F
F	T

where p is a 'sentence' in the language of the statement calculus or sentential logic.

Notions such as 'truth' are irrelevant; the truth tables are
definitions. The tables defining the connectives are:

for $\lor$			for $\land$			for $\rightarrow$			for $\leftrightarrow$		
p	q	$p \lor q$	p	q	$p \land q$	p	q	$p \rightarrow q$	p	q	$p \leftrightarrow q$
T	T	T	T	T	T	T	T	T	T	T	T
T	F	T	T	F	F	T	F	F	T	F	F
F	T	T	F	T	F	F	T	T	F	T	F
F	F	F	F	F	F	F	F	T	F	F	T

where p and q are constituent sentences.

It is to be noted (1) that so-called sentential connectives are
defined by these tables, (2) that 'statements' are actions or

linguistic utterances whose fundamental property is that they are 'true' or 'false' and that 'sentences' are not necessarily written sentences or other forms of conventional symbolic utterance.

But the reader may object 'In using truth tables, are you not destroying the distinction between psychology and logic?' The answer would be that we are concerned here with *assignment* of T or F to statements, not with valid consequences of statements nor with inference based on tautologies as laws. We are concerned with tracing the roles of T and F through repeated use of tables as organized for the general purpose.

Moreover, we are concerned with assignment not just in the purely formal sense of the classical statement calculus, which assumes that with each initial 'sentence' there is associated exactly one member of T, F, which one of T and F being irrelevant. We are concerned here with assignment as expressing a basic distinction in *behaviour*, by which actions are categorized by individuals, the very distinction which makes it possible for men to devise formal games and even build machines for grinding out truth tables indefinitely out of the tables defining the connectives. The difference between the purely formal and the behavioural is a reflection of the distinction between a formula and a statement. A formula becomes a statement when a symbol x it contains is replaced by the name of an *object*: but the 'symbol' is a symbol which does not symbolize (!) unless the formula has already become a statement. It does not matter what x is called in the absence of the *discrimination* inherent in its symbolizing an object.

A formula is a declarative utterance which does not really declare, although we can of course make *statements* which refer to the formula itself. The x in a 'formula' does not even discriminate between x's-not-symbolizing and x's-symbolizing, whereas in the case of a statement the object symbolized could be x's-not-symbolizing or x's symbolizing. So it is F that a formula is either T or F and T that a statement is either T or F.

In short, with our hierarchical organization of values in view, it is essential for us, in our concern with the behavioural aspect of formal patterns, instead of the pure formal patterns themselves, to base our discussion of truth tables on what can be regarded as rudimentary truth tables, viz.:

F,	T	p	$\sim p$	'one member of'
		T	F	$\{T, F\}$
		F	T	
defining: formula	statement	negation		assignment

(Technical terms of the statement calculus.)

To effect the conversion to the contrast system it is necessary to identify certain aspects of the previous system with the T and F of the truth table system. First use is made of the contrast between the confusing mode and the discriminating mode referred to earlier. The confusing mode is identified with F, the discriminating mode with T, as indicated below.

Since the level 1 relational structure is composed of the original element, the four conditions obtaining in the use of the element apply in the structure. To identify other aspects of the relational system with aspects of the truth table system, use is made of these four conditions.

Application of Conditions obtaining in use of Element for Conversion
The first two simple conditions apply directly, regardless of whether an element is in isolation or in a combination. It thus follows immediately from the above that in the conversion: condition 1, 'the element may operate in the confusing mode' is identified with F; condition 2, 'the element may operate in the discriminating mode 'is identified' with T.

To identify the more complex conditions 3 and 4 with the features of the truth table hierarchy it is necessary, since the elements are in combination, to return for the moment to the level 1 relational structure symbolized by

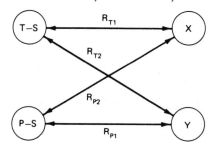

Applying condition 4, 'no static position is allowable', X must become more and more clearly defined as a thing or as a person, similarly for Y. Neither can remain partly thing and partly person. Thus in the conversion, condition 4 is identified with the rule 'One member of $\{T, F\}$', i.e. with assignment.

Condition 3 states that if the element is not operating in the confusing mode it must operate in the discriminating mode and vice versa. The above application of condition 4 to the level 1 relational structure implies that if R_{T1} operates in the confusing mode R_{P2} must operate in the discriminating mode and vice versa, which is the statement of condition 3 as applied in the structure. A similar statement can be made of R_{P1} and R_{T2}. Thus condition 3, as applying in the structure, refers to the possibility of interchanging the confusing and discriminating modes. Thus in the conversion condition 3 is identified with the table for negation.

Alternatively, with conversion the level 1 structure may be symbolized by

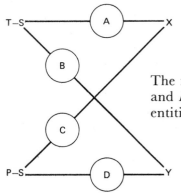

The relations R_{T1}, R_{T2}, R_{P1} and R_{P2} have become the behavioural entities A, B, D and C respectively.

Remembering that in the conversion the confusing mode has been identified with F and the discriminating mode with T, condition 3 may now be stated as 'if A is F, C must be T (if D is F, B must be T) and vice versa', which may be viewed as a statement of negation.

Summing up we have:

Condition 1	Condition 2	Condition 3	Condition 4
confusing mode	discriminating mode	confusion expressed in possibility of interchange of the confusing and discriminating modes	fixation in the sense that one combination of modes must be fixed upon

corresponding in the conversion to the rudimentary truth tables

F	T	table for $\sim$	'One member of $\{T, F\}$'

defining:

formula	statement,	negation,	assignment

Referring to the discussion of 'normative distinctions' in the introduction it can now be seen that the distinction between action and act is the distinction between F and T and the distinction between person and object as a thing is the distinction between the table for negation and the rule 'one member of $\{T, F\}$'.

See section headed 'Conversion' in Chapter 8 for detailed exposition of this conversion.

While F and T refer to behavioural entities they do not yet refer to *contrasting* behavioural entities; the table for negation nevertheless expresses the possibility[2] that T and F may be interchanged. In the terms of the Chapter 7, referring to the mode of functioning at stage one, symbolized by $S_1 \leftrightarrow O_1$, this interchange possibility, symbolized by the table for $\sim$, relates to conflict implicit in choice-making at this stage; nevertheless one alternative has to be fixed upon, as is symbolized by 'one member of $\{T, F\}$'. But at this stage, the final choice is made only in direct action, it is not yet verbalized in conventional language signs, only in action occasioning immediate dissatisfaction and satisfaction can the choice be made and conflict resolved.

[2] The ambiguity of the self-explanatory gesture.

In the above the relational structure associated with level (1) is used to effect the conversion to the rudimentary truth tables. Analysing the movement through the successive structures associated with levels (2) to (5) it is possible to effect the conversion to truth tables associated with higher levels. Space does not permit the display of the analysis. An important point which emerges from the analysis is that F and T at these higher levels are not independent. They are now interdependent in the sense that F underlies T or T overlies F. An everyday example is afforded by the fact that in a situation the term 'unfair' arises directly out of the overt situation, whereas the term 'fair' arises only when it has been suggested or imputed in some way that something of the situation is 'unfair'. It is significant in this respect that all of the Ten Commandments concerned with action are negative.

In the following section a formal hierarchy of dualities, expressing contrasts, is displayed in terms taken from expositions of logic. Unlike the usual approach to logic which is to maintain precise and sharp distinctions, our purpose is to display a structure expressing cumulative ambiguities. For the logician's purposes F and T must be seen as mutually exclusive alternatives neither having precedence, for our 'psychological' purposes emphasis is now placed on the growing interdependence of F and T based on the asymmetry of F underlying T.

Contrast Structure

GENERAL MOVEMENT: *Level (1)*. At level (1) F and T are distinct, being implicitly contrasted in negation and assignment. This duality is implicit in that the duality itself cannot be expressed formally; but it becomes explicit at level (2) in that the duality of the tables for $\vee$ and $\wedge$ with respect to interchange of F and T can be formally stated. The tables for $\rightarrow$ and $\leftrightarrow$ are shown below on page 146 to express the ambiguity and overlapping of $\vee$ and $\wedge$.

These tables for $\rightarrow$ and $\leftrightarrow$ express a new implicit duality, implicit in that no interchange within these tables can be formally stated. The interchange of the tables for affirmation and negation within the tables for $\vee$ and $\wedge$ leads to the tables for $\rightarrow$ and $\leftrightarrow$. Thus these tables represent the new form taken by assignment and negation at level (2), the table for 'affirmation' being the form taken by assignment in the repeated use of tables.

Thus the transition from level (1) to level (2) is marked by an implicit duality becoming explicit, which is expressed in turn by a new implicit duality.

Similarly the transition from level (2) to level (3) is marked by this new implicit duality's becoming explicit, and in this the 'biconditional', ↔, arising at the end of level (2) is basic in that the repeated use of truth tables is subject to formal laws, which are dual in that interchange of ∨ and ∧, involving interchange of F and T, gives rise to interchange of laws, e.g.

$$p \vee (q \vee r) \equiv (p \vee q) \vee r$$

is dual to

$$p \wedge (q \wedge r) \equiv (p \wedge q) \wedge r$$

in that this formal interchange is possible the duality is explicit.

Every move from level to level of the hierarchy is similarly characterized. The forms at successive levels symbolize the successive higher dimensionality of truth table usage, F and T being distinct at level (1), contrasted in tables at level (2), linking repeated inductive use of tables at level (3), give rise to two dimensions, as a relation of columns of pairs of tables at level (4), and interrelation of related tables at level (5). This successive higher dimensionality of truth table usage mirrors the successive structures of the relational system in the previous paper.

At each move, from level to level, a 'piece-meal' context of an entity becomes a *whole* new entity in its own new 'piece-meal' context.

DUALITIES OF TABLES AND MODES OF FUNCTIONING. Returning to the truth tablets we have at level (1)

F	T	Table for ∼	'One of $\{T, F\}$'
defining formula,	defining statement,	defining negation,	defining assignment.

Here, as stated above, F and T are independent, the tables for ∼ and 'One of (T, F)' expressing respectively the mutual exclusion and exhaustive alternation of F and T.

At level (2) duality emerges, the fundamental source of the duality being the fact that F and T are now mutually involved (F underlying T). Detailed consideration of this duality:

The tables for $\vee$, $\wedge$, $\rightarrow$ and $\leftrightarrow$ are

p q	p∨q	p q	p∧q	p q	p→q	p q	p↔q
T T	T	T T	T	T T	T	T T	T
T F	T	T F	F	T F	F	T F	F
F T	T	F T	F	F T	T	F T	F
F F	F	F F	F	F F	T	F F	T

The tables defining $\vee$ and $\wedge$ are different in that the two inner rows differ, and are similar in that the top and bottom rows are the same. These tables are dual, for interchange of T and F in these tables results in the interchange of the tables for $\vee$ and $\wedge$. The first two columns are unchanged but the third columns have been interchanged. The characteristic of the table for $\vee$ when contrasted with the table for $\wedge$ is that the last column is F only when the first two are F. The characteristics of the table for $\wedge$ when contrasted with the table for $\vee$ is that the last column is T only when the first two are T. The forms of the characteristics and the way in which they emerge indicate explicitly the duality of the two tables.

The tables for $\vee$ and $\wedge$, as interpretations of systems defined by normative distinctions, are regarded as behavioural entities. From the above they can be seen as contrasting behavioural entities.[3] The duality of the tables expresses the explicit conflict in choice-making at this stage, explicit in that the conflict is now verbalized; for example the connective $\vee$ can be interpreted as 'word' (emphasis on denotation) and $\wedge$ as 'name' (emphasis on connotation). Judgments are made and acted upon, albeit, the judgment can be made finally only in action.

The tables for $\rightarrow$ and $\leftrightarrow$ are dual, which follows from considering them as reduced to combinations of the tables for $\sim$, $\vee$ and $\wedge$. By repeated use of these tables we have the following extended table, in which incidentally the table

---

[3] The or/and ambiguity of meaning and word.

$$\frac{T \qquad T}{F \qquad F}$$

for 'affirmation' takes the place of the definition of assigment.

1	2	3	4	5	6	7
				$\to$		$\leftrightarrow$
p	q	$\sim p$	$\sim q$	$\sim p \vee q$	$q \vee p$	$(\sim p \vee q) \wedge (\sim q \vee p)$
T	T	F	F	T	T	T
T	F	F	T	F	T	F
F	T	T	F	T	F	F
F	F	T	T	T	T	T

Considering columns 1 and 2 the outer (top and bottom) rows give the table for affirmation, the inner two the table for negation. Considering columns 2 and 3 the outer rows now give the table for negation, the inner the table for affirmation; the tables have been interchanged. Considering columns 2, 3 and 5 the F of 2 and the F of 3 lead to the F of 5. Since this is the characteristic of the table for $\vee$ which is meaningless in the absence of the different characteristic for $\wedge$, this column 5 expresses the difference between the tables for $\vee$ and $\wedge$, and so is the form which the table for $\sim$ of level (1) takes at this stage.

Considering columns 2 and 4, once more the tables for $\sim$ and affirmation have been interchanged. The F's at the top of the columns 3 and 4 become T's in 5 and 6 and hence T in 7. Thus this T expresses the two F's. The bottom T of column 7 expresses the two T's at the bottom of column 3 and 4. Hence the two T's of column 7 express the similarity of the tables for $\vee$ and $\wedge$. The two F's of column 7 coming after F-T and the T-F of column 5 and 6 express the difference between the two tables. In this way column 7 expresses exhaustive alternation. This is the new form of the level (1) definition of assignment, new in form in that it incorporates the level (2) version of table for $\sim$.

The interchange of the tables for $\sim$ and affirmation in the extended table effects a switch from column 5 to 7 or vice versa and in this sense there is duality between the tables 5 and 7.

The duality implicit in the exhaustive alternation at level (1) having become explicit at level (2) in duality based upon the interchange of T and F, has now imposed upon it a new duality implicit in the general level (2) version of exhaustive alternation. The tables for $\rightarrow$ and $\leftrightarrow$ as interpretation of systems defined by normative distinctions are regarded as contrasting behavioural entities. Furthermore these behavioural entities incorporate the previous contrasting entities, the tables for $\vee$ and $\wedge$. Thus a second and more complex conflict in choice-making arises, implicit[4] but superimposed upon the first, explicit, conflict.

Referring to the modes of functioning at level 2 (Ch. 7) the contrasting behavioural entities for $\vee$ and $\wedge$ are associated with the functioning of S_2^1 symbolized by

$$S_2^1 \xleftarrow{\quad R_1 \quad} O_2^1$$

and the contrasting behavioural entities $\rightarrow$ and $\leftrightarrow$ are associated with the functioning of S_2^2 symbolized by

$$(S_2^1 \xleftarrow{\quad R_1 \quad} O_2^1) \xleftarrow{\quad R_2 \quad} O_2^2$$

It is to be noted that there is an exact correspondence between the behavioural entities for $\vee$ and $\wedge$ as included in the behavioural entities $\rightarrow$ and $\leftrightarrow$, and the inclusion of the mode of functioning of S_2^1 within the mode of functioning of S_2^2.

'Metamorphosis of entity' can now be recognized in the change from mere F and T at level (1) (associated with the functioning of S_1) to the characteristics $F\,F$, F and $T\,T$, T of $\vee$ and $\wedge$ at level (2) (associated with S_2^1). Similarly the 'integration of a unity' as used in Ch. 7 may now be recognized in the repeated use of tables leading to $\rightarrow$ and $\leftrightarrow$. Using truth tables as behavioural entities may appear peculiar but it is exactly what is done, when, for example, concerned with the motivation for the table for $\rightarrow$, a logician writes that we certainly wish that a true statement does not imply a false and this at least is secured by the table.

LEVEL (3). At level (2) connectives are defined. Now at level (3) aspects of truth table principle are defined as follows:

[4] The ambiguity of social relation and common task.

use of initial column	final column	use of final column	final column as link between initial columns
defining prime formula	composite formula	formula extended	inductively

The first two aspects 'prime formula' and 'composite formula' are defined by the use of an initial and final column of a table. The order inherent in prime-composite is the explicit expression of the source of the duality of ∨ and ∧ – the interdependence of F and T, F lying within T.

These two aspects of the principle of truth tables refer to the use of one basic truth table whether ∨ or ∧ or → or ↔. But the use of the tables can be repeated. As in the usual formulation of the statement calculus, a set of prime formulae can be extended by adjoining all the composite formulae that can be formed by repeated use of the various connectives, so that if p and q are members of the extended set so are $p \vee q$, $p \wedge q$, $p \rightarrow q$, $p \leftrightarrow q$, and $\sim p$, the truth value of a composite formula being defined inductively in accordance with the tables.

The level (3) 'connectives' (that is the principles of repeated inductive use of truth tables) could be formally expressed by the associative and other laws of the Boolean algebra of sets; but just as the latter are often represented by Venn diagrams so we use 'initial' and 'final' to represent the aspects of truth table principle.

Just as at level (1) the definitions of negation and assignment expressed, in an implicit duality, the mutual exclusion and exhaustive alternation of F and T, leading at level (2) to the explicit duality of ∨ and ∧ based on interchange of F and T, so at level (2) → and ↔ express the implicit duality of the difference and similarity of the tables for ∨ and ∧ which becomes an explicit duality at level (3). This duality is based upon the same difference and similarity of the tables for ∨ and ∧ but is now expressed as final and initial columns of a table. But this contrast of the difference and similarity of the tables was expressed via the contrast of the tables for negation and affirmation so the new implicit duality, at level (3), is formalized by the two-member set

$$\left\{ \left\{ \frac{F \mid T}{T \mid F} \right\}, \left\{ F, \ T \right\} \right\}$$

i.e. effectively by the two-member set

$$\left\{ \{F\}, \ \{F, \ T\} \right\} \qquad\qquad (x)$$

One member $\{F, \ T\}$ being an unordered pair,[5] the other member $\{F\}$ determining which member of $\{F, \ T\}$ is to be considered 'first', in short (x) represents an *ordered* pair $<F, \ T>$.[6]

Thus at level (3) there is irreversibility, unlike the form taken by the interchange at level (2).

The new form x of interchange at level (3) is expressed in the fact that a final column may be seen as an initial column in the extension of the table. In this the emphasis is on the unordered pair $(F, \ T)$. Inasmuch as, in induction, a final column is a step for further extension there is emphasis on the ordered pair (x).

At level (2) the tables for $\rightarrow$ and $\leftrightarrow$ express the difference and similarly for those for $\vee$ and $\wedge$. Now again the definition of formula extended inductively expresses the difference between the definitions of prime and composite formula, viz. $(F, \ T)$ as an unordered pair simply marking the difference between prime and composite, with the ordered pair (x) showing the similarity expressed in the included F.

So at level (3) there is, upon the explicit duality represented by the one-number set $\{F\}$ together with the two-number set $\{F, \ T\}$, which duality contains another explicit duality represented by T complementary to F, superimposed a further implicit duality,[7] that of the pair $F, \ T$, as unordered or ordered. This duality will become explicit at the next level (4).

With each of these dualities is associated a pair of contrasting behavioural entities which from the above may be expressed by

1. The duality represented by '$\{F, \ T\}$ or $\{T, \ F\}$'
2. The duality of the sets $\{F, \ T\}$ and $\{F\}$

---

[5] The ambiguity of the association of 'object' and 'meaning' in denoting.

[6] The ambiguity of 'attribute' and word, in connoting.

[7] The ambiguity of 'classifying' and 'group' formed.

3. The duality represented by $\left\{\ \ , \{F,\ T\}\right\}$ and $\left\{\{F\},\ \ \ \right\}$

Referring to the modes of functioning at stage (3) (Ch. 7) these contrasting behavioural entities are associated with the modes of functioning:

1. S_3^1 operating: $S_3^1 \xleftrightarrow{R_1} O_3^1$

2. S_3^2 operating: $(S_3^1 \xleftrightarrow{R_1} O_3^1) \xleftrightarrow{R_1} O_3^2$

3. S_3^3 operating: $(S_3^1 \xleftrightarrow{R_1} O_3^1) \xleftrightarrow{R_3} (S_3^2 \xleftrightarrow{R_2} O_3^2)$

Note the correspondence.

In Chapter 7 it is stated that through R_3, S_3^3 is identified with

$$(S_3^1 \xleftrightarrow{R_1} O_3^1) \quad \text{and} \quad (S_3^2 \xleftrightarrow{R_2} O_3^2)$$

conjointly. The role of the blank spaces in duality 3 above is to express the aspects implied by 'conjointly'.

LEVEL (4). At level (3) aspects of truth table principles were defined. Now at level (4) different relations are defined, 'relations' in the sense of relationships between columns of pairs of tables involved in the extended use of tables. Whereas at level (3) the emphasis was on extension as relative, as successive columns, at level (4) we are concerned with relationships between columns seen as aspects of principle. Thus at level (4) columns are not considered piece-meal but as ordered pairs in combination.

A relation is defined by an open sentence $P(x, y)$ in which $P(a, b)$ is either T or F for any ordered pair (a, b) belonging to a product set $A \times B$, and a relation R in a set A is called 'symmetric' if $(a, b) \in R$ implies $(b, a) \in R$ and 'antisymmetric' if $(a, b) \in R$ and $(b, a) \in R$, implies $a = b$. R is 'transitive' if $(a, b) \in R$ and $(b, c) \in R$ implies $(a, c) \in R$.

R is 'reflexive' if for every $a \in A$, $(a, a) \in R$.

Summing up:

| $\begin{aligned}(a, b) \in R &\rightarrow\\ (b, a) \in R&\end{aligned}$ defining symmetric | $\left.\begin{aligned}(a, b) &\in R\\ (b, a) &\in R\end{aligned}\right\} \rightarrow a = b$ defining anti-symmetrical relation | $\left.\begin{aligned}(a, b) &\in R\\ (b, c) &\in R\end{aligned}\right\} \rightarrow (a, c) \in R$ defining transitive relation | $(a, a) \in R$ for every $a \in A$ defining reflexive relation |

Considering the symmetric relation, assigning either value T or F to a column, then in changing from $(a, b) \in R$ to $(b, a) \in R$ the relation, per se, remains unchanged but its value changes. Thus there is an explicit[8] duality in that the interchange of the columns a and b leads to the interchange of T and F for R.[9]

Thus considering the definition of the symmetric relation

$$(a, b) \in R$$
$$(b, a) \in R$$

if the first is T, the second is F and vice versa.

With respect to the antisymmetrical relation, in the considering of (a, b) as table values rather than column values it is essential to consider the question of order. Here a second explicit duality[10] is formally expressed by the definition of antisymmetrical relation.

With $a \neq b$ there is order

if $(a, b) \in R$ then $(b, a) \notin R$ and R is T.

With $a = b$ there is no order, and R is F.

Thus with the change from $a \neq b$ to $a = b$ there is a change in the value of R.

A relation, as defined by an open sentence $R(x, y)$ in which $R(a, b)$ is either T or F for any ordered pair (a, b) belonging to the set $A \times A$ expresses formally the contrast between column value and table value. This gives a third explicit duality[11] at level (4). The level 1 implicit duality, of the mutual exclusion and exhaustive alternation of F and T, expresses that it is F that a formula is either F or T and T that a statement is either F or T. This duality is now present at level (4) in the sense that the definition of relation, of which symmetrical and antisymmetrical relations are aspects, is a definition of a statement by means of ordered pairs of formulae. The definitions

---

[8] The ambiguity of denotation (class) and denoting.

[9] Of course the relation still holds after the interchange (P is 'either F or T') but we are particularly concerned here with the role of F-T which originated in the level (2) duality with respect to interchange.

[10] The ambiguity of abstraction and connoting.

[11] Now the or/and ambiguity becomes fully explicit in the ambiguity of denotation and abstraction.

of symmetrical and antisymmetrical relation are respectively two new forms of F and T.

Moreover there is a new implicit duality[12] at level (4) in that the formal definition of transitive relation emphasizes the terms of the relation whereas the definition of reflexive relation emphasizes relation itself. This duality will become explicit at the next level, (5).

With each of these dualities is associated a pair of contrasting behavioural entities which from the above may be expressed, bearing in mind that a relation is a set, by

1. The duality represented by $\left\{\{a, b\} \text{ or } \{b, a\}\right\}_{R_s}$

2. The duality of the sets $\{a, b\}_{R_a}$ and $\{a\}_{R_a}$

3. The duality represented by $\left\{\{a, b\} \ , \ \right\} \text{ and } \left\{ \ , \ a\right\}$

4. The duality represented by

$$\left\{\left\{\{a\text{-}, b\}, \ \right\}, \ \right\} \text{ and } \left\{ \ , \left\{ \ , \{ a\right\}\right\}$$

Note the correspondence with the modes of functioning at level (4) (Ch. 7).

1. S_4^1 operating: $\qquad\qquad S_4^1 \xleftrightarrow{R_1} O_4^1$

2. S_4^2 operating: $\qquad\qquad \left(S_4^1 \xleftrightarrow{R_1} O_4^1\right) \longleftrightarrow O_4^2$

3. S_4^3 operating: $\quad \left(S_4^1 \xleftrightarrow{R_1} O_4^1\right) \xleftrightarrow{R_3} \left(S_4^2 \xleftrightarrow{R_2} O_4^2\right)$

4. S_4^4 operating:

$$\left[\left(S_4^1 \xleftrightarrow{R_1} O_4^1\right) \xleftrightarrow{R_3^A} \left(S_4^2 \xleftrightarrow{R_2^A} O_4^{2A}\right)\right] \xleftrightarrow{R_4} \left[\left(S_4^1 \xleftrightarrow{R_1} O_4^1\right)\right.$$
$$\left.\xleftrightarrow{R_3^B} \left(S_4^2 \xleftrightarrow{R_2^B} O_4^{2B}\right)\right]$$

LEVEL (5). At level (5) the previous 'relations' become related to each other through being 'between' members of a set called a domain or universe of discourse.

At level 5 we have

| The technical definition of predicate | The technical definition of term | The technical definition of universal quantifier | The technical definition of existential quantifier |

[12] The ambiguity of induction and deduction.

Individual variables are classified in the predicate calculus as 'terms', the 'universal quantifier', often written as $(\forall x)$ may be read as 'for every x', the 'existential quantifier', often written $(\exists x)$, may be read as 'there is an x such that', an n-place predicate', $P(x_1, x_2, \ldots, x_n)$, is an expression such that on an assignment of values to the variables $x_1, x_2, \ldots, x_n$ from a domain, a statement results. It is assumed that a non-empty set D called the 'domain' is given, such that each individual variable ranges over D, also that a 'logical function' f on D^n into $\{F, T\}$ is assigned to each predicate letter P and that to each distinct free variable ('free' in that its occurrence is not within the scope of a quantifier) is assigned a value in D. Then if $P(y_1, y_2, \ldots, y_n)$ is a prime formula obtained by substitution of any variables in a predicate P and f is assigned to $P(x_1, x_2, \ldots, x_n)$ and a_i is assigned to y_i; the truth value of $P(y_1, y_2 \ldots, y_n)$ is taken as $f(a_1, a_2, \ldots, a_n)$. Also the truth tables of the statement calculus hold; and for a given assignment of values to the predicates and free variables of $(\forall x)P$ the truth value of $(\forall x)P$ is T if and only if the value of P is T for every assignment to x, whereas for a given assignment of values to the predicates and free variables of $(\exists x)P$, the truth value of $(\exists x)P$ is T if and only *if* the value of P is T for at least one assignment to x.

Just as, at level (4), table values were generated out of column values, so at level (5), out of table values are generated n-dimensional tables represented by columns $P_1, P_2, \ldots, P_n$ in which all possible alternative combinations of values of T and F are assigned. Table values as a recurring array are connected by a relation $P((a, b), (c, d), \ldots, (m, n), \ldots)$ in which (a, b) and (c, d) are ordered pairs but in which the order (a, b), (c, d) is not significant with respect to the general form of P.

Dualities
1. This is inherited from the symmetric relation of level (4). The ordered pairs (a, b) and (c, d) may be interchanged without changing the general form of P although in a particular case the final column would be changed.[13]
2. This is inherited from the symmetric relation of level (4). In that (a, b) and (c, d) are in themselves ordered pairs, this

[13] The ambiguity of 'object' and meaning, in denoting, now becomes fully explicit as 'psychological control'

second duality expresses on the one hand this order and on the other the lack of order when two or more column values are the same.[14]

3. In the generation of n-dimensional tables by the use of recurring table values to form all possible arrangements the order of the table values is significant; just as, at level (4), order was significant for table values. Hence the 'terms' in $P(x_1, x_2, \ldots, x_n)$ where x_i stands for a set of ordered pairs. The 3rd duality is expressed by the values of the ordered pair ranging freely over the domain embodying in the order aspect the previous antisymmetry, the free ranging over the domain embodying the previous symmetry.[15]

4. In the building up of all possible alternative arrangements the previous implicit duality of the reflex and transitive relations is now explicit as a duality of unorder and order in the sense of the contrast between the independent repetition of the free variables as values taken by any term and on the other hand the ordered succession of terms $x_1, x_2, \ldots, x_n$.[16]

5. The definitions of the universal and existential quantifiers are associated respectively with dualities 1 and 2 arising out of $P((a, b), (c, d), \ldots, (m, n), \ldots)$ and dualities (3) and (4) arising out of $P(x_1, x_2, \ldots, x_n)$. In this way duality 5 expresses the complex order–unorder oppositions constituting the first two pairs of dualities, namely the contrasting of unorder imposed upon order with order imposed upon unorder.[17]

With each of these dualities is associated a pair of contrasting behavioural entities which from the above are expressed, bearing in mind that the domain is a set, by

1. The duality represented by $\{(a, b), (c, d)$ or $(c, d). (a, b)\}_P$
2. The duality of the sets $\{(a, b), (c, d)\}_P$ and $\{(a, b)\}_P$

---

[14] The ambiguity of denoting and denotation (class) has now become fully explicit as 'conforming individual'.

[15] The ambiguity of attribution and word now becomes fully explicit as 'differentiation of social classes'.

[16] The ambiguity of abstraction and connoting has now become fully explicit in 'economic function' where 'economic' refers to the oreered relations of production.

[17] The ambiguity of induction and deduction has given way to the quantitative distinction between universal and particular in a universe of discourse.

3. The duality represented by

$$\{\{m_j, n_j\}_{xi} \quad \text{or} \quad \{n_i, m_j\}_x\} \quad \text{and} \quad \{\{m_j, n_j\}_x \quad \text{and} \quad \{m_j\}_{x1}\}$$

4. The duality represented by

$$\{\{\{m_j, n_j\}_{x1} \quad \text{or} \quad \{n_j, m_j\}_{x1}\}, \dots \}$$

and

$$\{ \qquad\qquad , \{\{m_j, n_j\}_{x1} \quad \text{and} \quad \{m_j\}_{x1}\}\}$$

5. The duality represented by

$$\{\{\{\{m_j, n_j\}_{xi} \quad \text{or} \quad \{n_j, m_j\}_{xi}\}, \qquad\qquad \}, \qquad\qquad \}$$

and

$$\{ \qquad\qquad , \{ \qquad\qquad , \{m_j, n_j\}_{x1} \quad \text{and} \quad \{m_j\}_{x1}\}\}\}$$

Note the correspondence with the modes of functioning of level (5) (Ch. 7).

1. S_5^1 operating: $\quad S_5^1 \xleftrightarrow{R_1} O_5^1$

2. S_5^2 operating: $\quad \left(S_5^1 \xleftrightarrow{R_1} O_5^1\right) \xleftrightarrow{R_2} O_5^2$

3. S_5^3 operating: $\quad \left(S_5^1 \xleftrightarrow{R_1} O_5^1\right) \xleftrightarrow{R_3} \left(S_5^2 \xleftrightarrow{R_2} O_5^2\right)$

4. S_5^4 operating:

$$\left[\left(S_5^1 \xleftrightarrow{R_1} O_5^{1A}\right) \xleftrightarrow{R_3^{AB}} \left(S_5^2 \xleftrightarrow{R_2} O_5^{2B}\right)\right] \xleftrightarrow{R_4^{BD}}$$
$$\left[\left(S_5^1 \xleftrightarrow{R_1} O_5^{1A}\right) \xleftrightarrow{R_3^{AD}} \left(S_5^2 \xleftrightarrow{R_2} O_5^{2D}\right)\right]$$

5. S_5^5 operating: $\quad M \xleftrightarrow{R_4} N \quad$ where M is

$$\{\left[\left(S_5^1 \xleftrightarrow{R_1} O_5^{1A}\right) \xleftrightarrow{R_3^{AB}} \left(S_5^2 \xleftrightarrow{R_2} O_5^{2B}\right)\right] \xleftrightarrow{R_4^{BD}}$$
$$\left[\left(S_5^1 \xleftrightarrow{R_1} O_5^{1A}\right) \xleftrightarrow{R_3^{AD}} \left(S_5^2 \xleftrightarrow{R_2} O_5^{2D}\right)\right]\}$$

and N is

$$\{\left[\left(S_5^1 \xleftrightarrow{R_1} O_5^{1B}\right) \xleftrightarrow{R_3^{AB}} \left(S_5^2 \xleftrightarrow{R_2} O_5^{2A}\right)\right] \xleftrightarrow{R_4^{AC}}$$
$$\left[\left(S_5^1 \xleftrightarrow{R_1} O_5^{1B}\right) \xleftrightarrow{R_3^{CB}} \left(S_5^2 \xleftrightarrow{R_2} O_5^{2C}\right)\right]\}$$

Comments

The above treatment gives rise to fifteen pairs of behavioural entities corresponding to the fifteen modes of functioning referred to in the previous paper. At each level one of the dualities is implicit becoming explicit at the level above, the other dualities being explicit. As in the previous paper, if corresponding pairs of behavioural entities of two successive levels are compared, the pair at the higher level incorporates, with metamorphosis of entity, the pair at the lower. Further, at a particular level the more abstract pairs of behavioural entities incorporate the less abstract.

Each pair of behavioural entities is associated with a particular mode of functioning as described in Ch. 7. Where the duality is explicit it relates to the conflict explicit in the decision-making involved in a particular mode of functioning. Where the duality is implicit it relates to the conflict implicit in the decision-making involved in the corresponding mode of functioning.

The nesting (in the incorporation of the one within the other) of pairs of behavioural entities within a pair of behavioural entities along a level and between levels constitutes a hierarchial system of choice-making as referred to by Miller and illustrates the increasing complexity of judgment-making occurring as an individual develops and the contexts within which judgments are to be made become progressively extended.

Discussion

The hierarchy of decision-making developed above is expressed in very abstract terms, necessarily so, since the concern is with the formal representation of such a hierarchy. With the complexities of an individual's social context and further complexities arising from the extensions of this context through higher social organization this abstract structure is not clearly evident in everyday life. As Miller remarks, in everyday life people tend to organize their values hierarchically. Nevertheless the form of the organization is not immediately evident except in so far as interjections such as 'bad' or 'good', 'unfair' or 'fair', 'wrong or right', 'ineffective' or 'effective', 'inexpedient' or 'expedient' and many others seem to express some ordering which has not been explicated and precisely stated. Nor, in the making of judgments in everyday life is it necessary to do so. It only becomes necessary to produce a formal representation of such ordering when the purpose is the study of judgment-making itself – psychology.

Characterization of Levels and Dualities
Level (1)   Characterized by the ambiguity of self and *umwelt* growing out of each other (Ch. 7) from which all further ambiguities emerge. It is the level of the ambiguity of the self-explanatory gesture, 'choice' is made in direct action. The duality is on the one hand that of the separation inherent in that attention is directed towards one of many possibilities, and on the other hand of the bringing together inherent in the taking or leaving of an object.
Level (2)   Duality 1. On the one hand the individual is related to another individual through the object and on the other hand the individual is related to the object through another individual. In this the self-explanatory gesture becomes explicated in the ambiguity of meaning and conventional word. Choice-making is now made indirectly, i.e. through another person. Thus the choice is made in an extended context (duality 2); extended in that the second person is now explicit and another object introduced.
    Duality 2. This is the ambiguity of social relations and common task. The former expresses the ambiguity of meaning and word in separating them and the latter the ambiguity of meaning and word in bringing them together. Meaning and word are separate in the first case in the sense that an individual communicates that of which the second individual has no experience. In the second case meaning and word are brought together in that in the common task there is a mutual modification of individuals' experiences.
Level (3)   Dualities 1 and 2. The ambiguity of social relation and common task becomes explicated in the ambiguity of class and that of defining property in a further extension of context involving the introduction of another individual. In the former, duality 1, an object is related to another object through an individual. This is the ambiguity of the association of object and meaning in denoting (different as objects/similar with respect to meaning). In the latter, duality 2, an object is related

to an individual through another object. This is the ambiguity of the associations of attribute and word in connoting (similar in defining property/different with respect to use). Duality 3. With the introduction of the other individual at this level order is introduced. This individual is common to two pairs of individuals, each pair being related by an object. On the one hand the other two individuals are related to each other through him and on the other hand the common individual is related to the other two through the objects. This is the ambiguity of classifying and group formed (separation and bringing together of class and defining property. Intuitively non-contradiction and excluded middle). Level (4) Dualities 1 and 2. With extension of context in the introduction of a further object the ambiguity of classifying and group formed is explicated in the ambiguity of empirical generalization, in the sense of a class of ordered pairs. As a class of pairs there is the ambiguity (duality 1) of denotation and denoting (class/association of object and meaning). As ordered pairs, order being a new defining property, there is the ambiguity (duality 2) of abstraction and connoting (property as an attribute of something/attribution of the property).

Duality 3 is a higher duality having, as its aspects, duality 1 and duality 2. Now the or/and ambiguity of level (2) becomes fully explicit in the ambiguity of denotation and abstraction (word for a class/meaning of a property).

Duality 4. The objects hitherto introduced as members of a class were the same as objects. The introduction of the further object at this level makes possible the ordering of pairs of objects. Whereas in the introduction of the further individual at the previous level, an individual fulfils the ordering role (final cause), at this level the further object fulfils this role (effective cause). This is the ambiguity of induction and deduction, duality 4 (relationship in the sense of pairs of individuals related by objects/polarity in the sense of pairs of objects as related by individuals). Level (5) Duality 1. One aspect of induction is systematized in 'psychological control' in the sense of objects as related through other objects, with the extension of context to external objects as such. The ambiguity of object and meaning in denoting is now fully explicit.

Duality 2. The other aspect of induction is systematized in 'conforming individual' in the sense of objects as relating other objects. The ambiguity of denoting and denotation is now fully explicit.

Duality 3. One aspect of deduction is explicated in 'differentiation of social classes' in the sense of individuals as related through other individuals. The ambiguity of attribution and word is now fully explicit.

Duality 4. The other aspect of deduction is explicated in 'economic function' in the sense of individuals as relating others. The ambiguity of abstraction and connoting is now fully explicit in the ordered relations of production.

Duality 5. Dualities one to four are possible only in that, with extension of context to external objects as such the individual as such has become fully realized in interrelated individuals.

The ambiguity of induction and deduction has given way to the quantitative distinction between the universal and the particular in a universe of discourse (statistical dispersion/average).

Through this last duality the theoretical work is linked back to the experimental data which originally served as its basis.

10

Development of Truth Tables and 'Levels'

R. O. Gibson

I should like to make some remarks about how I came to use truth tables for the 'levels'. For any reader of the book, one just 'does it', the only possible justification being the sort that was given by Isaac and O'Connor in their theoretical paper; but of course there is a personal history to it.

For several years I argued and discussed with John Isaac not only theoretical points but all sorts of matters – aspects of the organization at Brunel, current political matters, other staff members' general positions, points arising from our teaching of physics and maths, etc. etc.

About 1961 Isaac, who was already thinking of doing some research along the line which led to his work with Brian O'Connor, asked myself and some others each to write an essay on 'levels of abstraction'. He was conducting a sort of experiment, so would give us only minimal hints as to what he wanted. My essay was to be on geometry. Isaac hinted that he expected only a few 'levels of abstraction' to appear in each essay. So I tried to find some clue from somewhere which would give me, as a starting point, a rough idea of the number of levels.

Eventually I took my cue from Marx's division of the development of society into some half-dozen stages.

Next, I divided geometry up into:

(i) primitive shape;
(ii) the rule-of-thumb mensuration of the ancient delta-civilizations;
(iii) the pure geometry of the Greeks;
(iv) the co-ordinate and combinatorial geometry of the period stretching from the Renaissance to the end of the eighteenth century; and

(v) the differential geometry of surfaces and projective geometry which flowered from the beginning of the nineteenth century – Gauss, etc. (Just as Beethoven in music, Goethe in literature or Hegel in philosophy.)

I added a level (vi) at first – topology, which can be regarded as twentieth-century geometry, but later I dropped it as I came to regard topology as being precisely '*about*' the geometry of the five 'levels'. No matter what topologists might say on the point, in my view topology was doing in a precise and conventional way exactly what I was trying to do in simpler, more practical terms, as became clear once I has marked off the material in topology books into five stages characterized by greater and greater systematic organization.

So my first abstract formulation of the levels took the form of marking off the levels from each other simply by dividing up conventional topological axioms into five groups (guided intuitively by the ordinary geometrical division (i) to (v) referred to above).[1]

However, it was ridiculous to think that there could be any development from level to level in one subject in a simple linear form. Development could only be possible through aspects of a given subject getting more and more mixed up with, and coalescing with, aspects of some other subject or subjects. Hence the idea of the movement-across (the 'columns') as opposed to the movement-down (the 'levels'). Next, why *four* main aspects?

In thinking about levels of abstraction in geometry I spent an enormous amount of time on level (ii), feeling that once I had got things a bit clearer there I should be able to move upwards almost mechanically, and also move downwards to the more difficult level (i). Level (ii) was easier from my point of view compared with the nebulous level (i) in that it is already somewhat abstract and also one can always get clues from the history of the ancient Egyptians and their techniques, whereas the level (i) tribal stuff is hopelessly concrete and non-historic, even though to be able to write systematically *about* it – *writing about* a primitive is one thing, *being* a primitive quite another –

---

[1] Gibson, R. O. (1975): *Value judgement and dualism in geometry and arithmetic*; Mathesis Press, Ann Arbor, Michigan.

seems the very thing one is trying to do in 'levelling' (trying to 'know oneself').

So, with the ancient Egyptians, Babylonians and pre-Socratic Greeks in mind I considered at great length a simple measurement operation, outlined as follows.

A round shape and a straight shape, which are distinct at level (i), come together in contrast at level (ii) when a relatively straight object is taken as measuring rod to determine the distance between two relatively round things.

The (*a*) *rod* occupies (*b*) successive (temporal) (*c*) positions (spatial), which (*d*) are counted (numerical).

(Here, I had vaguely in mind Kant's four 'categories' of thinghood, temporal unity, spatial unity and causality.)

In that the rod is a lump whose positions are counted, the originally straight object now partakes of the round, whereas the round things A and B partake of straightness in that they are linked, one being 'carried into' the other by the rod. So the originally separate round and straight are now coming into contrast, the contrast between the *continuous*, the 'straight-edge' aspect of the rod, the rod's being moved along, and the *discontinuous*, the breaking up constituted by the rod's positions being counted.

However, no individual ever makes a single measurement, in utter isolation; he has a purpose. The measurement has a context, a figure which is at least triangular. So the rod goes from

to

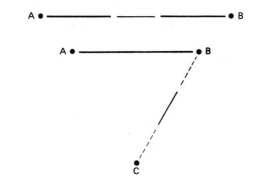

and in being swung from AB to BC it rotates about its end at B functioning exactly as a compass does. But the positions in AB and those in BC are linked (B) by the end-point of the rod which is functioning as compass-'centre'. Now we have four main aspects: 'straight edge' – 'measuring rod' as such – 'compass' – 'centre'.

Any further move takes us from the *piece-meal* context AB, BC, of the rod to a *new* level – marked by this piece-meal context giving way to *whole figures* (triangles etc.), themselves having a *new* piece-meal context made up of faces of polyhedra, and one can again come up with four aspects – a 'side' of a figure instead of a rod ('side' generating the figure instead of the rod's generating a line), an 'angle' as the discontinuity aspect; also a 'segment' and a 'vertex' (which express the contrast and overlapping of the concepts 'side' and 'angle').

This process can be continued to higher levels, giving a system of 5 levels and 4 'columns'.

Accordingly, I made a second division of topological axioms,[2] into a 5×4 grouping – to give me my fundamental abstract framework. The four columns correspond to the standard subjects:

(*a*) The open-set aspect of point-set topology.
(*b*) The filterbase aspect of point-set topology.
(*c*) The homology aspect of algebraic topology.
(*d*) The homotopy aspect of algebraic topology.

(*a*) and (*b*) differ from (*c*) and (*d*) as the local differs from the global.

Then I carried out a levels treatment of arithmetic,[3] using 'ideal theory' and theory of 'cardinals and ordinals' taken to be *about* levels of arithmetic, just as I had used topology for geometry; also levels in algebra (I used 'group-theory' as the abstract formulation) and levels in calculus (using the theory of vector-spaces and operators).

Then followed the levels treatment of branches of physics, of chemistry, grammar, music and very briefly, painting.

The next question which arose was: what is that which is

[2] *See* n. 1 above.
[3] *See* n. 1 above.

intuitively the pattern obviously common to these levels schemes?

I had already vaguely thought of roundness (a child's 'blooming confusion'), leading to the continuity of the straight-edge, as the (1) 'psychological', and the discrimination involved in straightness, leading to the quantitative, as the (2) 'logical', the psychological and logical being conceived as the distinction between oneself and something external; on the other hand it seemed that inasmuch as men are linked *angularly through* objects the piece-meal context was (3) socio- (4) economic. Here, after Marx's calling the economic 'basic' it seemed natural to me to see the fourth column, the stepping-stone at each level to the next level up, as the economic.

A propos the four main aspects, I realized that what I had pigeon-holed at each level was purely *static*. In seeking the dynamic, I came to regard the 4 'columns' as the 4 *jumps* from level to level. In doing this I was partly influenced by the fact that Hegel, in taking a synoptic view of the history of philosophy, made a four-fold division:

> Pure Science or Logic is divided into four branches. Logic of Being qua Being or ontology; Logic of Essence, in which Being is understood to be essentially dialectical; Logic of the Concept, in which the dialectical nature of Being becomes intelligible for itself; Logic of the Idea, in which all opposites are actualised in a teleological process. All opposites in reality are also opposites in philosophical reflection. Reality is in thought, thought is in reality. (Hegel: *Encyclopedia of Philosophy*.)

So now I had an admittedly vague interpretation of the four aspects, though reinforced by the consideration that any pattern which was common to the levels schemes in particular technical subjects *must* be socio-psychological or economic, since all these technical subjects, though concerning things, are nevertheless human activities.

So in my own mind I settled for:

'psychology – logic – the social – the economic'

Also, assuming the four-fold division would be reflected within each one, I tried to formulate levels treatments of these sub-jects as I had done for the others, vaguely proceeding as follows:

Psychology

   (i) asleep – awake – dream – surprise
  (ii) attention – cognition – emotion – sensation
 (iii) purpose – recollection – sentiment – idea
 (iv) self – faculty – mind – sense data (sensa)
  (v) self-realization – a merely functional self –
      unconsciousness – consciousness

'Economics':

   (i) satisfaction – need – rest – work
  (ii) supply – demand – division of lavour – commodity
 (iii) price – money as exchange medium – cost – money as
      unit of account
 (iv) interest – rent – wages – profit
  (v) capital – banking – distribution – investment

For the 'social' one I used statistical concepts. Then I gave up these attempts, as too vague.

Then I realized that this approach to: 'psychology – logic – social – economic' (I) was no good because there was a funda-mental difference between these subjects and the technical ones such as geometry, mechanics, or musical technique, a difference which one could express in two ways:

1. The subjects (I) had grown out of subjects which were concerned with *norms*, viz. aesthetics, philosophical logic (as opposed to formal logic), ethics of 'right', ethics of 'good'.
2. Whereas a science subject deals with an entity through context, each of the subjects (I) deals with context itself, through entities.

Once I had realized this, knowing:

1. That truth tables are concerned with *F-T*.
2. That, whereas in a subject such as topology, otherwise undefined terms acquire definition in the ways in which

they are used[4] (ways stated explicitly in axioms such as 'the union of any number of "open sets" is an open set'), in the statement calculus it is the connectives themselves which are defined by the tables.

I decided on the truth table approach, my purpose being to make an abstract scheme for the subjects (I) taken together, just as I had used topology for geometry.

Moreover, this decision was reinforced by two big considerations. First, I found that, imbued with trying to get from entity-via-context to context-via-entity, I was able purely by technical manipulation to switch from topological axioms defining their terms to schemes in which certain 'connectives' were given by tables *identical in form with truth tables*.[5]

Secondly, there were many ways in which my old 'psychology – logic – social – economic' seemed to fit in with the truth table hierarchy I devised. For example, taking my level (ii) geometry aspects as symbolic for any levels scheme, these four aspects seemed to correspond with the four fully fledged (unlike $\sim$) truth tables, for $\vee$, $\wedge$, $\rightarrow$, $\leftrightarrow$. The one for 'or' seemed to go well with: positions over which a measuring-rod, in its role of straight edge, moved, positions as *alternative*, the straight edge being a 'connective'. The one for 'and' seemed to go well with: positions brought together by the 'measuring-rod' *per se*. Similarly the swinging round (compass-wise) of the rod, from one side of a figure to a side which follows, seemed to fit 'implication'. Then thinking of 'or' as a new kind of 'falsity', no longer sharply separated from 'truth', 'and' as a new kind of truth no longer sharply separated from falsity, 'or' seemed 'psychological' whereas 'and' seemed 'logical' in the following way:

If someone said to me, 'The moon is made of cheese', my attention would be focused on the fact of his making the (false) statement, i.e. focused on his *behaviour*; whereas if he said, 'Mount Everest is higher than Mount Snowdon', my attention would go outwards, to *what* he said or talked about. (Here I refer to my own act of discrimination; however, just as falsity can be viewed as social, in the sense of 'negation',

---

[4] *See* n. 1, above.
[5] *See* n. 1, above.

so truth can be viewed as economic, in the sense of 'assignment'. As Dietzgen wrote: 'In so far as stray thoughts, giants, and brownies, lies and errors are really existing, though only in the imaginations of men, to that extent they are true. . . . All errors and lies are true errors and true lies, hence are not so far removed from truth that one should belong to heaven and the other to eternal damnation.') But the main reinforcement for using the truth tables came from language. I had attempted a levels essay in grammar or language (which I had divided – following the linguistics books largely – into (1) semantics, (2) morphology, (3) syntax and (4) phonology). I pigeon-holed 'meaning' and 'word' at level (ii) in semantics, taking them as belonging to my first two 'columns' in semantics (earlier I had settled for 'word' and 'name' but became dissatisfied with that). Afterwards 'meaning' and 'word' seemed to correspond exactly to 'false statement' and 'true statement' (considering 'meaning' as a level (ii) version of the confusing mode and considering ('God was the Word') – also my 'measuring-rod' covers positions in the way a word 'covers' its denotation.

Summing up: truth tables are admirably suited for our purpose, because apart from the above considerations the precision of the extended mechanical use of the tables rests on their utter generality. They are concerned only with the truth values of composite statements as depending on the assignments of values to the constituent statements. All that truth tables ever assert is 'if someone in some situation or other judges that . . . or classifies such and such statement as true or false, then according to convention it follows that . . .'

By 'convention' here one does not mean the adoption of a procedure in the sense of a game, but actual social convergence, inseparable from economic considerations.

However, if one started one's hierarchy with the tables for $\vee$, $\wedge$, $\rightarrow$, $\leftrightarrow$, this would leave out $\sim$, also even if one squeezed in $\sim$ somehow, one would get only the game-like formal manipulations of the textbooks, based on treating F and T as just equal alternatives. Also one needed to formalize *level (i)* somehow. To avoid formal games and to accommodate level (i) it was necessary to *depart from the 'logic' textbooks* by inventing 'rudimentary truth tables', now including the 'lost' table for negation and putting it in the 3rd 'column' of (i) because negation is *social*; i.e. in real life what is 'denied' is always what someone else has said.

With the 'rudimentary' truth tables, F and T are no longer simple alternatives neither having priority; they are alternatives, yet F *underlies* T. In this way, the 'round' underlies the 'straight', arithmetical 'unity' underlies 'multiplicity' and so on for basic contrasts in other subjects, e.g. a 'low' or 'high' sound; generally, the *unconscious* is basic, confusion underlies discrimination. As Ernest Dowson wrote (poetically of course):

> Out of a misty dream
> Our path emerges for a while, then closes
> Within a dream.

11

The Null Set

R. O. Gibson

It seems that methematical logicians are able to communicate with crystal-clear precision. However, at the basis of their involved though precise arguments lie the 'null' or empty set and the 'universal set'.

As regards the former, many logic books contain an attempted 'proof' of

$$\varnothing \subset A \tag{i}$$

Where $\varnothing$ is the null set and A any given set. Sometimes the author remarks that his proof is not absolutely convincing, maybe adding an alternative proof which could be accepted by the reader as satisfactory. Some authors do not attempt a proof, simply postulating that

$$\varnothing \subset A$$

perhaps adding that it is a formal necessity for the whole logical system.

As regards the universal set $\bigcup$, it is either taken for granted that in some sense it includes all sets, or this is established by (i) taken together with a principle of duality, thus obviating the need for a detailed proof of

$$\bigcup \supset A \tag{ii}$$

on the lines of the 'proof' of (i).

(i) and (ii) imply that

$$\varnothing \subset \bigcup$$

On the other hand, books on the classical statement calculus treat

$$F \text{ and } T \tag{iii}$$

as symmetrical in that they are simply alternatives, neither having precedence, mutually exclusive in 'negation' and exhaustive alternatives in 'assignment'; although the 'falsity' and 'truth' of everyday life which inspired the symbols (iii) are by no means symmetrical.

A 'statement' may be defined as that which results when, given a linguistic expression containing some x, x is replaced by the name of an object, or more precisely, in the language of the predicate calculus, a statement is a formula containing no variables outside the scope of a quantifier.

The step S_1 from the above definition of 'statement' to statement defined as that which is classifiable as F or T enables the step S_2 from statements as F or T to the formal laws of sets, in the following way.

The tables for $\vee$, $\wedge$, $\rightarrow$, $\leftrightarrow$, are characterized respectively by

(I)   A composite statement is F if and only if the constituent statements are F.

(II) A composite statement is T if and only if the constituent statements are T.

(III) A true statement cannot imply a false one.

(IV) The composite statement is T if and only if the constituents have the same value.

The shift from the first to the second definition of statement is bound up with the shift from 'formula' as a linguistic expression containing an x to a formula's being that which can take a 'truth value'.

In virtue of the characteristics of the tables for $\vee$, $\wedge$, $\rightarrow$, $\leftrightarrow$, and taking into account that F and T are now variables restricted to false and true statements respectively – *in the extended inductive use* of truth tables true statements can be regarded as elements forming a group with respect to the operation $\rightarrow$, T representing the whole group and F representing its identity element. The statements can be interpreted as 'sets' of objects, T being 'defining property', qualifying a given object for membership – for uses of the $\wedge$-table are linked by the characteristic II.

The very steps S_1 and S_2 are incorporated in the definition of 'relation', in its symmetrical and antisymmetrical forms, the incorporation being marked by the valuation procedure for the quantifiers of the predicate calculus, associated with F and T in that:

For an assignment of values to the predicates and free variables of $(\forall x)P$ the truth value of $(\forall x)P$ is F if and only if the value of P is F for at least one assignment to x; whereas for an assignment of values to the predicates and free variables of $(\exists x)P$, the truth value of $(\exists x)P$ is T if and only if P is T for at least one assignment to x.

Summing up, F *underlies* T in that S_1 enables the step S_2. The steps S_3 and S_4, to relation and thence predicate, are distinguished by a *predicate's* having a 'logical function on' D^n, where D is the domain. In this way negation underlies assignment.

In short, the steps S_1, S_2, S_3, S_4 are reflected in F, T, $\sim$, 'assignment', respectively.

So far we have used facets of standard textbook logic to represent S_1, S_2, S_3, S_4 by F, T, $\sim$, 'assignment', respectively.

Now we *invent* an arrangement of these facets, in a 5×4 matrix of 'levels' and 'columns'.

$$F \quad T \quad \sim \quad \text{'one member of } \{F,\ T\}\text{'}$$
$$\vee \quad \wedge \quad \rightarrow \quad \leftrightarrow$$

commutative and distributive laws   (x)

for $\vee$,	for $\wedge$,	$p \vee \sim p$ etc.	$p \vee \sim p$ etc.
symmetrical	antisymmetrical	trans.	reflex. relation
predicate	term	$\forall$	$\exists$

S_1, S_2, S_3, S_4 are the steps from level to level.

Since F represents a mere step, something empty, it is 'some x or other'.

Since T represents a second step it is 'a definite x'.

Since $\sim$ represents S_3 it is 'a context of some x or other' (given by a formula).

Since 'assignment' represents S_4 it is 'a defining context' (the formula has become a statement).

Next, 'some x or other' (F) is an undefined term, i.e. an 'object'.

The *behavioural* enters with T, for a definite x is an object as actually discriminated, i.e. a response-object.

Then a 'context' of an x is just a linguistic expression containing information; whereas 'context as defining' is basically a gesture.

Although we might regard F as a behavioural entity, in calling it a 'stimulus-object', – to match T – as it is a mere undefined term it is not behavioural. The undefined term acquires definition through its context, i.e. in the way in which it is 'used'. In mathematics otherwise undefined terms acquire definition through axioms, e.g. a 'set' satisfies certain axioms such as 'the union of 2 or more sets is a set'.

From the above section on the continued use of truth tables, false statements form a system which is *continuous* in the sense that the union, or the intersection, of any number of sets is a set, F being the null set and T the universal set (so 'F underlies T' corresponds to $\varnothing \subset \cup$). But true statements (level (ii)) form a system which is *discontinuous* in the sense of a system which (a) does not contain the null set, and of which (b) every finite intersection of sets of the system also belongs to the system. This contrast or duality of continuity and discontinuity is expressed by mutual-exclusion and exhaustive-alternation statements, i.e. propositions and terms as chains and links defined by *homomorphism* and *correspondence*. In fact, the columns of the matrix (x) are marked off from each other by: continuity – discontinuity – homomorphism – correspondence (after the level (i) mutual exclusion and exhaustive alternation of F and T in $\sim$ and 'assignment').

If, in accordance with the '*SR* and *FT*' paper, one starts with 'stimulus-object' and 'response-object' and builds up, relabelling the parts of (x), one ends up with 'predicate' and 'term' as 'differentiation of function' and 'n functions of differentiation', respectively, the *latter* being represented by n-valued logic, or probability ('valid consequence') as a result of the original F and T (*two* 'entities') having given way to 'truth-values' whereas the *former* is statistical.

Both are dual, but one is micro, the other macro; the former is 'member – of a social class', the latter is 'different social classes – of a system'.

As regards $\forall$ and $\exists$:

In that the four *steps* from level to level are reflected in F, T, $\sim$, and 'assignment' the levels-structure is independent, i.e. interpretable in any universe of discourse. The structure of levels itself is the sociological perspective ('term-predicate') of the present writer (∃) or of anyone (∃) who happens to agree with him, *'agreement' being defined by* a particular model or interpretation of the structure itself whether made up of words or symbols, observed objects or parts of an experimental process (∀).

In this, that an undefined term is defined by its context, or equivalently, '*F* underlies *T*', or '$\varnothing \subset \bigcup$' – can be expressed in all sorts of ways, e.g. 'one is just part of the infinite material world' or 'behaviour presupposes object' or Sartre's 'the nothingness which lies at the heart of man'.

Part D

Truth Tables and Levels of Abstraction

12

S-R and F-T

R. O. Gibson

Part I of this chapter presents a hierarchy of 'levels' of social-psychological development based on stimulus-response. The approach is a behaviouristicially unorthodox use of the conventional terms 'stimulus-response', rejecting as simplistic and mechanical those treatments of S-R which do not take sufficiently into account the social relation of the observer to a behaving subject. The admission, in this chapter, of that ambiguity which is inevitable in all human affairs permits us to link psychological stimulus-response with logical falsity-truth, by formally identifying the hierarchy of levels with a certain logical hierarchy.

Part II presents a truth table hierarchy based on falsity-truth. The presentation rejects as merely arid formal games, those kinds of logic which are based on a simple inductive distinction between 2-valued and n-valued logic failing to take into account that in virtue of 'truth-function' 2-valued logic already involves induction. With the admission of this involvement is bound up the utter generality of the stimulus-object with which Part I begins.

The hierarchies I and II are identical in form. The theoretical system is, moreover, independent, in the sense of its being interpretable in terms of any universe of discourse whatsoever.

The levels will be indicated by the marks (i), (ii), (iii), (iv), (v).

I

(i) We start by considering an individual I_1 whose essential characteristic is merely that he is not dead. 'Stimulus', as excitation of the system I_1, presupposes the introduction of some object or other as stimulus-object. I_1 being immediate and *unanalysed*, since the 'object' can be *anything*, stimulus is language in the most general sense. Our general 'object' is an *undefined* term which, however, acquires definition in that the stimulus, as total process, includes obvious discrimination of an object by the individual I_1 himself, for example by a hand. Let us call this discrimination, by the individual himself, a 'response' and the thing so discriminated a 'response-object'. Thus I_1 begins to be analysed.

But then, the individual is not alone in the world. An individual I_2 reacts to an object via another individual's (I_1's) observed act of discrimination. Object as stimulus-object and object as response-object discriminated by I_1 are distinct for I_2. We define this mutual exclusion of stimulus-object and response-object to be I_2's 'information'. However, in I_1's act of discrimination observed by I_2, that I_1 continues to touch the object or withdraws from it expresses that stimulus-object and response-object are bound up with each other as exhaustive alternatives; this exhaustive alternation defines 'gesture'.

(ii) Since he is not alone in this situation, each individual's reaction to an object is not a simple stimulus nor simple response. Inasmuch as there is 'information' and 'gesture' about an object or thing discriminated, each individual's response is compound. The components of each individual's compound response correspond to the two individuals as related by the object. If, and only if, each individual's stimulus-object is common, that is something in a common perceptual world, we define each individual's compound response to be a 'meaning'. The object is 'common' inasmuch as the level (i) response-object presupposed some individual or other; on account of the generality of the 'individual' the object is as yet unanalysed. On the other hand we now define each individual's compound response as a 'word' when each individual's response-object is a common response-object in the sense that a response is now made *through* another individual. (Discrimination of an object as response-object is now 'choice'.) In this way it is now the turn of the object, as a meaning, to begin to be analysed.

But as well as the common object, O_1, for either individual there can be another object O_2, there has to be an (uncommon) O_2 to make a *common* object possible; we now define each individual's compound response to be 'social' if it is (*a*) a 'meaning' and (*b*) one of its component responses is 'information'. Also we now define each individual's compound response to be a common 'task' if it is (*a*) a 'word' and (*b*) both components are 'social' – that is each individual's performance is discrimination in relation to meaningful information.

(iii) In virtue of an O_2, objects are linked *through* an individual, just as at level (ii) each individual's response was compound; so now each individual can perceive that there is such a thing as a common task, in that, for him: (*a*) components of a compound response are interchangeable with respect to meaning, corresponding to interchange of say I_1 and I_2, also meaning is distributive over the components of a word, as its 'denotation'; that is, since each individual is a link common to two pairs of individuals, each pair having an object, we now have, not simply a common object, but a 'class' of common objects or 'denotation', the linking 'word' being a new kind of stimulus. (*b*) components of a compound response are interchangeable with respect to word, also word is distributive over the components of a meaning, word as an 'abstraction'; that is, each one of the common objects is a link between pairs of individuals responding *through* each other, meaning thus becoming 'word as an abstraction'. (Discrimination is now a 'defining property' qualifying an object to be a member of a class.)

Let us call these two kinds of interchange-cum-distribution 'association' of meanings and of words.

But a class for one individual can be referred to by *another* individual; in short a defining property with respect to a class involves complementation and identity – on the one hand as a *classification* of common objects, the classes resulting from the activity of the classifier; on the other hand as an ordering by class *inclusion*, the emphasis being on the classifier. The division into classes being analysis of the denotation of a defining property, analysis has now returned to the individual.

In classification and class-inclusion there is a principle of duality in the sense that interchange of meaning and word is associated with interchange of stimulus-object and response-object; on the one hand the level (ii) object is common inasmuch as response-object presupposed some individual or other, on the other hand a response is made *through* another individual in that the level (i) object-in-general is possible only for a definite individual. That this duality arises as an implicit principle at level (iii) is possible through a further such duality, imposed by the two kinds of association, referred to above as 'class'and 'defining property', on meaning and word – the individual becoming indefinite, the object definite.

(iv) The principle itself is now made explicit, as an empirical generalization, in the sense of a class not of objects but of linking individuals, that is a class of pairs of common objects – giving rise on the one hand to a relation, and on the other hand to order. (Discrimination as purpose, that is an ordering which defines a given pair to belong to the relation.)

But, analysis returning to the object, object's being ordered gives a 'relationship', or induction, and on the other hand 'polarity' with respect to the relationship, in deduction.

In one's opposing relation as unordered pair to relation as ordered, 'relationship' and 'polarity' express duality itself, dualism, as the explicit *association* of meaning and word with stimulus-object and response-object respectively.

(v) This principle of double duality – the two kinds of association now correspond to the previously recognized duality with respect to interchange – is itself made explicit, as a class of individuals classified according to function, with respect to a system, that is a *functional differentiation*, inter-relating relations. The higher duality (of dualities) arises as the related relations themselves vary over objects in alternative orderings. Now, within and inseparable from the differentiation, discrimination has become function. There can be any number of functions (i.e. n 'dimensions') in the social differentiation (or 'space'), just as at a lower level these could be any number of defining 'properties'.

But now, in a system, 'objects' constitute a *universe of*

discourse. Through the systematization the previous 'relationship' and 'polarity' have given way to continuum and manifold.

Continuum underlies manifold. Stimulus-object underlies response-object in the sense that, as systematizing individual one is now enabled, by the principle of duality made explicit as a principle, to admit one's association of meaning and word with stimulus-object and response-object respectively.

Yet this utter circularity, as an expression of functional differentiation, is the realization of individual freedom.

LEVELS AND STEPS FROM LEVEL TO LEVEL. That there are four steps, from level to level of the hierarchy, is reflected in each level's having four main aspects (made up of two pairs separated by our 'But' above). The hierarchy is based on the double distinction: social object – for an individual – functioning as a member – of system.

Although the 4 'horizontal' aspects coalesce as one proceeds from level to level, the reader will find it convenient to visualize the hierarchy as a 5×4 matrix of 5 rows and 4 columns.

In virtue of our level (ii) 'meaning – word – social – task', we shall regard the four main aspects of each level as: psychology – the linguistic – the social – economics.

It is at level (ii) that the social relation of the observer to a behaving subject first becomes manifest, albeit in an unsophisticated expression.

II

In this section we outline a hierarchy based on truth tables which will mirror the 5×4 pattern of levels outlined above.

Understanding a statement to be a sentence which can be classified as either true (T) or false (F) but not both, truth tables are used in the classical statement calculus to display the truth value assigments to composite sentences, out of which a sentence is composed by means of certain connectives. A fundamental role is played by the table for 'negation', symbolized by $\sim$.

p	$\sim p$
T	F
F	T

where p is a 'sentence', in the language of the statement calculus or sentential logic.

In this calculus notions such as 'truth' are are irrelevant; the truth tables defining the connectives are:

p q	$p \vee q$	p q	$p \wedge q$	p q	$p \rightarrow q$	p q	$p \leftrightarrow q$
T T	T	T T	T	T T	T	T T	T
T F	T	T F	F	T F	F	T F	F
F T	T	F T	F	F T	T	F T	F
F F	F	F F	F	F F	T	F F	T

p *and* q being constituent sentences.

It is to be noted that (1) the called sentential connectives are defined by these tables, (2) 'statements' are linguistic expressions whose fundamental property is that they are T or F and that 'statements' or 'sentences' are not necessarily written sentences or other forms of conventional symbolic utterance.

We now outline the levels.

(i) Considering (*a*) that a 'statement' is a linguistic expression which can be classified as true or false, and that a 'formula' is a linguistic expression containing an x which becomes a statement when x is replaced by the name of an object; also (*b*) that 'negation' and 'assignment' are defined respectively by the mutual exclusion and exhaustive alternation of truth and falsity as values of a statement p – we replace x and 'object as named' by F and T respectively and then take level (i) of our hierarchy to be represented as follows:

$$F \quad , \quad T \quad , \quad \begin{array}{c|c} p & \sim p \\ \hline T & F \\ F & T \end{array} \quad \text{'one member of } \{F,\ T\}\text{'}$$

posited respectively by:

　　　　formula, statement, negation, assignment

('formula' and 'statement' correspond to 'stimulus' and 'response' in (I)).

We shall take the tables for $\vee$, $\wedge$, $\rightarrow$, $\leftrightarrow$, to represent the four main aspects of level (ii) of the part (I) hierarchy.

(ii) The tables for

$$\vee \qquad \wedge \qquad \rightarrow \qquad \leftrightarrow$$

are characterized respectively by:

∨ , the composite statement is *F* if and only if each constituent statement is *F*.

∧ , the composite statement is *T* if and only if each constituent statement is *T*. (*T* as norm, i.e. as 'true statement'.)

→, the table for $p \rightarrow q$ is equivalent to that for $\sim p \vee q$.

↔, the table for $p \leftrightarrow q$ is equivalent to that for $(\sim p \vee q) \wedge (p \vee \sim q)$.

It can be shown that the tables for → and ↔ express the ambiguity or overlapping of those defining ∨ and ∧. This is the level (ii) version of the fact that the definitions of 'negation' and 'assignment' expressed the mutual exclusion and exhaustive alternation of *F* and *T*; this implicit duality becomes an explicit duality in the sense that the tables for ∨ and ∧ are dual with respect to interchange of *F* and *T*. Truth tables are based on $\sim$ and assignment of *F* and *T* as alternatives. It is this implicit duality's becoming explicit that we use to mark the transition from level (i) to level (ii).

Then the implicit duality of → and ↔ becomes explicit in turn at the next level, (iii), when formal laws based on ↔ will arise, just as at level (ii) truth tables are based on assignment.

(iii) In the usual formulation of the statement calculus, in which a formula has a 'truth value', a set of initial formulae can be extended by adjoining all the composite formulae that can be formed by repeated use of the connectives, so that if *p* and *q* are members of the extended set, so are $p \vee q$, $p \wedge q$, $p \rightarrow q$, $p \leftrightarrow q$, and $\sim p$, the truth value of a composite formula being determined inductively in accordance with the tables.

In virtue of the characteristics of the tables for ∨ , ∧ , →, ↔, (→ is characterized by 'a true statement cannot imply a false one', and ↔ by 'the composite statement is true if and only if the constituents have the same value') and taking into account that *F* and *T* are now variables restricted to false and true statements respectively, in the *extended inductive use* of truth tables true statements can be regarded as elements forming a group with respect to the operation →, T representing the whole group and F representing its identity element. (Operation and group correspond to the 'classification' and 'inclusion' of I (iii).) The statements can be interpreted as 'sets' of objects, T being 'defining property', for uses of the ∧-table are linked by 'composite statement is T if and only if constituent statements are T' (intuitive principle of abstraction) whereas the characteristic for ∨ gives 'set' itself (intuitive extension).

Regarded as sets statements are subject to the four pairs of Boolean algebraic laws:

the commutative and distributive laws with respect to ∨ and ∧ (the norm as formal law or axiom);
the two corresponding sets of complementation and identity laws.

From these four pairs of laws the associative laws

$$p \vee (q \vee r) \equiv (p \vee q) \vee r$$

and
$$p \wedge (q \wedge r) \equiv (p \wedge q) \wedge r$$

can be deduced; so can the absorption laws.

The Boolean laws are characterized by the principle of duality: if ∨ and ∧ are interchanged and also F and T are interchanged in any law, then the new law is dual to the original one.

(iv) We are now concerned with 'relations', between columns of pairs of tables in the extended use of truth tables. In the following definitions, relations in a set will be based on 'grouping operation' (cf. the transitions from (i) to (ii) and (ii) to (iii)).

A relation is usually defined by: an open sentence $P(x, y)$ in which $P(a, b)$ is either T or F for any ordered pair belonging to a product set $A \times B$. A relation R in a set A is called 'symmetric' if '(a, b) belongs to $(\in)R$' implies $(b, a) \in R$ and 'antisymmetric' if '$(a, b) \in R$ and $(b, a) \in R$' implies $a = b$. (The norm as tautology. The usual statement calculus definition of 'tautology' is that a statement whose value is T, for all possible assignments of truth values to its prime components, is a tautology.) Also R is 'transitive' in A if '$(a, b) \in R$ and $(b, c) \in R$' implies $(a, c) \in R$. Fourthly, R is 'reflexive' if for every $a \in A$, $(a, a) \in R$.

An 'equivalence relation' is one which is transitive, reflexive and symmetrical, whereas a 'partial ordering' is a relation which is transitive, reflexive, and antisymmetrical, expressing the very interchanges made by the principle of duality.

On reflexivity and transitivity will be based:

(v) The technical definitions, belonging to the predicate calculus, of: predicate – term – universal quantifier – existential quantifier. (With 'terms' the norm has now become valid consequence. The usual definition of 'valid consequence' is that a statement Q is a valid consequence of statements $P_1, P_2, \ldots, P_n$, if and only if for every truth value assignment to each of the prime statements occurring in one or more of $P_1, P_2, \ldots, P_n$, Q receives the value T whenever every P receives the value T.)

'Terms' are individual variables; the 'universal quantifier' ($\forall x$) may be read as 'for every x', the 'existential quantifier' ($\exists x$) as 'there is an x such that', an 'n-place predicate', $P(x_1, x_2, \ldots, x_n)$, is an expression such that an assignment of values (not truth values) to the variables $x_1, x_2, \ldots, x_n$ from a domain yields a statement. It is assumed that there is a non-empty set D, the 'domain', such that each individual variable ranges over D, also that alternative logical functions f on D^n into $\{F, T\}$ are assigned to each predicate P and that to each distinct free variable ('free' in that its occurrence is not within the scope of a quantifier) is assigned a value in D.

Then if $P(y_1, y_2, \ldots, y_n)$ is a 'prime formula' obtained by substitution of variables in a predicate P and f is assigned to $P(x_1, x_2, \ldots, x_n)$ while a_i is assigned to y_i, the truth value of $P(y_1, y_2, \ldots, y_n)$ is $f(a_1, a_2, \ldots, a_n)$.

Also the truth tables of the statement calculus hold; and for an assignment of values to the predicates and free variables of $(\forall x)P$ the truth value of $(\forall x)P$ is F if and only if the value of P is F for at least one assignment to x; whereas for an assignment of values to the predicates and free variables of $(\exists x)P$, the truth value of $(\exists x)P$ is T if and only if P is T for at least one assignment to x.

That F (identified with the 'x' of level (i)) underlies T (identified with name of object, replacing the x), is now recognized in the sense that, through symmetry and antisym-

I

(Starts with stimulus-object underlying response-object but ends with universe of discourse)

(i) stimulus-object / stimulus	response-object / response	mutual exclusion / information	exhaustive alternation / gesture
(ii) meaning	word (response as choice)	social	task
(iii) denotation	abstraction (defining property w.r.t. class)	classification	class inclusion
(iv) generalization (for pairs)	empirical (purpose, as ordering)	relationship (induction)	polarity (deduction)
(v) differentiation of function i.e. members of a social class	n functions (of differentiation), i.e. n social classes of a system	universe of	discourse

freedom as 'awareness of necessity'

II

(Starts with undefined term replaced by name of object, but ends with quantifiers, defined by valuation procedure)

undefined x (F)	name of object (T)	table for $\sim$	one of $\{F, T\}$
formula	statement	negation	assignment
$\vee$ = false statement	$\wedge$ (norm as true statement)	$\uparrow$	$\leftrightarrow$
comm. & dist. for $\vee$	comm. & dist. for $\wedge$ (norm as formal law)	complementation & identity, such as $p \vee \sim p \equiv T$	the dual complementation & identity, such as $p \wedge \sim p \equiv F$
symmetrical relation	antisymmetrical relation (norm as tautology)	transitive relation	reflexive relation
predicate	n terms (norm as valid consequence)	universal quantifier	existential quantifier
	freedom from scope of quantifier		

metry of relations, a statement can now be viewed as a formula having no free variables.

The hierarchy started with undefined term but ended with quantified term defined by valuation procedure.

The reader is advised to compare the following with the end of Part I, particularly the two paragraphs preceding 'Levels and steps from level to level'. In 'two-valued logic', F *underlies* T in that the step from 'statement', as a formula containing no free variables, to statements being classifiable as F or T enables the step from statements as F or T to the formal laws of sets, a formula acquiring a 'truth-value', these very steps being incorporated in the definition of relation, in its symmetrical and antisymmetrical aspects, the incorporation marked by the valuation procedure for the quantifiers of the predicate calculus.

Yet the logic becomes n-valued in the probability of 'valid consequence'. Negation underlies assignment in that the further steps, to relation and thence predicate, are distinguished by a predicate's having a logical function on D^n.

In short, the steps from level to level are reflected in the four main aspects of level (i).

13

'Fermat's Last Theorem' as an Expression of Duality

R. O. Gibson

Introduction

In that the four *steps* from level to level are reflected in *F*, *T*, $\sim$, and assigment, the succession of levels, I or II, is independent, i.e. interpretable in any universe of discourse.[1] Duality arises implicitly in particular sciences or arts, at a certain stage of their development, or in everyday life and conversation. We shall now consider some examples, starting with one taken from mathematics.

It is well known that many professional and amateur mathematicians have attempted to prove Fermat's Last Theorem. This asserts that

$$x^n + y^n = z^n \ (n > 2)$$

has no non-zero positive integral solutions. It has never been proved for general *n*, although Fermat himself, in the seventeenth century, claimed to have devised a proof, which he did not reveal 'because there was not enough room in the margin' of the paper on which he was writing. Since then many fallacious proofs have been put forward for the general case, but the only successes have been those dealing with special values of *n*. Most modern serious work on the problem has been confined to special cases. For example Vandiver[2] in 1929 proved the theorem for $n < 307$.

On the basis of our '*S-R* and *F-T*' chapter, the following assertion will be made: that the impossibility of proving the parallel postulate in geometry entails the impossibility of proving Fermat's Last Theorem.

[1] By the same token the predicate calculus becomes statistics, i.e. quantifier comes within scope of quantifier.

[2] Vandiver, N., *Trans. Amer. Math. Soc. 31* (1929), 613–42.

Regarding parallels, Euclid included in his general axioms: If a straight line meets two other straight lines so as to make the interior angles on the same side together less than two right angles, then the straight lines will meet if produced, on the side of these angles.

The Greeks were not worried by parallels, but after their time doubts arose and eventually mathematicians felt that the parallels axiom should be capable of being proved. Saccheri (1667–1733) postulated that the parallels axiom should be susceptible of being proved. Many mathematicians tried to prove the parallels axiom from the other axioms of Euclid but every proof presented was found to be fallacious, usually by begging the question in some way. About the end of the eighteenth century Playfair formulated as a postulate: In a plane there can be drawn through a given point only one line which does not meet a given line. With the advent of non-Euclidean geometry in the nineteenth century, the question of whether it was possible to prove the parallel postulate was settled, negatively.

The independence of the parallel postulate was shown by constructing a geometrical system based on a set of axioms in which the parallel postulate is replaced by a contrary postulate, the consistency of such a system being established by renaming terms of Euclidean geometry so as to give a 'model' of the non-Euclidean system as a 'translation' of the system into ordinary Euclidean geometry.

Modern mathematics, with concepts such as 'open set' and 'ideals', transcends the geometrical or arithmetical difficulties referred to above.

As regards our assertion referred to above, a connection between the parallel postulate and Fermat's Last Theorem was first suggested by a consideration of the historical development of geometry and arithmetic. For example, in the geometry of the ancient delta civilizations the relatively round and straight 'shapes' of the barbarians had become implicitly arithmetical, in the advent of *measurement* of distances between things, the measuring-rod whose positions are *counted* being a straight object: on the other hand primitive counting had given way to *numerals*, which, as grouping systems, implicitly involved 'shaping'. By the time of Descartes this mutual involvement of geometry and arithmetic had become explicit, in algebraic geometry on the one hand and on the other hand in the representation of numbers in a positional notation. The numerals and rule-of-thumb geometry of ancient Egypt arose in men's dealing with very limited problems. The Greeks, dealing theoretically with a far wider range of practical problems, axiomatized geometry. The axioms, from which they deduced the merely empirical rules of their predecessors, were from their point of view self-evident truths, unlike the axioms of nineteenth-century mathematics which were consciously adopted assumptions.

In their arithmetical algorithms the Greeks' use of letters of the alphabet to mark off units, 'tens', and so on, was implicitly but only implicitly a positional notation, becoming explicit very much later.

The Connection between the Parallel Postulate and Fermat's Last Theorem

It follows from Chapter 12, '*S-R* and *F-T*', part II (i), (ii), (iii), that false statements (level (ii)) form a system which is *continuous* in the sense that the union, or the intersection, of any number of sets is a set, F being the null set and T the universal set; whereas true statements (level (ii)) form a system which is *discontinuous* in the sense of a system which (*a*) does not contain the null set, and of which (*b*) every finite intersection of sets of the system also belongs to the system. This contrast or duality of continuity and discontinuity is expressed by mutual-exclusion and exhaustive-alternation statements, i.e. propositions and terms as chains and links defined by *homomorphism* and *correspondence*.

At level (iii) we have the contrariety of: set – defining property, expressed in: operation – group closure.

At level (iv) the principle of duality is made explicit in symmetric and antisymmetric relation, this in turn being expressed by transitivity and reflexivity.

Next we replace the general 'false statement' and 'true statement', 'exclusion' and 'alternation' statements etc., by suitable specific terms from elementary geometry and arithmetic to give *models* of the systems characterized abstractly at our levels (ii), (iii) and (iv), models as interpretations on the one hand of different kinds of duality and on the other hand as expressions of those dualities. There is no question of our replacing the level (i) 'formula' and 'statement' by anything for they simply posit an 'object' and an object as named. At level (ii) in geometry some straight object is taken as measuring-rod in determining a distance. We replace 'false statement' by the 'straight-edge' aspect of measuring-rod and 'true statement' by 'measuring-rod' *per se*. The 'exclusion' and 'alternation' statements are replaced by arithmetical 'base' and 'numeral', which express the duality of straight-edge and measuring-rod itself. In the discontinuity aspect of the use of the measuring-rod successive positions are counted, in the continuity (straight-edge) aspect of the use of the rod the rod is merely moved along.

The rod is used in a context, a rectilinear figure, for the measurer has some purpose. Similarly the level (iii) 'side' is part of a figure having *its* context. In the wider context the straight-edge is metamorphosed to a 'side', in that aspect of pure geometry concerned with congruence of figures; on the other hand the measuring-rod as such is metamorphosed to 'angle', a new form of discontinuity, in that aspect of pure geometry concerned with similarity of figures. These contrasting aspects of pure geometry are expressed by the Euclidean algorithm and by integral solutions of: a square number as a sum of squares. (Here it is essential to bear in mind that just as things are grouped as similar so are numbers, that at level (ii) a 'base' is not yet something necessarily fixed throughout successive 'base-numeral' steps, and that at level (iii) members of sets are the same, or different, according to how they are actually grouped.)

Widening the context again, taking axes of reference for a Cartesian curve, the opposition of 'side' and 'angle' is metamorphosed to 'parallels' and to the invariance or equidistance aspect of Cartesian coordinates, represented abstractly by symmetrical and antisymmetrical relations. On the other hand, this Cartesian opposition is expressed by the 'Euclidean algorithm' (i.e. the symbolic version of our old elementary-school H. C. F. process) and by integral solutions of $x^2 + y^2 = z^2$, but now as respectively the factorization aspect and similar-sets aspect of a positional notation for a 'natural number'. Just as the parallel postulate, which is equivalent to the postulate of invariance, is essential to pure-geometrical dimension, the arithmetical index cannot be greater than 2 because a positional notation cannot absolutely jump over a position but has to proceed from position to position; transitivity has to be based on simple *relation*.

On the basis of our (*a*) having replaced an 'object' *x* by *F* and an object-as-named by *T* and then (*b*) replacing false and true statements in our hierarchy of truth tables by specific elementary mathematical terms, we conclude that Fermat's Last Theorem is an expression of the parallel postulate, so that the impossibility of proving the latter from Euclidean axioms entails the impossibility of proving the former for ordinary Archimedean arithmetic.

One source of trouble in dealing with Fermat's Last Theorem is the attitude 'God created the natural numbers.' Not to admit that a 'natural number' is invented, at level (iv), as Cartesian locus is invented, constitutes failure to recognize one's own activities. In the very step of solving his level (iii) problem by admitting duality, the individual at level (iv) has a new problem in failing to recognize the duality as his, i.e. as 'dualism'.

Duality in Subjects other than Mathematics

Duality made explicit is recognition of one's lower-level activities. Duality is not confined to geometry and arithmetic, of course, but arises in calculus and algebra and in subjects other than mathematics. As an expression of explicit duality a counterpart of Fermat's Last Theorem arises at level (iv) (historically the era of Cartesian dualism) in various science subjects: for example, the question of gravitational and inertial mass in mechanics, or the problem of tonality in music, once pitch-key and diatonic harmony have been introduced (a problem originating in the contrast between 'intervals' of a scale and the overtones of a vibrating string).

We could assign mechanical meanings to 'false statement' and 'true statement' and so on, starting with 'balance-scale' and standard 'weight', at level (ii):

(ii) A balance-scale is defined as such by its use in the continuity aspect of a weighing process, the process of addition of instalments of 'heaviness' to the scale-pan until it descends, pulling up the other pan.

(iii) In the wider context of a mechanical system it is metamorphosed to a 'force'.

(iv) Then in the context of Newtonian mechanics it becomes 'inertial mass'. The inertial frame of reference is the mechanical counterpart to Cartesian axes of reference.

(v) Then, in a holonomic dynamical system, inertial mass is metamorphosed to 'degree of freedom'.

As in the case of geometry, we can match this series of metamorphoses with another:

(ii) In the weighing context, a body is taken as standard weight. It is defined as such by its use in the discontinuity aspect of weighing, the aspect concerned with the counting of units of weight.

(iii) In the formulation of the principle of the balance a 'weight' is metamorphosed to a 'moment' of a force.

(iv) Then in the context of Newtonian mechanics, inertial mass is matched by 'gravitational mass' – to which 'moment' has been metamorphosed.

(v) Finally, the metamorphosis of inertial mass to degree of freedom is matched by the metamorphosis of gravitational mass to a general 'constraint'.

Now let us follow up the above matched series by considering similarly the technical side of an 'arts' subject, namely the pitch aspect of music.

A musical scale is a step-wise, ordered arrangement, for the purposes of vocal or instrumental practice, of the notes belonging to the music of a particular stage of development of a society – starting, historically, from the beginnings of the ancient delta civilizations.

We have on the one hand an object, such as a vibrating stretched string of a certain length and tension, taken to give a standard note, and on the other hand this object used to produce notes *varying* in quality and forming a note-series.

In the case of musical pitch our matched metamorphoses through successively wider contexts are as follows:

(ii) scale	(ii) note
(iii) mode	(iii) tetrachord
(iv) pitch-key	(iv) diatonic harmony
(v) unrelated keys	(v) chromatic harmony

These series could be matched by series corresponding to other aspects of music, e.g. rhythm. More generally, it will be evident to the reader that it is possible to mark out similar schemes of metamorphoses with extension of context in subjects other than those dealt with above; but such marking out is possible only if one has some familiarity with the subject considered.

As a final example, let us consider chemistry.

We take our cue from the ancient Egyptians' extraction of metals from their ores by smelting. This depends on the use of an agent, such as charcoal, which can be viewed on the one hand as a 'making' or extracting agent and on the other hand as a 'changing' or breaking-up agent, leaving a residue. Once again, further development, though now of a chemical context, gives us two matched series of metamorphoses, starting with:

(ii) making-agent	(ii) changing agent
(iii) substance	(iii) property

Such a 'substance' is the Greek element 'earth'; in mentioning this aspect of chemistry here it is vital to remember that whether it is the chemistry of an ancient Egyptian, Greek, or modern chemist, he actually makes something out of *minerals*.

We continue our matched series for levels (iv) and (v) as follows:

(iv) a 'chemical element' in the sense of Boyle	(iv) a 'pure' compound
(v) atoms	(v) molecules

What is common to these examples is that, out of 'objects' at level (i), duality of the continuous and discontinuous arises at level (ii), becoming explicitly recognized at level (iv). In the case of mathematics level (iii) is characterized by 'axioms', in contrast with which level (iv) is characterized by 'postulates'; it is the 'independence' of the parallel postulate with which mathematicians have been concerned. However, in each subject explicit duality is postulational in that two aspects of the subject are recognized *as* aspects, neither being *derivable* purely from the other, although this very recognition is not yet itself recognized.

In accordance with part (I) of our '*S-R* and *F-T*' chapter the four main aspects of our scheme of levels (e.g. set – property – operation – group) can be called: psychology – language – the social – the economic.

In these terms the 'Fermat's Last Theorem' question, as one expression of duality, is a social manifestation of psychological conflict.

Mathematical Addendum

The argument in the text mirroring 'Fermat's Last Theorem' in the parallel-postulate is based on the impossibility of sharply separating social from natural science. The bare bones of the argument are

1. Invention of a 5×4 matrix composed of parts of textbook logic.
2. This logical scaffolding gives rise to a hierarchy of dualities characterizable in conventional logical terms, or in terms of linguistics.
3. The hierarchy involves a 5×4 structure of axioms, e.g., the conjunction of two or more 'statements' is a 'statement'.
4. Assignment of (*a*) geometrical, and (*b*) arithmetical, meanings to the undefined terms in the hierarchy of axioms, to give two different models of the hierarchy.

We shall now present the argument in more directly mathematical form, but it will be noted that the last step of the argument is *linguistic*.

We start with an outline of Kummer's famous attempt to prove 'Fermat's Last Theorem', based on the account given in[1]. Since Euler had proved the theorem for exponent 4, one may restrict consideration to

$$x^l + y^l = z^l \tag{1}$$

where l is an odd prime, x, y, z being assumed relatively prime. Kummer connected F.L.T. with decomposition into factors by noting that if ζ denotes a primitive lth root of 1 then (1) may be written

$$\prod_{k=0}^{l-1} (x + \zeta^k y) = z^l \tag{2}$$

[1] Borevich, Z. I. and Shafarevich, I. R. (1966): *Number Theory*, translated from the Russian; NY, Academic Press.

If a product of pairwise relatively prime rational integers is an lth power then each of the factors is an lth power. The factors on the L.H.S. of (2) belong to the algebraic field $R(\zeta)$ of degree $l-1$ over R, the cyclotomic polynomial being irreducible over the field of rational numbers.

Assuming unique prime factorization in the ring $D=\{1, \zeta, \ldots, \zeta^{l-2}\}$, the maximal order of the field $R(\zeta)$, and assuming that x, y, z, are not divisible by l, it can be proved that

$$x+\zeta y=e\alpha^l$$
and
$$x-\zeta y=e_1\alpha_1{}^l \qquad (3)$$

where e and e_1 are units of D, $\alpha \in D$, $\alpha_1 \in D$.

Using certain lemmas concerning the ring $D=Z[\zeta]$ over the rational integers, also assuming, for $l \geqslant 5$ (F.L.T. for $l=3$ having been proved separately), that (1) has integral solutions, then equations (3) lead eventually to a contradiction, of certain congruences mod. l.

Hence F.L.T. would be proved *if factorization into primes were unique* for $R(\zeta)$.

By a further argument involving the integers of this field, Kummer showed that, under the assumption of unique prime factorization, the case of F.L.T. in which precisely one of x, y, z is divisible by l also holds.

Kummer, making an unwarranted assumption of u.p.f., thought at first that he had proved F.L.T. But in the above account u.p.f. is taken as an explicit assumption, which means that the contradiction obtained proves that it is the *composite* proposition, 'that there are integral solutions of (1) *and* u.p.f. holds', which cannot be true. But these 2 propositions can be put together in the following way. Considering that the numbers of the ring $Z[\zeta]$ can be mapped onto the rational integers, in virtue of the theorem that an enumerable set of enumerable sets is enumerable, we see that when Kummer systematically invented 'units', 'integers', 'primes', etc., in D he was in effect talking about the system of rational integers, which constitute a u.f. domain, thus restoring u.p.f. in the sense of a mapping onto the rational integers. Since he was thus able, in the argument, to get together the propositions (*a*) integral solutions exist for (1), and (*b*) u.f.d., *by linguistic translation*, it is impossible to *prove* F.L.T.

Just as in the Riemann and Klein models of elliptic and hyperbolic non-Euclidean geometrical systems the consistency of the latter were established by renaming terms of Euclidean geometry, so Kummer in effect showed the impossibility of proving F.L.T.

The models, geometrical and arithmetical, arose at the stage of social development characterized by philological comparison and etymological derivation, but the geometrical case is easier to see, because in geometry, originating in surveying and construction, we can visualize structures and relations of objects whereas arithmetic, originating in chronometry and dividing out things, is more abstract in requiring awareness of social differentiation.

14

The 'Two Cultures' and 'Levels of Abstraction'

R. O. Gibson

At the end of the previous chapter we referred to Fermat's Last Theorem as one social manifestation of psychological conflict. Marxists would regard the psychological, as well as the strictly social, as part of the cultural superstructure, reflecting the economic 'basis'. However, when one has already made the *distinctions* between the psychological, the linguistic, the social, and the economic, it is difficult to see that anything is added by referring to one of these as 'basic'; although, in the light of the treatment of duality in the previous chapters we can accept psychological conflict as reflecting the socio-economic in the sense that explicit duality is expressed in an implicit duality, which in turn becomes explicit.

This duality or conflict has been referred to in various ways by different authors, as, for example, Cartesian dualism, or theories of psycho-physical parallelism or interaction, or, in more recent times, as 'the problem of the two cultures'.

Let us consider this last.

Is there a 'problem' of the 'two cultures'? Ever since C. P. Snow coined the phrase it has been bandied about, often lightly or vaguely, in conversation, newspaper articles and books. Yet, no matter how vague the uses of the phrase, its various interpretations do seem to have some connotation in common. They seem to imply the existence of some fundamental cultural separation or split which is undesirable, moreover a split which, once correctly diagnosed, could be healed by suitable treatment, maybe painlessly. It has recently been suggested in a newspaper article that in British education and technology one symptom of trouble is that engineering has for long been looked upon as a second-class intellectual activity.

Perhaps the easiest way for us to get some idea of the implied cultural distinction is to start by recalling the separation which was made in one's schooldays between 'arts' and 'science' subjects. It was popularly supposed that you needed 'brains' for science but not for classics, even at the schools where classics were treated as sacred. Yet long after leaving school one has so often found that in conversation on important topics, such as economic or social or political matters affecting our daily lives, arts graduates are broader in outlook and more articulate than science graduates; also one notes that some big firms recruit graduates for responsible jobs irrespective of whether they are arts or science graduates. In fact, the 'liberal studies' vogue some years ago was the outcome of an educational programme concerned with liberalizing the over-specialized Meccano-set-minded boffin who might be as 'green as grass' outside the intricacies of his special technical field in the sense that in his mind the developments in this field were separated from their social implications, or at least were related by him to the social in a naïve manner. So we had the spectacle of more than one individual, having played a vital part in the production of atomic weapons, rushing to sign a manifesto against their use. Also we witnessed the phenomenon of atomic weapons specialists who, though having come to the conclusion that the real problem was social, had such an over-simplified interpretation of the 'social' that they went off carrying secrets to the other camp, the Communists'.

In recent years it has been widely noted that there has been a great increase in the percentage of students who have opted for the social sciences. This is much to the surprise of certain members of our population, for example the writer of a letter to a certain newspaper suggesting, during student disturbances, that the London School of Economics should be shut down and reopened as a school for plumbers, plumbers being important and scarce.

The man in the street views psychologists as mad and cannot understand how a lot of money could be spent on a sociological research project which resulted in the conclusion: that people in high-rise flats prefer blocks of flats in which the lifts work to those in which they do not.

The man in the street tends to regard with suspicion not

only psychologists, but also statisticians and economists. He is painfully aware of the contradictory predictions of economists. He may compare them with 'proper' scientists such as chemists or physicists, whose work he regards as precise – overlooking the possibility that it may be in the nature of the case that precision, in the sense of objective agreement, is something not inherent in social studies. Perhaps this attitude is not surprising when one considers that on the one hand many psychologists themselves are intent on a down-to-earth aping of the physical sciences while on the other hand we have the guru type of psychologist belonging to the charismatic religious era which has produced phenomena such as Jesus Christ Super Star.

In considering this point, one can at least note that, whereas the physicist, in studying certain processes, makes judgments, the psychologist studies judgment-making. Similarly a psychologist has been jocularly defined as a man who goes to a nude show and watches the audience.

'Judgments' lead us to consider another characteristic of psychology, a characteristic relevant to our above remark that imprecision may be inherent in the nature of social studies. Nowadays the term 'behaviour' is used widely in psychology, but in a way which contrasts sharply with the dictionary definition of behaviour as moral conduct. Today the social sciences assume a very technical outlook. In the past social and political studies were closely related to the ethical norms of 'Good' or 'Right'. For example, Plato's *Republic* opens in effect with the question 'What is Justice?' In the nineteenth century it was conventional to divide philosophy into (*a*) metaphysics, which consists of two parts – one the study of pure being, or existence as such, and the other the theory of knowledge, concerned with the question of the relation between things and ideas, and the question of which is basic, which derivative; and (*b*) the three normative studies – ethics, aesthetics and logic, called 'normative' because ethical, aesthetic and logical judgments seem to involve reference to some ideal or standard of goodness, beauty and truth respectively, thus being concerned with an 'ought' and not merely with 'is' as in the natural sciences.

As I. A. Richards has pointed out (in *Principles of Literary Criticism*) the history of aesthetics is a history of confused theories. The question of the aesthetic standard, of beauty, brings us to consideration of art, in the sense of 'fine art'. The term 'art' has been used in all sorts of ways. For some people 'art is something fundamentally associated with primitive societies whereas science is seen as 'modern'. For others 'art' can emerge only at a certain level of development of productive labour, art being something which has ceased to be directly related to practical life; 'art' often means the fine arts belonging to classical, Renaissance or post-Renaissance cultures.

Closely related to the opposition of 'science' and 'art', an opposition is often made between 'pure' or 'applied' science or between the 'quantitative' and the 'qualitative' approaches in scientific work. For example, one sometimes hears it said that chemistry really began as a science only with the advent of the quantitative approach at the time of Lavoisier. But this brings us back again to the question of how man was able to progress from an artistic or qualitative knowledge of things to a scientific or quantitative study of concrete things, and how such progress was related to development from a primitive social level to that of industrial society.

As regards the inner conflict manifested in modern society, between management and labour and so on, the theory has been put forward that all this is due simply to a 'failure of communication', just as wars are 'misunderstandings', and that if everybody could get together and 'talk it over' the problem would be solved.

Although the phrase 'two cultures' has been widely used in ways which might suggest that it refers to something almost self-evident – maybe upper- and lower-class 'life styles' – we have said enough to show that the question of the 'two cultures' is anything but clear, at the level of daily-life common sense.

In making a closer scrutiny with a view to making a *formulation* of the problem of the two cultures, we shall invoke our system of levels.

According to the second of the four main aspects of each level of the hierarchy as discussed in '*S-R* and *F-T*', our levels could be called 'levels of abstraction'. Our term 'levels' was originally suggested by 'levels of abstraction'. This term has been widely used by semanticists, e.g. S. Hayakawa,[1] and by psychologists, and related to levels of social development.

On the other hand, in contrast with our 'abstraction', considering the other aspect of the duality as made explicit at a given level, that is the first main aspect of the level (meaning, class, symmetrical relation) we shall say that an individual now 'recognizes' his previous-level activity, recognizes the entities as his constructs.

In the '*S-R* and *F-T*' chapter we characterized the four main aspects of a subject at a given 'level' as: psychology – language – the social – the economic.

What about the levels themselves? One could characterize the levels (i) to (v) as follows, in religious and philosophical terms, but understood as behavioural. In doing this one is not committed to any religious or philosophical positions which have been put forward but one does accept them as historical. That is, we recognize them as parts of ourselves, exhaustive alternation passing into compound response (v. *S-R* and *F-T*).

(i) Level (i) is the level of primitive animism, in that stimulus-object underlies response-object. For example, tribal behaviour is reciprocal because it is arbitrary.

(ii) Level (ii) is the level at which the sharp reciprocity of stimulus and response, within the merely biological functional differentiation characterizing level (i) society, has given way to a no-longer-sharp distinction, in differentiation of function as the subordination of individuals to a common task. This is the *religious* level, symbolized in the truth-tables by defining 'connectives'; the tables for ∨ and ∧ symbolize a normative distinction which is a condition for social equilibrium consequent on the breakdown of the reciprocity of stimulus and response, which was implicit in primitive society.

Our 'religious' includes the ancient delta civilization despotisms but excludes the philosophical aspect of Christianity, the theology of which originated in Greek philosophy.

At level (iii), the level of formal principles, society is characterized by positive laws directed against individual acts prejudicial to it. Level (iii) is the level at which *philosophy* arises, in that the ambiguity of the religious norms has given way to

[1] Hayakawa, S. (1964): *Language in thought and action*; NY, Harcourt Brace.

explicit duality. Moreover, it is the level of idealist philosophy in that stimulus and response now appears as meaning and word.

In this new function as classifier an individual now recognizes his former subordination to a task.

For example, philosophy, as distinguishable from religion, arose in the roughly three-level ancient Athenian society (slaves, nobility, trading class), the ultimate realities discussed by the philosophers being change, regarded by most as illusory, and the eternal 'forms', constituting a hierarchy culminating in the Form of the Good, the source of all truth and beauty. When, through the development of functional differentiation, the internal stresses of society have developed sufficiently, unreflecting custom leads to positive laws holding together a society in which the original tribal reciprocal relations had broken down, to be followed by normative distinctions; the original reciprocity of common arbitrary behaviour in a relatively undifferentiated society having given way to the religious norms of men living in a condition of incomplete harmony, these social norms lead in turn to explicit laws. Philosophy reflects the laws in that the philosophers are spokesmen for those who now recognize the opposition of the religious norms of the post-tribal but pre-city-state society, that is the norms of the despotic level at which men had begun to recognize themselves in a somewhat organized world (temples, irrigation, etc.). The philosophers recognize the lack of harmony of the older religious norms within their own social structure but at the same time they crave for that very harmony. *Juxtaposed* to their philosophy were arcane rites originating at the tribal level.

Level (iv) is the level of categories, as universal principles of relation of sense-data (e.g. causality). It is the level of mechanical materialism, 'materialism' in that meaning and word have been replaced by classes of things experienced as having a defining 'property', 'mechanical' in that empirical generalizations are regarded as rigid laws. The individual now recognizes the level (iii) laws as such. Yet in his relationships he postulates the 'freedom' of related individuals (the norm as tautology). Also he not only recognizes the two sides of the duality posited by an individual operating at level (iii) but recognizes the dualism itself.

As an example: Cartesian dualism was formulated in a society at the roughly level (iv) stage at which labour itself (not 'labouring') becomes a commodity, made possible by accumulation of merchant capital. This dualism led to the two main lines of development usually called 'mechanical materialism' and 'subjective idealism'.

One might call level (iv) the level of *natural science*. Historically it is the level at which many empirical generalizations were made; e.g. Boyle's Law, Galileo's laws of motion, or certain generalizations in descriptive chemistry.

Level (v) may be called the level of *social science*. It is the level at which there is theoretical systematization of empirical generalizations, which are now seen as 'explained', for example explanation of an empirical law by a far-reaching generalization such as the principle of conservation of energy or the atomic theory of matter. The empirical laws are 'subsumed' under the principle from which they are regarded as derived (the norm as valid consequence).

Level (v) is the level of 'dialectics'; the valuation procedures for the universal and existential quantifiers (see '*S-R* and *F-T*', part II) symbolize the conflict of external and internal relations of a system. For example, the philosophy of dialectics, arising historically with the advent of state or capitalist monopoly, recognizes the opposite confusions of mechanical materialism and subjective idealism.

Of those people who call themselves philosophers of dialectics there are two main types: those who emphasize the contradiction of opposites (the external) and those who emphasize the unity of opposites (the internal).

In relation to our scheme of levels, we now make the formulation:

The problem of the two cultures is man's struggle through levels of abstraction to become aware of necessity, in the sense of recognizing that he himself has replaced

(1) 'object', as some object or other, and
(2) object as discriminated,

by (1) meaning, and (2) word.

Part E
Discontinuity Theory in Human Activity

15

Stratified Depth Structure of Bureaucracy

Elliott Jaques

Bureaucratic systems are divided into a hierarchy of horizontal strata and tend to be pyramid-shaped. These hierarchical strata do not at first sight appear to be established in any uniform way, there being variations in the number of manifest strata in different organizations and in different parts of the same organization. Work with time-span measurement, however, has revealed that underlying this conglomeration of manifest strata there is a consistent and definable depth structure[1] from which neither the manifest nor the extant structure can depart too far without collapsing. This underlying system of organizational strata appears to be universal and constitutes one of the fundamental properties of bureaucratic hierarchies.

Once the fine pattern of these strata is grasped, a general view of bureaucratic organizational structure can be obtained which is like looking into the symmetrical and regular structure of a crystal. The time-span structure of these strata is a fundamental quantitative characteristic of bureaucracy.

Consequences of ' Too Many' Levels of Organization

It is an almost universal disease of bureaucratic systems that they have too many levels of organization. This disease manifests itself in a number of commonly known symptoms. Among these familiar symptoms are: the occurrence of much by-passing because of excessively long lines of command; uncertainty as to whether a person's manager is really the next one up on the organization chart, or the one above him, or even the

[1] In the sense defined in Chapter 2, pp. 42–3, of Jaques, E. (1976): *A general theory of bureaucracy*; London, Heinemann Educational Books; New York, Halsted.

one above him; uncertainty as to whether a manager's subordinates are really just the ones immediately below him on the organization chart, or perhaps the ones below them as well; too much passing of paper up and down too many levels – the red tape phenomenon; a feeling on the part of subordinates of being too close to their managers as shown on the chart; a feeling of organizational clutter, of managers 'breathing down their subordinates' necks', of too many levels involved in any problem, of too many cooks, of too much interference, of not being allowed to get on with the work in hand.

Consideration of these symptoms raises the question of just how many levels there ought to be in a bureaucratic hierarchy. Another way of asking the same question is to consider what ought to be the length of the vertical line joining two roles in manager–subordinate relationship. Scrutiny of the literature makes it apparent that no general rules have been formulated. Controversy has been framed in terms of the advantage of 'flat' organization as against 'steep' organization, but in none of these arguments has the question even been asked, much less resolved, of how many levels there ought to be.

Three or four levels may be realistic, or even five or six or seven. But most people would consider a hundred levels or even fifty, or perhaps even twenty, to be surely too many. Why? What is it that determines how many levels there ought to be in any given hierarchy? In considering this question of number of levels it is essential to state what kinds of level or stratum. The usual meaning is that of so-called grades. Grades are strata used for ascribing status to individuals, for stating payment brackets, and for advancing individuals in pay and status. These grading systems commonly become used also for describing the organization of work and management. This second use occurs uncritically and by default. It is a source of enormous confusion. In discussing bureaucratic levels, therefore, we shall confine our attention to work-strata – the strata concerned with work organization and managerial levels.

True Managers, Quasi-managers and Bureaucratic Levels
This problem of how many working levels there ought to be can be illustrated by reference to a number of different types of bureaucratic hierarchy. Here, for example, are descriptions

of four lines of command (examination will show them to be based upon gradings) as set out in the manifest organization charts in a factory, in a civil service department, in a hospital nursing organization, and in the infantry. Let us examine each in turn in terms of one factor: namely, who is experienced as manager of whom.

Group Exec.	First Dep. Sec.		Major-General
Man. Dir.	Second Dep. Sec.	Chief Nursing Off. (10)	Brigadier
Prodn Dir.	Under Sec.	Principal Nursing Off. (9)	Colonel
Fact. Mgr	Principal Ex. Off.	Sr Nursing Off. (8)	Lt-Colonel
Works Mgr	Sr Chief Ex. Off.	Nursing Off. (7)	Major
Dept. Supt	Chief Ex. Off.	Ward Sister (6)	Captain
Foreman	Senior Ex. Off.	Staff Nurse (5)	Lieut.
Asst. Foreman	Higher Ex. Off.	Grade 4	2nd Lieut.
Supervisor	Ex. Off.	Grade 3	Sergeant
Charge Hand	Clerical Off.	Grade 2	Corporal
Operator	Clerical Asst.	Grade 1	Private

In the factory, if you ask the operator who is manager, he will probably ask if what you mean by his manager is his 'boss'. He will then want to know whether you mean his 'boss' or his 'real boss'. The distinction here is between what the operator would call 'my real boss' – the one from whom he feels he stands a chance of getting a decision about himself – and the 'middle-men' or 'straw bosses' who are pushed in between him and his real boss, and through whom he must go if he wants to see his boss. The operator would then probably pick the assistant foreman or foreman as his real boss, with the charge hand and supervisor (and possibly the assistant foreman) as middlemen or straw bosses.

The same phenomenon occurs higher up as well. For

example, the invoice department manager might well refer to the accounts office manager as his manager for 'administrative purposes', but the chief accountant as his direct manager where 'real accounts work' is concerned. Or the vice-presidents of a corporation might work with the deputy president as being their 'co-ordinative' manager, the president being the real immediate manager who meets directly with them all in the planning and control of corporate activities. Nowhere in the line of command is it possible to predict whether or not a subordinate will experience the next up on the organization chart (the manifest situation) as his real manager (the extant situation).

From the manager's point of view a mirror image is obtained. He may wish to appear well organized, and emphasize that his immediate subordinates are those shown immediately below him on the chart. But he too will admit that it does not necessarily always work quite that way, and that he must often make direct contact with subordinates two and three levels down 'in order to get work done'. This by-passing is seen as necessary even though it might not make good management theory!

In a department in the Civil Service the same answers can be obtained, perhaps couched in slightly different terms. A Senior Executive Officer (SEO) says, 'The CEO is my manager, and I am the manager of the HEOs. But what you probably cannot understand is that in the Civil Service we work in teams. It's not like in industry. The CEO, the HEOs and myself all pitch in together and work as a team.' The meaning of this statement becomes clear when further analysis reveals that the extant situation is that the SEO is really a staff assistant to the CEO and helps him to control and co-ordinate his (the CEO's) HEO subordinates; that is to say, what is manifestly

is extantly

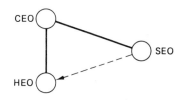

Again, as in the industrial example, the same kind of unclarity can be found at any or all levels in the system.

In a nursing organization, a Chief Nursing Officer (CNO) of a hospital group describes her relationship with her manifestly subordinate Principal Nursing Officers (PNOs) as one in which 'I am really the co-ordinator of a group of colleagues and not really their manager. You can't work in nursing with these strong managerial relationships. You all have to work together in the interests of the patients.' The extant situation is that of the CNO's being a co-ordinative colleague, in contrast to the manifest manager–subordinate relationship.

And again, in a military organization – in this case the infantry – it is easy to draw the organization chart as shown.

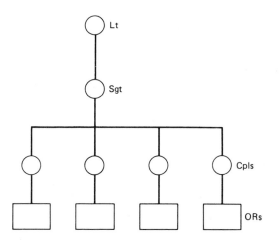

But what does it mean? A corporal – whatever the manifest organization – is not extantly accountable for the performance of the soldiers in his section; he is really an assistant, like a leading hand or a charge hand – someone who helps the real commander to control the platoon. Similarly, the platoon sergeant is not the platoon commander, however the organization chart is drawn. He is an assistant to the platoon commander. It is the platoon commander who is directly accountable for the performance of everyone in his platoon, including the sergeant and the corporals. This accountability is indicated in the distinction between being a commissioned officer as against a non-commissioned officer. The manifest situation might be drawn as above, but the extant situation is more nearly –

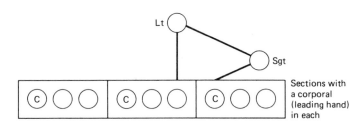

Sections with a corporal (leading hand) in each

Equally, higher in the line of command it will never be found that a lieutenant-colonel battalion commander has majors as direct fighting subordinates, who in turn have captains, who in turn have lieutenants, who in turn have second lieutenants, and so on down into the NCO levels. They would all be killed while trying to sort out who was giving orders to whom. It is only in managerial textbooks (and, unfortunately, increasingly in military training now that it is incorporating managerial theory) that military organization takes on this manifest form.

The conclusion from these and other experiences of bureaucratic organization in some twenty different countries including Eastern Europe, is that it is never possible to tell from an organization chart just who is manager of whom: in effect, it is a wise manager (or subordinate) who knows his own subordinate (or manager).

Just how confusing it can all become can readily be seen the moment the concepts of deputy and assistant are introduced. Is a deputy president, or deputy secretary, or deputy works manager, or deputy catering officer, or deputy engineer,

or deputy accountant, and so on ('assistant' can be substituted
for 'deputy' in each case) at genuine managerial level,

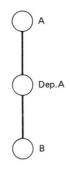

or is he a managerial assistant,

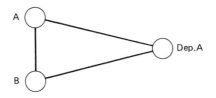

or is he merely someone who acts for the manager when he is
away?

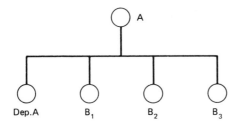

It is usually difficult to know just what is the extant situation –
the occupants of the roles being confused. Organizational confusion of this kind is tailor-made for buck-passing, everyone
willing to be manager in accord with the manifest organization chart when everything is going well, but retreating to the
extant situation when things are going badly.

Time-span Boundaries and Managerial Strata
The manifest picture of bureaucratic organization is a confusing one. There appears to be no rhyme or reason for the structures that are developed, in number of levels, in titling, or even in the meaning to be attached to the

linkage. That there may be more reason than meets the eye, however, in the underlying or depth structure of bureaucratic hierarchies became apparent from an accidental series of observations, hit upon quite separately and independently in Holland and in England during 1957 and 1958.[2] The findings were accidental in the sense that they were discovered in the course of studies being carried out for other purposes. The same findings have since been obtained in many other countries and in all types of bureaucratic system including civil service, industry and commerce, local government, social services, and education.

The findings may perhaps best be described as follows. The accompanying figure on page 217 shows a series of lines of command in which time-spans have been measured for each role. The diagram is schematized to show the time-span bands within which each role falls. It will be noted that as one moves higher up the hierarchy there is a fanning out of the time-spans, a phenomenon which occurs universally. The arrows from each role denote the occupant's feeling of where his real manager is situated as against his manifest manager.

What might at first sight appear to be a rather messy diagram reveals on closer examination the following interesting regularities: everyone in a role below 3-month time-span feels the occupant of the first role above 3-month time-span to be

[2] In Holland by F. C. Hazekamp and his co-workers at the Dutch General Employers Confederation, and in England at the Glacier Metal Company.

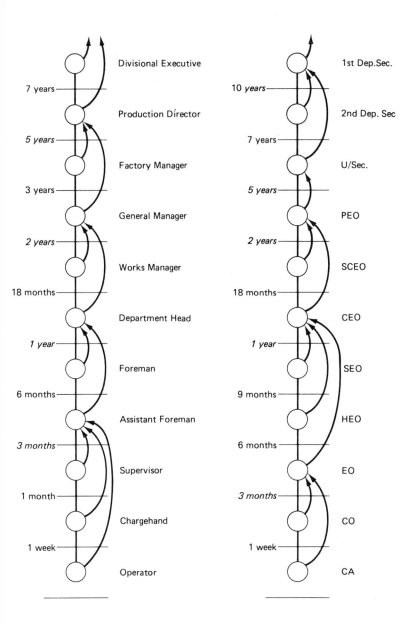

	Divisional Executive	1st Dep.Sec.
7 years / 10 years	Production Director	2nd Dep. Sec
5 years / 7 years	Factory Manager	U/Sec.
3 years / 5 years	General Manager	PEO
2 years / 2 years	Works Manager	SCEO
18 months / 18 months	Department Head	CEO
1 year / 1 year	Foreman	SEO
6 months / 9 months	Assistant Foreman	HEO
3 months / 6 months	Supervisor	EO
1 month / 3 months	Chargehand	CO
1 week / 1 week	Operator	CA

his real manager; between 3-month and 1-year time-span the occupant of the first role above 1-year time-span is felt to be the real manager; between 1- and 2-year time-span, the occupant of the first role above the 2-year time-span is felt to be the real manager; between 2- and 5-year time-span, the occupant of the first role above the 5-year time-span is felt to be the real manager; between 5- and 10-year time-span, the occupant of the first role above the 10-year time-span is felt to be the real manager. Sufficient data have not been obtained to show where the cut-off points are above 10-year time-span, but preliminary findings suggest a boundary at the 20-year level.

This regularity – and it has so far appeared constantly in over 100 studies – points to the existence of a structure underlying bureaucratic organization, a sub-structure or a structure in depth, composed of managerial strata with consistent boundaries measured in time-span as illustrated. The data extend to over 15-year time-span, and there has been the suggestion of a boundary at 20-year time-span in some very large employment systems, although this finding has not been confirmed by measurement.

Time-span	Stratum
	Str-7
(?) 20 yrs	
	Str-6
10 yrs	
	Str-5
5 yrs	
	Str-4
2 yrs	
	Str-3
1 yr	
	Str-2
3 mths	
	Str-1

The data suggest that this apparently general depth structure of bureaucratic stratification is universally applicable, and that it gives a formula for the design of bureaucratic organization. The formula is easily applied. Measure the level of work in time-span of any role, managerial or not, and that time-span will give the stratum in which that role should be placed.

For example, if the time-span is 18 months, that makes it a Str-3 role; or 9 months, a Str-2 role.

If the role is a managerial role, not only can the stratum of the role be ascertained, but also how many strata of organization there should requisitely be, including shop- or office-floor Str-1 roles if any. Measure the level of work in time-span of the top role of the bureaucratic hierarchy – say, chief executive of the hierarchy, or departmental head of a department within the hierarchy – and that time-span will give the stratum in which that role will fall, and therefore the number of organizational strata required below that role. For example, if the role time-spans at 3 years, it makes the bureaucracy a Str-4 institution, and calls for four levels of work organization including

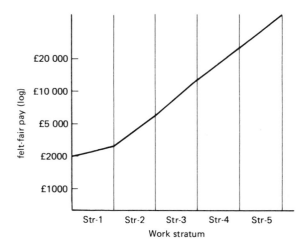

the top role and the shop- or office-floor if the work roles go down to that level. If the bottom work role, however, is above the 3-month time-span – say, for example, 6 months, as may be the case in some times of professional institution – then the institution will require only three levels of work organization, namely, Str-4, an intermediate Str-3, and the bottom professional Str-2.[3]

---

[3] The progression of the time-span boundaries of strata has an interesting geometric–logarithmic quality; above 3-month time-span they occur at 1 year, 2 years, 5 years, 10 years, 20 years; that is at approximately equal

*One-stratum Distance and Optimum Manager–Subordinate
Relationships*

The occurrence of too many levels in bureaucratic systems
creates difficulties, both for the staff members personally and for
the effectiveness of the institution. These difficulties can be
illustrated by reference to the self-explanatory conception of
roles being within the same stratum, or at one-stratum distance
(in contiguous strata), or at more-than-one-stratum distance.

Optimum manager–subordinate relationships require that
the time-spans of the two roles be such as to place them in
contiguous strata – the *one-stratum distance hypothesis*. When the
actual differences in level of work between manager and subordinate posts deviate from this pattern of one-stratum distance,
certain effects can be observed. Thus, for example, if B is set
up as the manager in charge of C, and they both fall within
the same stratum rather than within contiguous strata (there is
less than one-stratum distance between them), then a full-scale
manager–subordinate relationship will not occur. The subordinate will be found to have a great deal of contact with his
manager-once-removed. Regular by-passing of the manifest
immediate manager occurs. At salary review time it is the
manager-once-removed rather than the immediate manager
who reviews the subordinate's performance and decides the
assessment, taking recommendations from the manifest
manager. Similarly, when it is a matter of appointing somebody to the subordinate role, the manager-once-removed tends

---

logarithmic intervals. This progression suggests the operation of a fundamental psychological process in line with the Weber–Fechner law (to produce the psychological experience of arithmetically equal increase in sensation the stimulus must increase geometrically).

If we treat each executive stratum as one arithmetic unit of responsibility,
the equitable work-payment scale can then be plotted against those units (*see*
Figure on page 219). A possible interpretation of the straight-line geometric
progression from 3-month time-span is that logarithmic increases in responsibility input as represented by the logarithmically increasing felt-fair pay are
necessary to produce the experience of arithmetic increases in responsibility
as represented by each work-stratum. If this interpretation could be validated
it would help to explain the shape of the equitable work-payment scale and
would strengthen the notion that all work-strata are arithmetic unitary
equivalents from the psychological point of view.

to involve himself not only in setting policy for the selection but also in the selection itself. In such circumstances the manifest manager is in the difficult 'middleman' or 'straw boss' situation. He may try to make up for his muddied authority by throwing his weight around in order to gain a semblance of authority, or else he may just retire into doing the minimum necessary and staying out of trouble. The manager-once-removed (who is the extant manager) is also in trouble in that he cannot have the untrammelled contact he requires with his extant subordinates. He does have a natural scapegoat in the apparent manager, should anything go wrong. As for the subordinate, his manifest immediate manager is not his real manager. He will be in an uncomfortable relationship with that manager if he attempts to by-pass him, and tied up with red tape if he does not. He will not be able to have much confidence in his manifest manager's assessment of his performance.

Some of the worst features not only of red tape in bureaucracy but of autocratic dominance and rigidity, or of *laissez-faire* withdrawal, are created by the widespread occurrence of this less-than-one-stratum distance situation. If this analysis is correct, then many of the social psychological studies of managerial or supervisory behaviour and styles[4] may need to be looked at again in terms of whether the managers and supervisors were extantly in a manager–subordinate relationship with their so-called subordinates, or only manifestly so. The latter is the most likely, unless proved otherwise.

In short, something less than a full-scale manager–subordinate relationship will be found extantly to exist between the apparent manager and subordinate. But because the manifest situation calls for the apparent manager to act as though

[4] There are countless such studies: for example, to mention only a few: French, Jr, J. R. P., and Snyder, R. (1959): 'Leadership and interpersonal power', in Cartwright, D. (Ed.), *Studies in social power*; Ann Arbor, University of Michigan, Institute of Social Research. Lippit, R., *et al.* (1952): 'The dynamics of power'; *Hum. Rel. 5*, pp. 37–64. Lawrence, P. (1958): *The changing of organizational behaviour patterns*; Boston, Graduate School of Business Administration, Harvard University. Kahn, R. L. and Katz, D. (1953): 'Leadership practices in relation to productivity and morale', in Cartwright, D. and Zander, A. (Eds.), *Group dynamics*; Evanston, Ill., Row, Peterson.

he were manager, it can only encourage non-responsible management. Fortunately most people are sufficiently constructive in orientation to work to get on in spite of these organization-stimulated difficulties.

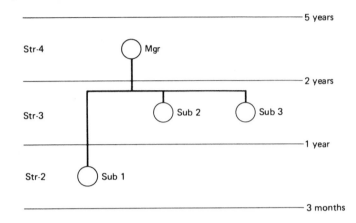

If, on the other hand, as in the diagram, the manager and his subordinate Sub_1 are in non-contiguous strata (and therefore, more than one-stratum distance), Sub_1 is not experienced as being in the same category as the manager's other subordinates, Sub_2 and Sub_3, who are in the contiguous stratum. Typical of the situation of more-than-one-stratum distance between manager and subordinate roles is the relationship between a manager and his secretary or his personal assistant, the level of work in whose role may be two or more strata lower than that of the manager and one or more strata lower than that of the team of immediate subordinates. Secretaries and personal assistants are not conceived of as part of the immediate command. They are not considered to be full-scale colleagues of the manager's other subordinates. They are assistants to that manager in helping him to do detailed parts of his own tasks such as typing, gathering information, conveying his instructions, etc. – which he would have to spend a lot of time doing himself if he did not have such assistance.

But it can happen that a manager's extant operational subordinates are at more than one-stratum distance. If they are, they will feel too far away from him; he will have to get down to too much detail in order to manage them; he will wish that he had an interposed manager between himself and them – and that is in fact the requisite solution to the problem. On the subordinate's side, the manager appears too distant also; he seems impatient, and expects too much and too quick understanding; the subordinate feels it difficult to cope.

In summary, then, what is postulated is the existence of a universal bureaucratic depth structure, composed of organizational strata with boundaries at levels of work represented by time-spans of 3 months, 1 year, 2 years, 5 years, 10 years, and possibly 20 years and higher. These strata are real strata in the geological sense, with observable boundaries and discontinuity. They are not mere shadings and gradations. Requisite organization of bureaucracy must be designed in such a way that manager–subordinate role relationships will be established at one-stratum distance (except for personal assistants of various kinds).

The question, then, is why this postulated depth structure should occur. Where does it come from? What is it caused by? What can be the source of these boundaries and the discontinuous stratification which they create? These questions are taken up in the succeeding chapters.

16

Stratification of Work and Organizational Design

Ralph Rowbottom and David Billis

To try to deepen an understanding of what hierarchies of management levels are about, a descriptive theory is offered of the existence of a natural stratification of the work to be done in organizations. It is based on action-research over a number of years in Social Services Departments in England and Wales. It appears that the first five successive organizational levels are concerned with what may briefly be categorized as: prescribed output *work*, situational response *work*, systematic service provision *work*, comprehensive service provision *work, and* comprehensive field coverage *work. Examples are quoted of how this conceptual framework has been used in practice (a) to clarify and simplify existing managerial structures, and (b) to help design total organization according to the quality of response to the environment which is required.*

What is the hierarchy of management levels in organizations *about*? In keeping with the spirit of their age, the earliest writers on management, the so-called 'classical' school – the Fayols, Taylors and Urwicks – simply took them for granted. These people were not so much concerned with why management levels were there, as how to strengthen them and improve their efficiency. In a different way the subsequent Human Relations writers also took them for granted, in their case by largely ignoring the 'formal' system in the pursuit of supportive, participatory processes. It was not until the advent of the later, more sociology-minded and systems-minded researchers, that managerial systems as such came under stern and critical review. Generalizing very broadly, two models were identified. The first was a conventional or traditional model variously described as 'hierarchical', 'bureaucratic', 'mechanistic', and 'authoritarian'. The second was a new, emerging model, by implication more suited to the turbulent social environment of the twentieth century, and variously described as 'non-hierarchical', 'antibureaucratic', 'organic', 'responsive', and 'democratic'. [We might take as key works here those of McGregor[1] (1960), Burns and Stalker[2] (1961) and Emery and Trist[3] (1965).] But a whole host of other names could be added to the founders of, and subscribers to, this now-dominant ideology – Argyris, Bennis, Blake and Mouton, Katz and Kahn, Lawrence and Lorsch, etc.

However, in spite of the general enthusiastic espousal of the second vision, not only by the academics and commentators but by many of the more lively and forward-looking managers themselves, strong elements of hierarchical structure still manifestly and stubbornly abound in most real-life organizations, public as well as private. The men at the top (or more modishly, the 'centre') still seem to carry significant extra increments of power and authority, not to speak of pay and status.

In this chapter we shall be examining a detailed thesis which serves to explain this persistence of hierarchical structure on the general grounds that there are different kinds of work to be carried out in organizations which can quite reasonably be described as 'higher' and 'lower'. Although we shall not be concerned with how these different kinds of work might justify differences in pay or status, we shall be very much concerned with what they imply in terms of authority. We shall also be concerned with the question of how the existence of work at a variety of levels is related to differing capacities amongst organization members and, more especially, to the way in which the capacity of any one individual member may develop through time. Here we may note the considerable influence on the ideas expressed in this chapter of the theories and findings of Elliott Jaques on these same subjects.[4] We may also note,

---

[1] McGregor, D. (1960): *The human side of enterprise;* New York, McGraw-Hill.

[2] Burns, T. and Stalker, G. M. (1961): *The management of innovation;* London, Tavistock.

[3] Emery, F. E. and Trist, E. L. (1965): 'The causal texture of organisational environments', *Human Relations,* 1965, *18,* 21–32.

[4] See Jaques, E. (1965a): 'Preliminary sketch of a general structure of executive strata', in W. Brown and E. Jaques, *Glacier project papers* (London,

without further pursuing, the links at this point with more general issues of 'social stratification'.[5]

Origin of the Work-stratum Model

The ideas to be described arose from an action-research programme which has been in progress since 1969 in the new Social Services Departments (SSDs) in Local Authorities (Social Services Organisation Research Unit[8]). In the course of work with a number of these Departments one of the recurrent problems noted was that of the precise role within the hierarchy of certain particular groups of senior staff. Time and again in field or seminar discussions members of Departments would spontaneously refer to the difficult organizational position of social work 'team leaders' or 'seniors', in relation to the members of their teams; or of 'homes advisers' in relation to the

---

Heinemann Educational Books); (1965b): 'Speculations concerning level of capacity', op. cit.; (1967): *Equitable payment* (2nd ed.) (Harmondsworth, Penguin); (1976): *A general theory of bureaucracy* (London, Heinemann Educational Books). His own initial conception of the stratification of work was based on empirical observations of a natural spacing of managerial tiers in terms of 'time-span' measures of levels of work. If the two approaches, his and the one described here, are consistent (as it is assumed they are) then his critical time-span boundaries between strata – 3 months, 1 year, 2 years, 5 years, and 10 years – will correspond to the boundaries between successive strata of work identified in the qualitative terms used below. In the various descriptions of work-strata offered below the links may also be noted with the idea of the 'perceptual – concrete' nature of the lowest stratum of human capacity; the 'imaginal – concrete' nature of the second stratum, and the 'conceptual – concrete' nature of the third stratum (ibid., 1976).

[5] For the general terms of the social-stratification discussion see the Davis and Moore versus Tumin debate (Bendix and Lipset[6] and also Dahrendorf[7]). Specifically, the issue may be noted of how far in general, differences in power, status and wealth in society may be explained or justified either in terms of the need to have a variety of different social functions carried out (which bears an obvious relation to the present discussion of 'work-strata'), or in terms of the existence of a given 'natural' distribution of human abilities (which bears an obvious relation to Jaques' notion of 'capacity').

[6] Bendix, R. and Lipset, S. M. (Eds.) (1953): *Class, status and power;* London, Routledge.

[7] Dahrendorf, R. (1968): 'On the origin of inequality among men'. *Essays in the theory of society;* London, Routledge.

[8] Social Services Organisation Research Unit (1974): Brunel Institute of Organisation and Social Studies, *Social services departments: Developing patterns of work and organisation;* London, Heinemann Educational Books.

heads of the various residential homes for children that they were expected to supervise; or of 'specialist advisers', 'principal officers' and the like at headquarters in relation to teams of social workers at Area Offices; or of 'deputy directors' in relation to 'assistant directors'.

Although each of these groups of staff were shown 'higher' on the charts than their counterparts, and were often indeed in more highly graded posts, analysis often revealed considerable uncertainties or disagreements about the extent of their managerial authority. There would be doubt as to how far they had the right to set policies or general authoritative guides for work which were binding on their counterparts, or to make authoritative appraisals of their performance, their suitability for promotion, etc. There would be doubt as to how far it would be right to describe them as accountable for the work of their counterparts.

By contrast, none of these same doubts would usually exist to any significant extent for certain other posts in the hierarchy – 'area officers' in relation to 'team leaders'; 'heads of homes' in relation to the staff of the home; 'assistant directors' in relation to 'principal officers'; or indeed directors of departments in relation to any or all other staff.

The attempt to probe further into why these distinctions should arise (and the answer was obviously more general than that of the personal strength or weaknesses of particular individuals) led to a general consideration of the *kinds* of work carried out in these various positions, and whether any significant stratification in the work itself might be observable. Clearly these 'kinds' of work would be perceived as not just different, but themselves as 'higher' or 'lower' in responsibility. However, there would be no need to deny as well the presence of some continuing scale of responsibility within each discrete kind or category. Hence, what we should be seeking to identify would be a series of discrete, qualitatively different *strata* of work, superimposed on a continuous scale of work of increasing responsibility from bottom to top of the organization.

In the attempt to identify these various work-strata some immediate observations appeared relevant. Ignoring the manifest hierarchy of authority and grades it was noteworthy:

(*a*) that certain social workers talked of 'their' caseload, and apparently carried a full measure of responsibility for each case within it;

(*b*) that others – students, trainees, and assistants, for example – did not talk in quite the same way and apparently did not carry full case responsibility, but carried out work under the close supervision and direction of some of the first group of staff; and

(*c*) that there were others again – more senior social workers, area officers, and specialist advisers, for example – who often spoke with regret about being unable at this stage of their careers to carry a personal caseload, and who seemed to be more concerned with general systems of provision and general procedures for work, training, administration, etc., than getting involved in particular cases.

Gradually from these beginnings a general thesis grew; and as it grew it seemed that it might be applicable not only to Social Services Departments but to a much wider range of organizations. In essence the thesis was this:

1. that the work to be done in organizations falls into a hierarchy of discrete strata in which the range of the ends or objectives to be achieved and the range of environmental circumstances to be taken into account both broadens and changes in quality at successive steps;

2. that the work at successively higher strata is judged to be more responsible, but that significant differences of responsibility are also felt to arise *within* strata; i.e. that these qualitative strata form stages within a continuous scale of increasing levels of work or responsibility;

3. that at least five such possible strata can be precisely identified in qualitative terms; in successive order and starting from the lowest: *prescribed output, situational response, systematic service provision, comprehensive service provision,* and *comprehensive field coverage;*

4. that these strata form a natural chain for delegating work and hence provide the basis for constructing an effective chain of successive managerial levels within the organization; and

5. that the understanding of these strata can also provide a practical guide to designing new organizations (or part-organizations) according to the kind and level of organizational

response required in relation to the social and physical environment in which the organization is to operate.

One important proviso needs to be added to the fourth point just made. It is assumed there (and for the rest of this paper) that managerial relationships are not for any reason inappropriate in principle. It should be noted that there are some situations in which the development of full managerial relationships (in the precise sense in which 'managerial' is defined later in the paper) appears for good reasons to be specifically excluded – as, for example, in the organization of medical consultants (Rowbottom[9]). However, even in these situations the question of the various levels or kinds of work to be done still remains, as well as the question of who is expected to carry them out.

This descriptive model of the natural hierarchy of work in organizations outlined above has been tested and developed over the year or so since its first formulation in a series of seminar discussions with groups of senior staff from social services throughout the country.[10] More specifically it has been employed in a series of exploratory projects during this period (some of which are described below) undertaken within specific Social Services Departments, and has already been absorbed into executive action in several of these projects.

The main features of each stratum of work in the model are summarized in Table I and elaborated one by one below. Illustrative examples are taken from the project work described in social services, but since the thesis is in such general terms, tentative illustrations have been offered as well drawing upon recent work in the field of health services (Rowbottom *et al.*[11]) and certain other material from the authors' combined experience. In addition precise definitions of the boundary between strata are given in clear-cut terms of the kinds of decisions which

[9] Rowbottom, R. W. (1973): 'Organizing social services, hierarchy or . . . ?' *Public Administration, 51*, 291–301.

[10] The Social Services Organisation Research Unit at Brunel has been running a continuing series of research conferences and seminars now in its sixth year, specifically with the purposes of disseminating and simultaneously testing organizational theories emerging from its field project work.

[11] Rowbottom, R. W., Balle, J., Cang, S., Dixon, M., Jaques, E., Packwood, T. and Tolliday, H. (1973): *Hospital organization;* London, Heinemann Educational Books.

TABLE I. Summary of Work-strata

Stratum	Description of Work	Upper Boundary
1.	*Prescribed output* – working towards objectives which can be completely specified (as far as is significant) beforehand, according to defined circumstances which may present themselves.	Not expected to make any significant judgments on what output to aim for or under what circumstances to aim for it.
2.	*Situational response* – carrying out work where the precise objectives to be pursued have to be judged according to the needs of each specific concrete situation which presents itself.	Not expected to make any decisions, i.e. commitments on how future possible situations are to be dealt with.
3.	*Systematic service provision* – making systematic provision of services of some given kinds shaped to the needs of a continuous sequence of concrete situations which present themselves.	Not expected to make any decisions on the reallocation of resources to meet as yet unmanifested needs (for the given kinds of services) within some given territorial or organizational society.
4.	*Comprehensive service provision* – making comprehensive provision of services of some given kinds according to the total and continuing needs for them throughout some given territorial or organizational society.	Not expected to make any decisions on the reallocation of resources to meet needs for services of different or new kinds.
5.	*Comprehensive field coverage* – making comprehensive provision of services within some general field of need throughout some given territorial or organizational society.	Not expected to make any decisions on the reallocation of resources to provide services outside the given field of need.

the worker at any level is or is not expected to make in the course of his work. (These boundary definitions provide the ultimate test in practice in classifying the kind of work required in specific given jobs.)

Stratum 1 – Prescribed Output

At the lowest stratum of work the output required of the worker is completely prescribed or prescribable, as are the specific circumstances in which this or that task should be pursued. If he is in doubt as to which task to pursue, it is prescribed that he take the matter up with his immediate superior. Work consists of such things as rendering given services, collecting given information, making prescribed checks or tests, producing predetermined products. What is to be done, in terms of the kind or form of results to be achieved, does not have to be decided. This will (either) have been specifically prescribed for the occasion or (frequently) have been communicated during the process of induction to the job as the sorts of response required when certain stimuli are experienced. If there is any doubt about the result required it can be dispelled by further description or demonstration to the point where more detailed discrimination becomes irrelevant to the quality of result required. What does need to be decided – and this may not necessarily be at all straightforward – is just how to produce the results required, that is, by what method and also with what priority. Thus, greater or lesser exercise of discretion is necessary – the work is far from being prescribed in totality.

The personal qualities called for within this stratum include possession of knowledge of the range of demands to be expected in daily work, knowledge of the proper responses called for, skills in carrying out these various responses and, not least, appropriate attitudes to the work in question and the people to be dealt with.

And so within this stratum we have the typical work of those in Social Services Departments described as social work assistants, care assistants, cleaners, cooks, drivers and clerks. More generally, it may be assumed that most artisans and craftsmen work within this stratum, and also those professional trainees and apprentices destined for work at higher levels who are as yet in some early and preparatory stages of their career.

Stratum 2 – Situational Response

Within the second stratum the ends to be pursued are again in the form of results required in specific situations, but here the output required can be partially, and only partially, specified beforehand. The appropriate results or output must now depend to a significant degree on assessments of the social or physical nature of the situation which presents itself and in which the task is to be carried out. The work is such that it is impossible in principle to demonstrate fully beforehand just what the final outcome should look like – this could only be established by actually going through the task concerned. However, by way of limit, no decisions, that is no commitments to future action, are called for in respect to possible future situations which may arise. The work is still concerned with the concrete and the particular.

Rather than collecting given information, or making prescribed tests or checks as in Stratum 1, the task would now be redefined in Stratum 2 in the more general form of producing an appraisal or making an assessment. Rather than rendering a prescribed service or making a prescribed product, the task would now be redefined as producing a service or product of a certain kind but shaped according to the judged needs of the particular situation. The 'judged needs' might, for example, be those of a person in distress (Social Services), or a child at school (Education), or a customer (Commerce). Within this stratum 'demands' can never be taken at their face value: there is always an implicit requirement to explore and assess what the 'real' needs of the situation are.

Thus in addition to the technical skills of the Stratum 1 worker, the worker in Stratum 2 must have the ability to penetrate to the underlying nature of the specific situations with which he finds himself in contact. Indeed it is this latter ability, based on some body of explicit theoretical knowledge, which perhaps distinguishes the true 'professional' in his particular field from the 'craftsman' or 'technician' who is only equipped to work within the first stratum described above.[12] However, this is not to imply that only members of the acknowledged pro-

[12] The introduction of ideas of discrete work-strata into theories of occupation and profession presents intriguing prospects. Apart from the possible distinction of 'craftsmen' and 'technicians' from 'professionals', just described,

fessions may work at this stratum or higher ones. The ability itself is the thing in question, not any body of explicit theory.

Within this stratum the sort of managerial roles can be expected to emerge which carry full accountability for the work of Stratum 1 workers and duties of assessing their needs and capabilities in allocating work and promoting their personal development. (In contrast, what might be called 'supervisory' roles may exist in the upper reaches of Stratum 1, but those in them will not be expected to make rounded appraisals of the ability and need of subordinate staff, but rather to carry out such prescribed tasks as instructing staff in their work, allocating specific jobs and dealing with specific queries.) However, it is not at all necessary to assume that all roles within this stratum have a managerial content, and indeed the kind of definitions proposed here and below surmount the problem of being forced to describe higher-than-basic strata of work in a way which automatically links them to the carrying of managerial or supervisory responsibility. The example of the experienced social worker who takes full responsibility for cases but works without subordinates has already been cited.

Stratum 3 – Systematic Service Provision
At Stratum 3 it is required to go beyond responding to specific situations case by case, however adequately. It is required to envisage the needs of a continuing sequence of situations, some as yet in the future and unmaterialized, in terms of the patterns of response which may be established. Relationships of one situation to another and the characteristics of the sequence as a whole are crucial. In order to design appropriate responses some general specifications of the *kinds* of services which are required must be available.

Thus, in Social Services Departments an example of Stratum 3 work would be the development of intake and assessment

---

it also draws attention to the likely presence of many different strata or levels within any one occupational group – or, putting it another way, of finding social workers, teachers, doctors, etc. within any one of Strata 2, 3, 4, etc. This stratification *within* occupational groups is usually obscured by a sociological habit of treating each group as if its members had one unique status or prestige level – treating the house-surgeon as identical with the President of the Royal College of Surgeons, for example.

procedures for all those clients who apply to, or are referred to, a particular Area Office; or the development of standard assessment procedures for the range of children being referred by existing fieldwork services for residential care. In Health Services an example might be the development of systematic accident and emergency services in a particular hospital. In Education, it might be the development of a general curriculum for all the infants who present themselves at a particular school for primary education. In manufacturing, it might be developing a system for handling orders for a particular kind of product.

Within this stratum, however, work is confined to dealing with some particular flow or sequence of situations which naturally arises from the given organizational provision. The work does not extend to considering and dealing with various situations of need that do not, without further investments of resource, yet manifest themselves in any particular organizational or territorial society – for example, needs for social work that might be manifested were additional local offices to be opened in new districts. Although staff working within Stratum 3 may draw attention to the possibilities of such new investments, they will not be expected to make any *decisions* about them.

Stratum 3 work is essentially concerned with developing systems and procedures which prescribe the way future situational-response work is to be carried out. There is seemingly similar work in Stratum 2 which consists of laying down general rules, methods or standards. However, this, if it is indeed within Stratum 2, will be pitched in terms of the totally prescribed responses required in completely specifiable circumstances. Thus at Stratum 3 the first genuine policy-making type work emerges: that is, the laying down of general prescriptions which guide, without precisely specifying. In using the word 'system' here we are referring to prescriptions of this general type. Characteristically, the work involves initial discussions and negotiations with a number of fellow workers and co-ordinating with them the introduction of new schemes. Necessarily, it involves some use of conceptualization, both of types of situations likely to be faced and of appropriate kinds of response.

Within SSDs it has become clear that many 'specialist advisers' and 'development officers' work at this level; and also the 'area officers' in charge of large local offices containing several teams of social workers and ancillary staff.

Stratum 4 – Comprehensive Service Provision

At Stratum 4 the definition of the aims of work and the environmental situation to be encompassed takes a decisive jump again. No longer is it sufficient to stay passively within the bounds of the succession of situations with which contact arises in the normal course of things. Now further initiative is required. It is required to take account systematically of the need for service as it exists and wherever it exists in some given society, territorially or organizationally defined. However, within this stratum the identification of the need to be met is still limited by a particular conception of the kinds of service which the organization is understood to be legitimately providing. Let us elaborate this last point.

At Stratum 2 the identification of need which can be met is limited both by the existence of certain given systems and procedures and the existence (or non-existence) of substantive organizational resources with which to carry out work at a given point in the broader society concerned. At Stratum 3 the former constraint disappears but the latter remains. But at Stratum 4 both these constraints disappear. The only constraint on developing new services or proposals for new services is the constraint of given policy, explicit or understood, on the particular kind of services which will be regarded as well-established, sanctioned and legitimated.

The starting question at Stratum 4 is: what is the extent of the need for services of these kinds throughout the given territorial or organizational society? New information about the various ranges of past situations encountered is not enough. More information must be fed in, of the kind that can often only be discovered by systematic survey or deliberate 'intelligence' work.

Thus, in Social Services the starting point may be all those in a given county or borough, known or unknown, needing advice or material aid or other specific services because of their physical disabilities; or all those who could benefit, for one reason or another from, say, 'meals on wheels' or 'home help' services. In commerce, it might be all those in some given regional, national or international territory who would be potential customers for certain established ranges of product or service. Within any given organizational society, it might be the internal needs for facilities to carry out various kinds of personnel, administrative or financial work.

At Stratum 4 then, the essence of the work is concerned with developing comprehensive provision of services or products of a specified kind throughout some defined society. Financial investment in plant and buildings and, in general, recruitment and training programmes are a natural concommitant. Since new capital investment of any significant size is always a sensitive matter, the final sanction for it may often rest at higher organization levels, or indeed within governing bodies of various kinds. Organization members within Stratum 4 may not themselves have authority to make the final decision on investment therefore, but at least they will need some degree of authority to reallocate existing resources so as to cope with emerging or as yet untapped areas of need within the society concerned.

Within this Stratum are to be found in SSDs various 'assistant directors' and 'divisional directors'. In Health Services it is presumed that most of the new community physicians, the chief nurses, and the administrators at Area and District level are also working within this stratum. It appears unlikely that any people within this fourth stratum can carry out their work without assistance; all appear to need access to subordinate or ancillary staff.

Stratum 5 – Comprehensive Field Coverage
At Stratum 5 need has to be considered again in its complete incidence throughout some given territorial or organizational society, but the scope is broadened by moving from a framework of accepted, specified and sanctioned kinds of service on offer to a framework which simply defines some general field of need. The work consists essentially of developing whatever comprehensive provision may be required within this given general field. Thus, in Social Services Departments, in moving from Stratum 4 to Stratum 5, the focus changes from things

like needs for homes for the elderly, casework with problem families, provision of home help, to the general question 'how can social distress in this district, in all its forms, best be prevented or alleviated?' In Health Services the question changes from 'what sorts of hospital, general practice, and public health services are needed throughout this district?' (with the meanings that these terms already attract) to 'what are the basic health needs of this district, group by group, and how may they best be met in any combination of old or new services?' Other general fields of need in the public sector whose nature would imply potential Stratum 5 work would include education, leisure, housing, physical environment, transportation, etc., where similar questions might be posed. In industry, needs in Stratum 4 terms for things like 'overcoats', 'telephones' or 'calculators' would presumably become redefined as needs for 'clothing', 'communication systems' and 'data processing', respectively, in Stratum 5 terms.

Thus there is an important distinction to be observed here between what we have called *particular kinds of service* and *general fields of need*. As we are using it, the phrase 'particular kinds of service' is one which at a given point of cultural development would conjure up a precise picture of what the services comprised and what kinds of physical facilities and staff were needed to provide them. On the other hand, a field-of-need description would convey no such precise image. (Presumably, in the normal course of social development many terms, which initially imply little more than fields of possible need, later acquire much more concrete connotations. Think, for example, of the now specific connotations of such phrases as 'general medical practice' or 'social casework' or 'television services' or 'life insurance' compared with their imprecise significance at earlier points of social history.)

Work within this stratum involves much interaction with directing and sponsoring bodies of various kinds – boards of directors or other governing bodies, financial bodies, trusts, public authorities and the like. Inevitably, staff within this stratum spend much time 'outside' the immediate operational zone of the organization.

Within this stratum then, we should expect to find the chief officers of at least the major departments in local authorities, some senior executive posts (as yet not altogether clear) in the new health authorities, and the chief executives of many large commercial operating organizations, free-standing or part of larger financial groupings.

Possible Higher Strata

So far we have described five discrete strata of work but there seems no necessary reason to stop here. Jaques (see Chapter 15), for example, has assumed on the basis of his own observations of viable managerial structures in a number of varied organizational settings that at least seven distinct levels can be identified. There is evidently further work above the fifth stratum concerned with the interaction of many fields of need at local, regional, national or even international levels. There is the need within local authorities to produce plans which intermesh the whole range of public services – education, social services, planning, leisure, etc. – provided at local level. The same intermeshing of various broad fields of public service, together with nationalized industries, arises at national level. In the private sector there is the increasing growth of national or multi-national conglomerates bringing together operating divisions or subsidiaries in many broad fields. For the moment the existence of such higher-level work is noted, but no definite classification can be advanced.

'Zooming' and 'Transitional Phases'

Before passing on, however, two important elaborations of the thesis which have been developed in discussions of its applicability to Social Services Departments must be mentioned. The first is the idea of 'zooming'; the second what might be called the 'transitional phase'.

It is evident that staff at Stratum 3 and upward are not able to spend, and do not spend, all their time simply considering extended ranges of work and needs, as it were, in abstraction. Stratum 5 staff will frequently get involved in discussions of the comprehensive provision of existing kinds of services, the establishment of specific systems, or the correct handling of the specific and perhaps quite crucial cases; Stratum 4 staff will quite frequently get involved with particular systems or they too with particular cases; and so on. Such phenomena may be described as 'zooming' (Evans[13]). There may be a variety of causes: direct externally given requirements, such as insistence by the governing body that the head or director of a public agency looks into a particular case; or the need to help some subordinate in difficulty; or a laudable aim to get the 'feel' of lower-level and more concrete realities, from time to time; or even perhaps the occasional attempted flight from higher demands!

Does this mean that more senior people commonly act at several different levels of work, concurrently or in rapid sucession? To assume this would in fact be to assume that they experienced rapid expansion and contraction of personal capacity, one moment only capable of seeing aims and situations in a narrow context, and the next far more broadly – which seems implausible. On the contrary, it is readily observable that when people capable of operating at high levels get involved in work which is at *apparently* lower levels, that they tackle them in crucially different ways, ways which constantly exhibit the characteristics of the higher-level approach. Where people with Stratum 3 capacity become involved in concrete situations needing their attention, these specific situations are rapidly seized on as illustrative instances of a general problem demanding a more systematic response. Where Stratum 4 people become involved with particular ailing systems or procedures their interventions inevitably lead to considerations of how the benefits might be extended comprehensively throughout the organization concerned.

An actual illustration of this process which has come to our notice is that of the industrial chief executive who asked his secretary to prepare and to maintain in an up-to-date state an organization chart of his company for the wall of his office. Given the written, highly explicit accounts of jobs and organization which were current in this particular company, this task would appear to have been straightforward enough, but nevertheless the chief executive found himself dissatisfied in this instance with the results of his secretary's work. As anyone knows who has tried to draw charts of the detailed and complex relationships, however well established, in large

[13] Evans, J. S. (1970): Managerial accountability – chief officers, consultants and boards. Unpublished paper, Brunel University.

organizations, the sheer job of charting itself is not so simple as it might seem. The chief executive grappled with it for several hours – indeed all evening. What he began to devise was not simply an answer to his immediate problem (Stratum 2) but the outlines of a general system of organizational charting (Stratum 3). Moreover, having devised such a system he proceeded to think about, and later to act upon, the possibility of its useful employment throughout the company (Stratum 4). (Whether he proceeded to any further action which indicated a Stratum 5 or higher outlook is not known; however, the point is made.)

What this suggests then is that 'zooming' is a normal or proper part of executive work, and must be thought of as not simply a 'zoom down' into a lower stratum of work (leaving apart, that is, the case where the person concerned is not in fact capable of operating at the higher stratum) but also properly a subsequent 'zoom up', or return, the total sweep in fact providing valuable concrete experience for the more abstract work to be carried out.

The second phenomenon which must be taken into account is that of the *transitional phase*, which is to do with the observable development in people's abilities as they approach the points in their careers where they are ready to take on work at the next higher stratum. Now it is possible, as described above, to define a completely sharp boundary between strata in terms of certain kinds of decisions which may or may not be made, but it is not easy to believe that human capacity develops in the same completely discontinuous way. One does not go to bed one night unable to think beyond the case in hand and wake up next morning unable to do other than see cases as illustrative of whole ranges of work to be tackled accordingly. There

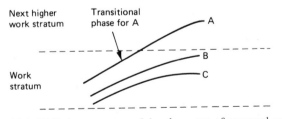

FIGURE 16.1. Differing patterns of development of personal capacity

is evidence that personal capacity to do work at various levels develops in a continuous pattern over time though at different rates for different people – as A, B and C in Figure 16.1 (Jaques, op. cit., 1967). Moreover, for those like A who are on their way to achieving not merely a higher ability within a given stratum, but ability of a different and higher kind (and only for those people), observation now suggests that they begin to show evidences of this higher ability in a nascent form well before it has reached its fully realized state. The 1- or 2-year practical post-qualification experience in 'responsible positions' required by many professional bodies, before full-professional registration is awarded, is no doubt a particular recognition of this phenomenon at the Stratum 1–2 boundary.

The organizational consequences of this phenomenon are as follows. Whereas the manager within the next higher stratum, say, for example, the *systematic service provision* stratum, Stratum 3, may involve A, B and C, who are all at this moment of their careers in Stratum 2, in discussion about new policies (say, the introduction of new systems or procedures) he is likely, it seems, to get contributions of a different quality from A than from B or C. Such discussion may help to train A for his forthcoming leap. Indeed, he may be asked to do such things as chairing working parties to produce ideas for new policies, though at this stage of his career he will not be judged quite ready to take full responsibility for the final formulation of such policies or responsibility for their implementation following approval.

Applications of the Model
Having now laid out the model, at least in its present stage of development, the remainder of the paper is devoted to the uses to which it can be put. We shall consider:

(*a*) how the ideas can be used to clarify roles and organizational structure within existing organization; and

(*b*) how the ideas may help to design new organizations considered as total systems from which a particular quality of response is required in relation to their environment.

Illustrations of both applications will be given from actual developmental project work that has been carried out in particular Social Services Departments.

The Clarification of Existing Organizational Roles and Structure
As has been noted, the theory under discussion grew out of observations of the equivocal position of certain apparently managerial posts in many SSDs. Such posts seemed regularly to attract conflicts about their status and authority in a way not true of other posts within the hierarchy. Earlier studies in manufacturing and nursing organizations had revealed similar phenomena (Brown;[14] Rowbottom *et al.*[15]). Generalizing, it seems that if a hierarchy is set up in any organization on the basis of all the various different grades of post which may exist or be required in the given organization, then not all of them will turn out in practice to carry the same relationship to those beneath them. Moreover, to the extent that this phenomenon is denied officially, or by those in the particular posts concerned, certain inevitable and quite painful stresses and conflicts will result.

Let us start with a definition. Let us describe the strongest, most secure, most authoritative posts in the hierarchy as 'fully managerial' or simply 'managerial'. We shall associate these with unquestioned rights to set or sanction general aims and guides for subordinates, and with rights to appraise their performance and capacity in practice and to assign or reassign work to them accordingly. Then we may pose a simple proposition: that no more than one of these managerial posts can be sustained in any one stratum of work (as here defined) within the hierarchy. Thus, knowing the range of strata of work to be carried out within any organization, we can readily compute the maximum number of viable managerial posts in the hierarchy. In the case of Social Services Departments for example, assuming the desire to carry out work at all five of the strata identified above, there would only be room for four such managerial posts in any strand of the hierarchy.

However, as it happens, there are something of the order of 10 or 12 main *grades* of post in SSDs, and indeed it seems quite usual for organizations to generate many more steps in their grading hierarchies than can be justified in terms of the basic

[14] Brown, W. (1960): *Exploration in management;* London, Heinemann Educational Books.
[15] op. cit.

managerial hierarchy required. What is the position of the people in all these other posts? Judging from project work in various fields that has been quoted, the answer, it appears, is that they will in reality tend to carry roles which are less than, and crucially different from, full managerial roles as they have just been described. At least four possible alternative roles have been identified in these various fields of project work – 'co-ordinating roles', 'monitoring roles', 'staff-officer roles' and 'supervisory roles' (Brown, op. cit.; Rowbottom *et al.*, op. cit.; Social Services Organisation Research Unit, op. cit.). Each has its distinct qualities, but in general none of these types of role carries authority to set general aims and guides for those in posts of lower grade, or to appraise their performance and capacity, or to assign or reassign work accordingly.

In other words, these other people will not naturally and readily be identified as the 'boss'. It will be more natural and satisfactory to have a 'boss' who is (and is capable of) working at the next higher stratum of work, and one who is therefore able to make a radical adjustment to the whole *setting* within which work is carried out when major problems loom. What is unsatisfactory and a constant source of tension is a supposed boss who goes through some motions of appraising performance and setting general aims and guides, even though in reality he is only carrying out work of essentially the same kind himself, and therefore needs to refer any major difficulties requiring radical readjustments in work or circumstance to some further point still in the hierarchy. This is indeed 'bureaucracy' with a vengeance!

Some Examples from Social Services

Let us briefly illustrate how this idea of linking managerial roles with different strata of work has been applied in actual projects in SSDs.

One project (still in hand) is concerned with the managerial structure of an Area Social Work Office and in particular with the role of the Team Leader, which has been felt in this Department as elsewhere to raise considerable problems. There are four teams in this particular Office and each Team Leader is 'in charge' of a team of up to a dozen or so people. Manifestly, the hierarchy is as shown in Figure 16.2 (2.1). On the surface it appears that all members of the team are managed, directly or indirectly, by the Team Leader. Collaborative analyses, using these ideas of discrete strata of work and managerial and other roles, have revealed a very different situation, one much closer to the model of Figure 16.2 (2.2), which, now it has been made

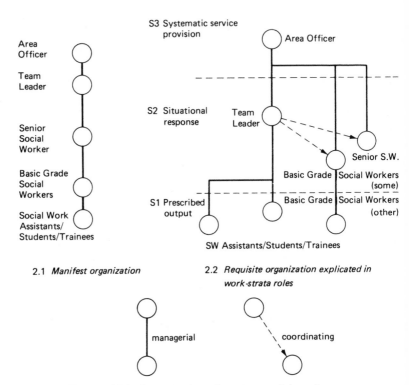

2.1 *Manifest organization*

2.2 *Requisite organization explicated in work-strata roles*

FIGURE 16.2. Organization of an area social work team

explicit, seems to command considerable approval. In reality it appears that Team Leaders, Senior Social Workers and certain of the more experienced Basic Grade workers are all working within the same 'situational response' stratum – they are all carrying full 'professional' responsibility for their cases, drawing only on voluntary consultation with colleagues as and when they require it. Moreover, when large issues appear on the scene, they all tend to look directly to the Area Officer for guidance rather than the Team Leader. In respect of the other workers at this second stratum then, the Team Leader has essentially a *co-ordinative* role – co-ordinating the daily flow of work, co-ordinating duty arrangements, chairing team meetings, etc. – though in addition he provides advice to his colleagues, when asked. In contrast, the social work assistants, the trainees and students, and other of the Basic Grade social workers, both unqualified and newly qualified, are still working in Stratum 1, although many of them, particularly the students and newly qualified social workers, may be expected to be within the 'transitional phase' leading to Stratum 2. This latter group clearly requires special treatment. However, since none of these people have actually realized a Stratum 2 capability, they can all be expected to find it acceptable to see the Team Leader (or perhaps one of the other Stratum 2 workers to whom they may be attached for training purposes in the case of students) in a managerial role—in conventional social work terminology as a realistic and accepted 'supervisor'.[16] Thus, what could easily be seen and interpreted (or misinterpreted) as a long, complex hierarchy within the Area Office can now be seen in a much clearer, simpler and more functional form, with only one intermediate management level, and that not applying to all staff within the Office.

Another project has been concerned with helping the top management group of an SSD to redefine and clarify their own roles and relationships. One issue concerned the role of the Deputy Director. His position was publicly portrayed as in Figure 16.3 (3.1). His role was generally described in terms like 'doubling for the Director' and 'dealing with day-to-day matters', but carried some specific areas of responsibility as well. Although on examination the roles of the Assistant Directors revealed clear Stratum 4 work, examination of the Deputy's role failed to reveal the same. The new organization (Figure 16.3 (3.2)) which was introduced made specific use of the idea of work-strata, and failing to find room for any intermediate

---

[16] It may be noted that the term 'supervisor' as used in social work practice implies in fact a range of authority and accountability commensurate with a 'managerial' role, as defined above. However, the term 'supervisor' in the Glacier Project (Brown, op. cit.) and later work was used, in keeping with industrial and certain other practice, to define a role with precisely *less* than full managerial characteristics.

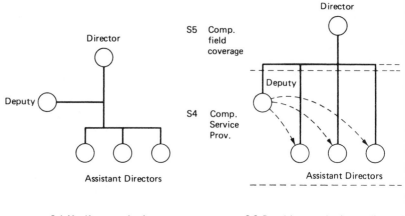

3.1 *Manifest organization*   3.2 *Requisite organization explicated in terms of work strata and roles*

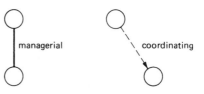

FIGURE 16.3. Top management structure of a social services department

managerial level between the work of the Director (Stratum 5) and his Assistant Directors (Stratum 4), the Deputy was assigned a senior Stratum 4 post, with responsibility in this case for the comprehensive provision of all 'fieldwork' services. Although a significant co-ordinative role was also recognized in relation to his other Stratum 4 colleagues, it was clearly established that all these people were to regard the Director and not the Deputy as their immediate manager.

A third project (supported by seminar work of the kind described above) has been concerned with the nationally important question of the future role and organization of the Education Welfare Service, at present usually attached to Education Departments but with strong links to SSDs. The distinction between Stratum 1 and Stratum 2 definition of the role of the Education Welfare Officer turns out to be of central significance. In a Stratum 1 conception, his work is describable in terms like enforcing school attendance, providing specific information to parents, and providing or arranging specific material aids. In a Stratum 2 conception his work becomes redefinable in terms such as dealing in a flexible, responsive way with problems of non-attendance and their social causes, with a view to promoting a situation in which the child can best benefit from the educational facilities available. The indications are that the strong preference will be for the second definition of the role – a decision with profound implications for the training and deployment of staff – with perhaps recognition of the need for the provision of ancillary staff at Stratum 1 as well.

Other projects have applied similar analyses to the kind of work required of heads of homes in residential social work – whether it should be at Stratum 1 or 2 (Billis[17]); to the kind of work required of so-called 'training officers' – whether it should be at Stratum 2 or 3; and to the kind of work required of those developing new types of social work with disturbed adolescents known as 'intermediate treatment' – again, whether at Stratum 2 or 3.

Designing New Organizational Structure
The examples quoted so far have all been of situations where staff and organization already exist and the problem is to clarify the levels of work to be done, and the consequent managerial and other role structure called for. In a more fundamental application, the theory can also be applied to the design and establishment of new organizations by posing the question: what strata of work is the organization as a whole required to encompass?

A current example from our own project work is that of the setting up, or rather re-establishment, of hospital social work organization following the recent transfer of hospital social workers *en bloc* from Health Authorities to Social Services Departments. We have become involved in helping in this task of integration in three Departments. Nationally, the difficulties of integration have been much exacerbated by uncertainties about relative gradings. Although the same sort of grade-titles have traditionally been used in both hospital social work and

[17] Billis, D. (1975): 'Managing to care', *Social Work Today*, 6, 38–43.

local authority services – 'principal', 'senior', and 'basic' grade – the actual associated salary scales have been lower for workers in hospitals. There has been considerable argument as to whether this in fact betokens less responsibility, grade-title for grade-title; or whether it simply reflects the continuous history of comparative underpayment of hospital workers.

Here, the Work-stratum theory has provided a useful cutting edge in project work. Separating and leaving aside for the moment any questions of grade and pay, it has been possible to expose the basic issue: what kind of work is required to be carried out in hospital settings of various types? The answer from the field has been unanimous on the need in all hospital settings for work of at least Stratum 2 – the total 'situational response' of the fully responsible caseworker. The remaining issue is then seen to be whether to provide on site, in any hospital or group of hospitals, an organization capable of carrying out systematic provision of social work services (that is, Stratum 3 work), or to leave the on-site organization as one merely capable of co-ordinated Stratum 2 work, the necessary higher-level work being done by others not specifically associated with the particular hospitals concerned.

Given this analysis, the three project Departments concerned are now in processes of making explicit choices, and seem in fact to be opting for full Stratum 3 organizations in the larger hospitals or hospital groups, and Stratum 2 individual posts or teams in the smaller hospitals. Questions of appropriate grading can properly follow, starting with the question of whether there could be any justification for lower grades for the same stratum of work in one setting or the other.

Thus, the Work-stratum theory appears to offer a new way, not only of deciding the design of extensions to existing organizations, but of designing organizations from new. It is a way which starts from the question of the *kind* of impact which is required on some given social and physical environment. At the same time it is a way which does not seek to deny the fundamental reality of the stratification of authority in many situations. Such stratification is justified in defensible terms of higher and lower kinds of work to be performed, rather than in such crude arguments as the inevitability of having those who direct and those who obey.

It may be stressed that the quality of organizational impact on, or response to its environment can be a matter of *choice*. As Silverman[18] and Child[19] separately observe, organizations are the creation of conscious decision-taking actors, not simply a product of a 'causal' environment. Much has been written about the correlations between various kinds of organizational structure and organizational environment, but not a lot has been said about the precise mechanisms by which managers might create so-called 'organic' or 'mechanistic' organizations. Apart from some of the Tavistock work on detailed systems design, using ideas of 'primary tasks' and 'sentient groups' (see, for example, Miller and Rice[20]), the literature is content for the most part to rest at broad descriptive or ideological levels; or to observe empirical correlation in certain organizational and environmental characteristics. But the levers of change are rarely revealed.

The Work-stratum model, as described here, offers one very concrete way in which organizations may be designed to react in various ways, or various degrees of depth, to their environment. Thus, a Stratum 3 system will respond in quite a different and perhaps more 'organic' way than a Stratum 2 system. Conversely, the model also offers a precise way of categorizing the various possible stages of evolution of any given organization from the Stratum 1 'solitary-jobber' type of organization, capable only of a prescribed response to its environment, right through to the fully mature Stratum 5 type of organization. (This may be compared with other published descriptions of organizational evolution such as those of Chandler;[21] Jaques, op. cit.; Greiner.[22])

From this viewpoint the Stratum 5 organization with its fully realized capability for self-development emerges as the system

[18] Silverman, D. (1970): *The theory of organizations;* London, Heinemann Educational Books.

[19] Child, J. (1972): Organisational structure, environment and performance: The role of strategic choice', *Sociology, 6,* 1, 2–22.

[20] Miller, E. J. and Rice, A. K. (1967): *Systems of organisation;* London, Tavistock.

[21] Chandler, A. D. (1963): *Strategy and structure;* Cambridge, Mass., M.I.T. Press.

[22] Greiner, E. L. (1972): 'Evolution and revolution as organisations grow', *Harvard Business Review, 50,* 4, 37–46.

of special interest. It appears to offer one concrete answer to the general problem posed by Schon[23] of how society is to produce organizations, both public and private, capable of coping with the demands of an increasingly unstable world. The increasing establishment of Stratum 5 organizations at the 'periphery' (in Schon's term) seems to offer a means of getting away from a society dominated by the exclusive development of new ideas at the 'centre', and their diffusion on a 'centre periphery' model, with all the attendant problems he so ably identifies. It offers a means of retaining coherent organizational structure. At the same time it does not exclude the possibility of basic political and legal control from the centre. Thus, to stick to the examples quoted extensively in this paper, the current establishment in Britain of new organizations at local level in the fields of both Social Services and Health Services, capable of working to the most general, i.e. Stratum 5 terms of reference, while still subject to the overall legal–political control of central government, seems a development to be welcomed.

At this point the thesis leaves us with some large questions: Are there other public services which could benefit from establishment in Stratum 5 organizations, either by extension or reduction of their present structure? What is the justification for the many large national public services which presumably require more than four-level executive structures, but with a brief which suggests only a Stratum 4 definition of need, such as providing comprehensive national rail services or a national supply of coal? What is the social justification for the existence of larger-than-Stratum-5 industrial and commercial organizations? How far might we see the proliferation of these as symptomatic of a society over-obsessed with advantages of the economy of size and scale, and neglectful of the needs for more convivial institutions in which men can live and work?

[23] Schon, D. A. (1971): *Beyond the stable state;* London, Temple Smith.

17

Assessment of Individual Capacity

Gillian Stamp

The research described in this chapter arose in response to the need to provide qualitative psychological content to complement the experimental work of J. Isaac and B. O'Connor[1] described in Chapters 4, 5 and 6 and to extend Professor Jaques[2] theories of time-span and capacity into formulations which could be used in the assessment of managerial capacity in organizations.

Elliott Jaques' theory of time-span as an instrument for measuring levels of work in organizations has produced a great deal of evidence for the existence of at least five qualitatively different levels of work. This, in turn, has led him to an hypothesis about the distribution of the capacity to do work.

The universality of this pattern of levels of work in organizations in a number of different countries suggests that the regularity of this discontinuity is a reflection of the distribution of a particular kind of human capacity in the population as a whole. This capacity is not expressed in quantitative, continuous increases or decreases in information, skill or ability, but in qualitatively different ways of organizing action and experience into structured wholes, total ways of viewing the world and responding to it.

This hypothesis about the nature and distribution of work-

---

[1] Isaac, D. J. and O'Connor, B. M. (1969): 'Experimental treatment of a discontinuity theory of psychological development, *Human Relations*, vol. 22, pp. 427.

Isaac, D. J. and O'Connor, B. M. (1973): 'Use of loss of skill under stress to test a theory of psychological development', *Human Relations*, vol. 26, p. 487.

Isaac, D. J. and O'Connor, B. M. (1975): 'On a discontinuity theory of psychological development', *Human Relations*, vol. 29, No. 1, pp. 41–61.

[2] Jaques, E. (1976): *A general theory of bureaucracy*; London, Heinemann Educational Books.

capacity led to ten years of work by J. Isaac and B. O'Connor. Their aim was to test the proposition that, in a given situation, an individual will behave in one of a number of qualitatively different ways. Aware of the limitations of a method which relies on observations of behaviour, they devised a series of experiments structured in such a way as to provide quantitative measures of behaviour. Their work thus used quantitative variates to discriminate discrete levels of behaviour in contrast to other approaches which used qualitative variates of behaviour to discriminate stages or levels.

The results of their experiments provide clear, quantitative evidence for the existence of five discrete hierarchically integrated levels of functioning. Each level shows an increase in complexity and scope and includes the lower level or levels as a component integrated at a higher level. At the lowest level there is only one component, at the second two, at the third three, etc.

Since their work was intended to be of a general nature and did not originate from systematic observation of behaviour but from quantitative experiment, Isaac and O'Connor were not able to give a descriptive account of these levels of functioning.

In describing the implications of their work Isaac and O'Connor refer to the very general nature of the problems used in their research and explain the instability of individual scores on this basis. However, they suggest that, if a more specific problem or problems were used, the scores provided by individuals would be consistent in the sense that they would fall into the same mode for each problem. They write, '. . . it now becomes reasonable to design experiments aimed at characterising the modes of functioning in terms of described behaviour.'

For the purposes of psychological research into individual differences in the modes of functioning it was necessary to design a task which provided an extended stretch of behaviour in which individual differences could be carefully observed and which reflected as closely as possible specific real-life working situations. For these reasons the card-sorting task used by Isaac and O'Connor and described in Chapter 4 was extended and made more complex; subjects still had to discover the nature of the problem for themselves and to construct the solution through time but the number of variables was increased and a new element was built in by the introduction of a blank card. This card was introduced in order to include uncertainty and ambiguity within the problem-defining and solving situation. Subjects were told that this card was to be used if they wished to discard but that there would be no response from the administrator when it was used, unlike the response to the placing of other cards when the subject would be told whether he was right or wrong.

In order to extend the range of information about strategy construction, on completion of the task each subject was asked about the details of some of the strategies observed and was encouraged to talk about the relationship between the task and a real-life working situation.

This card-sorting task was used with male and female subjects in a number of large London-based companies and in a university – with a total of 536 subjects in all. In some cases information from the card-sorting task was used as a check on in-company staff appraisal systems and results were matched with the company's own long-term assessment of capacity; in others the information was used as an adjunct to interviewing in selection situations and the results were matched against short-term assessment.

Objective scoring of the number of trials to solution of this more complex problem produced a multi-modal distribution of scores for each level of problem complexity which closely matched the multi-modal distributions obtained by Isaac and O'Connor in all their experimental work. The pattern of these scores in fact extended the histograms which they had obtained into the five-mode distribution which they had predicted in their paper 'A Discontinuity Theory of Psychological Development' (Chapter 7).

At the beginning of this work matching was sought only on level of capacity but, in the course of interviewing the managers of people who had completed the card-sorting task, descriptions of styles of working emerged which were systematically associated with scores on the task. That is to say, each of the modal groups appeared to be associated with a type of capacity or style of approach to problems.

As the work progressed this finding was tested both by feeding results back to subjects during interview and by asking managers or interviewers to comment on type as well as level. This finding on type of capacity has shown a consistently high face validity in relation to both subjects and managerial assessment and is now established as a means of assessing style of capacity. Assessment of level of capacity is arrived at by the analysis of individual differences in strategy as observed in the card-sorting task and from further information regarding strategies for constructing solutions which are described in the interview. These assessments matched both long- and short-term managerial evaluations of level of capacity very closely. Cases in which there was disagreement on level were particularly interesting because, after discussion, it always became clear that the interviewers had focused on candidates' technical knowledge and had made their estimate of capacity on that basis rather than in terms of the overall competence to construct strategies.

As a result of this work it is now possible to make clear descriptive statements about the characteristics of five qualitatively different levels of approach to a problem and five different modes of approach.

Levels of Approach
Statements about levels of approach are derived from observation and analysis of the qualitatively different ways in which people organize their fields of attention and action in relation to a particular task. They can be divided into five discrete clusters of increasing order of complexity and increasing capacity to manage ambiguity and uncertainty.

The different levels of approach are discriminated on the basis of qualitative differences in:

(a) perception of the rules of the situation;
(b) the focus and flow of behaviour;
(c) the handling of ambiguity and uncertainty;
(d) the response to the person administering the task;
(e) concrete behaviour;
(f) use of information;
(g) patterns of language.

LEVEL 1
(a) Action is firmly anchored in the rule.
(b) Abstract shapes on the cards are related to concrete objects

and the cards are then sorted accordingly; work is focused on one dimension at a time.

(c) The task is taken as it stands; ambiguity is not perceived and uncertainty is strictly limited by translating the abstract into the concrete.

(d) The person administering the task is perceived to be in control of both the definition of the problem and its solution.

(e) Piles of cards are physically blocked with the hands in an effort to reduce confusion and to handle each pile separately.

(f) Information from the cards can only be used when it has been translated into the concrete and the familiar.

(g) In discussion with subjects there is frequent use of the exclusive either/or when talking about solutions to problems. The task is disliked because of its very limited relevance to concrete work situations.

LEVEL 2

(a) The rules are seen as clearly limiting the context within which judgment and action will be taken.

(b) The focus of behaviour is on each pile of cards separately and not across the display as a whole. There is a tendency to assume magic solutions – to feel that it is something that, if it worked once, will not work again.

(c) An awareness of ambiguity emerges but the capacity to tolerate uncertainty is limited and ambiguity is handled by separating situations from each other and responding to each as a distinct event.

(d) The person administering the task is constantly used for feedback and redefinition of the situation.

(e) The cards are invested with an apparently magical significance and are tapped, mouthed and arranged in small separate piles on the table before being placed.

(f) Subjects often have difficulty in coping with the flow of information and pace it by long pauses in activity. Information is collated around each pile separately.

(g) In discussion subjects use both the exclusive and the alternative form of 'or' as well as 'and'. They often say that they have difficulty in getting away from what they have already done and in rethinking when they have found a solution and then learnt that it is not correct.

LEVEL 3

(*a*) Subjects tend to extrapolate from the given rule, perceiving it as a starting point for the development of systems of solution or for a serialist approach to the problem.

(*b*) The focus of behaviour is on the three illustrated cards and the fourth blank card is not perceived as a part of the whole display for some time. The cards are ordered by types and are used mainly in such a way as to set up a series of tasks. There is always an assumption that the solution will emerge in time with or without the involvement of the subject – 'Time will tell.'

(*c*) Uncertainty is handled only with difficulty; it is not seen as a potential resource for action but as defining the limits of the system for solution, 'I don't think about the ones I discard.'

(*d*) The person administering the task is seen as the originator of the rule and as largely in control of the information flow, 'As a consequence of what you have told me I have to work out the code.'

(*e*) The cards are usually handled in groups of ten or twelve at a time; they are often placed in quick succession and then the subject will pause for a while. The pack is frequently divided into three apparently more manageable parts and the cards shifted from hand to hand but not usually placed on the table before use. The blank card is often referred to as a 'dump'.

(*f*) The subject will always look for connections or trends. There is a tendency to reject a 'No' response and to work only with the 'Yes' response and to try to be right rather than wrong.

(*g*) In discussion subjects often use 'if–then' statements as a basis for a serialist solution to problems. They will make remarks like 'Once you've reached a conclusion you just have to live with it' or 'I had a logic but now you have confused it', 'Better to throw cards away than confuse by placing them', suggesting some difficulty in shifting from the serialist approach which they have set up.

LEVEL 4

(*a*) The subject searches for and then seeks to maintain the rule structure; he will frequently say, 'There is always a pattern in anything, it's just a matter of finding what it is.' He will often express an interest in whether or not the rules will change and will expect to perceive the rules as the task proceeds.

(*b*) The flow of behaviour is towards all four of the cards but the blank card is used only when a hypothesis has been developed and must be tested. Subjects frequently handle the problem first as a whole and then look for the detailed parts or structure the parts into a whole, and will often refer to the significance of part/whole relationships in structuring solutions to problems.

(*c*) Uncertainty is tolerated only when a system for solution has been developed; ambiguity is handled by structuring alternatives into matching pairs. The task is perceived as one in which one has to sort out rules of which one is unsure.

(*d*) The person administering the task is seen as part of the rule structure and always as being in control of whether or not the rules will change.

(*e*) The pack of cards is usually handled as a coherent whole and often held in one hand throughout the task.

(*f*) Negative information can only be used after a hypothesis has been developed and when it needs testing. There is always a search for information which will give hints of underlying themes or possibilities. Information is often structured in terms of the relationship between parts of the problem and the whole or vice versa.

(*g*) In discussion subjects tend to use phrases like 'as well as, not instead of', 'it's all right if you know the pattern tendency,' and to refer frequently to the concepts of pattern, order and organization.

LEVEL 5

(*a*) The subject will listen while the rules are described and will then define the situation for him/herself and will usually be inclined to think beyond the rules and to attempt to set his own criteria.

(*b*) All four cards are seen and used as resource material for the solution of the problem from the beginning of the task. Disorder may be deliberately induced in an attempt to create a new pattern.

(*c*) Uncertainty is welcomed as a resource, alternatives are readily generated.

(*d*) The person administering the task is seen and used as a resource for the development of theories about the solution of the problem.

	Rules	Behaviour Flow	Handling of Ambiguity
5	Rule-making Thinking outside the rules.	All cards used as resource. Patterns created.	Uncertainty as a resource Generate alternatives.
4	Search for and maintenance of rule structure. Interest in whether or not rules will change.	All four cards used but blank only for hypothesis testing. Tend to handle problem first as a whole then parts *or* structure parts into whole.	Uncertainty tolerated wh structure for solution developed Handle alternatives by matching pairs.
3	Extrapolation from a given rule.	Cards ordered by type. Three illustrated cards used mainly to set up a series of tasks.	Uncertainty defines the li of system for solution. 'Don't think about the on I discard.'
2	Rules limit context of judgment and action.	Each pile handled separately. Magic – 'if it worked once it won't work again'.	Ambiguity handled by separating situations from each other.
1	Action anchored in rule.	Relate abstract shapes to concrete objects. Work with only one dimension at a time.	Task taken as it stands. Ambiguity not perceived

(*e*) The cards are nearly always fanned out, there are attempts to shuffle and to select wanted cards rather than having to play meaningless cards unnecessarily.

(*f*) Subjects will often refer to the importance of the not known as a possible source of information and to the necessity of being as sensitive to things which do not happen and things which are not said as to the more obvious evidence. There is usually a very early move to seek negative information and a deliberate use of all sources, for example in a comment to the administrator, 'Your response came so fast that I knew the solution must be simple.'

(*g*) Subjects will ask 'Why is there only one answer?' or 'Is there another criterion for sorting which is correct but which is not yours?'

These descriptive statements about qualitatively different levels of approach to a task can be summarized as follows:

1. Rule-anchored.
2. Judgment and action within the rules.

Response to Administrator	Concrete Behaviour	Use of Information	Comments and Patterns of Language
l as part of theory ration.	Cards shuffled and fanned out. Attempt to choose 'wanted' cards.	Use of contradictory information. Use of all sources.	Why is there only one answer? Pay attention to what is left unsaid.
a as part of rule cture, controlling ible rule changes.	Pack of cards handled as a coherent whole.	'No' used when a hypothesis has been developed. Search for information will give hints of underlying themes.	There had to be an order. There always is a pattern in anything one has to tackle. As well as, not instead of.
ginator of rule. troller of rmation flow.	Cards handled in groups. Blank card a 'dump'.	Always look for connections. Reject 'No', work	'I had a logic but now you have confused it.' 'Time will tell.' If–then.
d for feedback and finition of ation.	Cards in separate piles. Mouthed, tapped and patted.	Pace flow by pausing. Information collated around each pile separately.	Interchange of exclusive alternatives 'or' & 'and'. 'I can't get away from what I've done.'
a as in control of problem and tion.	Separate piles. Piles often physically blocked in order to avoid confusion.	Translated into concrete before it can be used.	Dislike of task because of its very limited relevance to concrete work. Use of exclusive 'either/or'.

3. Extrapolation from a given rule.
4. Search for, and maintenance of, the rule structure.
5. Rule-making.

They can be summarized in the above table.

Links to other Work on Levels of Approach
Interest in the concept of discrete strategies or levels of approach to situations is growing in a number of disciplines ranging from mathematics and physics to the psychology of moral development. In examining the literature on this work it is interesting to note the very strong similarities not only in the five- or six-level hierarchy but also in the details of the distinctions in behaviour and approach at each level.

These findings are best summarized in tabular form (see p. 260).

The descriptive findings on qualitative differences in level of approach link particularly closely to Gibson's work on the use of truth tables to symbolize levels (*see* Chapter 10). At level

| | Individual Capacity | Mathematics | Social Analysis | Mathemat |
	Stamp	Gibson[3]	Jaques[2]	Bennett[4]
5	Rule-making	Empirical generalizations related by theory	Theory construction	Potentiality Initiative
4	Search for and maintenance of rule structure	Empirical generalizations based on relationships	Abstract modelling	Limitation c action withi organized framework
3	Extrapolation from given rule	Empirical generalizations based on connections	Conceptual scanning	Related syst interaction
2	Judgment and action within rules	Emergence of ambiguity	Imaginal Concrete	Polarity Dualism
1	Rule-anchored	Exclusive alternatives in action	Perceptual Concrete	Wholeness Single-term

1 in his model he demonstrates the sharp separation of *F* and *T*. At level 1 in the psychological model we have shown that action is always anchored in the rule, that the task is taken as it stands and that there is a strong tendency to work with only one dimension at a time. At level 2 in his model he shows how the use of the conditional and bi-conditional tables expresses the coming into contrast of *F* and *T*, the emergence of ambiguity and the mutual involvement of 'or' and 'and'. At level 2 in the psychological work there is the first emergence of an awareness of ambiguity and of the need to handle alternatives, subjects at this level also express the mutual involvement of 'of' or 'and' in their speech and in their tendency to handle ambiguity by separation or addition.

[3] Gibson, R. O. (1975): *Value judgments and dualism in geometry and arithmetic*, Mathesis Press, Ann Arbor, Michigan.

[4] Bennett, J. (1956–66): *The dramatic universe*; London, Hodder & Stoughton.

Education	Capacity in Mental Handicap	Moral Development	Organization Analysis
Bloom[5]	Macdonald[6]	Kohlberg[7]	Rowbottom[8] & Billis
Synthesis and new pattern	Flexible goal Flexible plan	Make law rather than obey it	Comprehensive field coverage
Form and pattern	Fixed goal Flexible plan	Law and order orientation	Comprehensive provision of service
Application of rules or procedures	Fixed goal Fixed plan	The majority is right	Systematic service provision
Comprehension responding	Goal externally set and plan initiative	Profit and loss calculations	Situational response
Receiving knowledge	Goal and plan externally set	Rules seen as external and eternal	Prescribed output

At level 3 in the truth table model associative laws for 'or' and 'and' emerge and a pattern of classification across the columns develops. Psychological level 3 is characterized by extrapolation, sequential solutions and an interest in connections and principles.

At Gibson's level 4 relations become relationships between columns of pairs of tables in their extended use. He points out that, whereas at the previous level the emphasis was on extension as relative or successive, the emphasis is now on relationship as something two-dimensional. The most significant char-

[5] Bloom, B. S. (Ed.) (1956): *Taxonomy of educational objectives*, Book 1; London, Longman.
[6] Macdonald, I.: To be published
[7] Kohlberg, L.: in Mischel, T. (1971): *Cognitive development and epistemology*, London, Academic Press.
[8] Rowbottom, R. and Billis, D. (1977): 'The stratification of work and organizational design', *Human Relations*, Vol. 30, No. 1, pp. 53–76.

acteristic of the psychology of level 4 is the search for an
assumed pattern or structure and the tendency to handle
alternatives by creating sets of polarities and developing the
relationship between them.

Level 5 in the truth table model is described as the level of
true dialectics in the sense that the dialectics are recognized
as belonging to the subject and not left to reside in the external
situation; at this level theory or a general structure of organization emerges. At level 5 in the psychological model behaviour
is characterized by the need to define the situation for oneself
and to use uncertainty as a resource for the generation of
theory.

Modes of Approach

Statements about the five different modes of approach arise
from the score achieved on the card-sorting task; objective
scoring of the number of trials to solution consistently produces
a multi-modal distribution of scores for each level of problem
complexity. A person's score is a remarkably consistent indicator of type of capacity or style of approach to a task. This
finding is always fed back to subjects on completion of the card-
sorting task and has a very high degree of face validity. The
five modes can be described as follows:

MODE 1: Proceduralists or Pragmatic Specialists – pragmatic
specialists are primarily concerned with active doing in relation to a carefully defined context. They can be described as
'doers'. People scoring in this mode are described as competent,
persistent and attentive to detail; they are frequently people
with professional or technical qualifications who are described
as very competent in their specialist field but unlikely to succeed
outside it. They are often seen as very important back-up men
to senior managers in the sense of providing essential specialist
information, e.g. statistics, patent law.

MODE 2: Practitioners or Pragmatic Generalists – pragmatic
generalists tend to base their active orientation to the solution of
problems on an understanding of the subtleties and complexities of situations, and particularly their human implications.
People scoring in this mode are described as pragmatic, good

at organizing both their own work and that of others. Not particularly imaginative but very successful at making the most of the current situation and at making quick decisions on the basis of information available.

MODE 3: System-setters or Theoretical Generalists – theoretical generalists are primarily network builders concerned with establishing connections between events and relationships between persons. People scoring in this mode are described as good at gathering and organizing quantities of information, at using others constructively, at creating a context in which others can work, as having a general ability which can operate across a wide field, and as having good planning ability.

MODE 4: Structuralists or Theoretical Specialists – theoretical specialists tend to focus on the construction and testing of hypotheses and show a particularly well-developed capacity to perceive or to discover patterns of events or relationships. People scoring in this mode are intellectually very able, subtle, creative and very self-contained in their work towards which they take an essentially theoretical approach; they are described as excelling in research and staff or consultancy roles.

MODE 5: Originators – originators tend to look for the unusual in any situation and to find ways of using it in order to create new patterns. The word most commonly used to describe people scoring in this mode is 'flair'; they are also described as poor at routine work, usually taking an original approach to a problem even when this may not be appropriate, and as having either an exceptional capacity for human empathy or as completely failing to relate to others and as a source of irritation to their colleagues.

Links to other Work on Modes of Approach
The findings about type of capacity are strongly supported by a number of pieces of research into cognitive strategies. There is now a good deal of evidence that a disposition to adopt one kind of strategy characterizes an individual over several areas of

activity. J. Bruner,[9] G. Pask,[10] E. Johnson[11] and J. Bieri[12] have all described and analysed the different strategies which people use in relation to either concept attainment or problem-solving tasks. Pask concludes that 'There are a small number of relatively consistent enduring modes of cognitive schematisation which characterise the behaviour of an individual across situations', and that the manner in which an individual structures and cognizes one realm of events bears a close relationship to how he structures another. Johnson's work shows that most subjects consistently use just one of a small number of strategies and that these can easily be distinguished by the use of multi-variate clustering techniques; he suggests that it is possible to identify a 'profound cognitive style' in the person which is immutable.

This evidence of consistency of cognitive style across different areas of activity is supported by the very high face validity of score on the card-sorting task as an indicator of type of capacity, i.e. style of approach to a problem.

In the course of collating the descriptive statements about level and type of capacity some common core characteristics emerged.

For example, level 1 is characterized as 'rule-anchored' and mode 1 as 'pragmatic specialist' or proceduralist, meaning a person whose dominant mode of orientation to a problem-solving situation involves action of a detailed and specific kind within a certain set of rules or within a particular professional framework.

Similarly, level 2 is described as judging the complexity of a situation and acting within the rules and mode 2 as 'pragmatic generalist' or practitioner, meaning a person whose preferred mode of response to a problem is action based on the assessment of the underlying dimensions of a situation.

Level 3 is described as an extrapolative, serialist approach and mode 3 as 'theoretical generalist' or a person with a

[9] Bruner, J. (1966): *Toward a theory of instruction*; W. W. Norton & Co., New York.

[10] Pask, G. (1975): *Conversation, cognition and learning*; Amsterdam, Elsevier.

[11] Johnson, E. (1971): *The Journal of Experimental Psychology Monograph No. 90*; pp. 167–96.

[12] Bieri, J. and Blacker, E. (1956): *Journal of Abnormal and Social Psychology*.

system-setting orientation to a problem in which connections between events are sought and established.

The level 4 approach is described as one in which hypotheses are developed to test for the underlying structure which is assumed to exist, and mode 4 as 'theoretical specialist' or structuralist, meaning a person whose approach to a problem is highly intelligent in the traditional sense of establishing and testing hypotheses in a predominantly deductive way.

Finally, level 5 is characterized as a rule-making approach and mode 5 as 'flair' or originator, meaning a person whose preferred mode of orientation to a problem is original and innovative, and who has an inclination to think outside the rules of situations.

Examination of these formulations suggested that the five levels could be equated with Isaac and O'Connor's model and that the five modes matched their pattern of components at each level. The match between the two sets of findings, one from quantitative, experimental data and one from qualitative, descriptive statements, can be clearly seen by comparing the diagrams on page 114 with the table on page 266.

Each type of capacity emerges as a component at a particular level; for example at level 1 there is only one component or type which is described as rule-anchored, at level 2 another type or component emerges so that, at this level, two components are available, i.e. the level 1 rule-anchored component or 'doing' type and the level 2 judgment and action within the rules component or 'practitioner' type. At level 3 three components are present: the 'doing' type, the 'practitioner' type and the 'system-setting' type. This suggests that a person whose level of approach is level 3 (extrapolation from a given rule) in principle has available three types of approach to a problem; in practice, however, our research and other work on cognitive strategies shows that people tend to have a dominant mode of orientation which they bring to bear on most problems.

As each higher level is achieved, the lower-level components or types are integrated within the context of the higher-level structure. The level 1 component ('doing' type) of level 3 is not identical to the level 1 component of level 2 because it is now part of a new pattern in which the three components are integrated.

	Doers Pragmatic Specialists Prescribed Output	Practitioners Pragmatic Generalists Situational Response	System-setters Theoretical Generalists Systematic Service Provision	Structuralists Theoretical Specialists Comprehensive Organisation of Services	Originators Flair Comprehensive Field Coverage
Level 5 Rule-making	D(5)	P(5)	SS(5)	S(5)	F
Level 4 Search for rule structure	D(4)	P(4)	SS(4)	S(4)	
Level 3 Extrapolation from given rule	D(3)	P(3)	SS(3)		
Level 2 Judgment of situation and action within rules	D(2)	P(2)			
Level 1 Rule-anchored	D(1)				

These statements about type and level of capacity are primarily about individual differences in the approach to work but they can also be seen as the basis of statements about the nature of work itself. Just as a certain pattern of structuring work suggested the notion of discrete levels of human capacity, so distinctions between different types of work at the same level could be a reflection of the distribution of types of capacity in the population as a whole. The emergence of particular kinds of work at certain levels in an organization – specialist advisory work at level 4 for example – could be a reflection of the emergence of the theoretical specialist component of individual capacity at that level.

The psychological work thus gives content not only to the theoretical context developed by Isaac and O'Connor from experimental work, but also, in its description of the relationship between different components of capacity at increasing levels of complexity, to the pattern of dualities developed by Isaac and Gibson in their use of truth tables in the analysis of human action.

We have shown that, with only one component available, at level 1 the prime approach is one of action anchored in the rule and that duality is implicit and not fully expressed until the next level. The orientation at this level is holistic, concerned with complete things as they are presented so that reasoning is not concerned with exposition or extrapolation but is purely inductive.

At level 2, with the integration of the rule-anchored level 1 component and the judgment within rules level 2 component, there is an emergence of ambiguity, arising from the awareness of the underlying dimensions of what is presented. Duality now becomes explicit. The emergence of duality expands the context of action in abstract terms and makes possible the development of deductive reasoning based on explicit duality.

At level 3 the level 1 component is integrated with the level 2 'practitioner' component and with the new 'system-setting' component of level 3. At this level the inductive approach emerges again, but now it is expressed in terms of a concern for connections, sequential solutions and extrapolation from a given rule. The level 1 and 2 components now contribute to the context in which the implicit duality of level 3 is expressed.

At level 4 the context of action becomes more extensive and more abstract with the emergence of a structural component. At this level there is a 'doing' component, a component concerned with underlying meaning and one which is expressed in connections and principles and the fourth-level component which expresses the explicit duality of structure. Deductive reasoning again becomes possible because of the emergence of explicit duality. The pattern of working is one in which hypotheses are developed and tested in order to explicate the functioning of structures.

At level 5 there are four interactive explicit dualities and one implicit – the fifth component, which represents 'flair' or the highest order of inductive thinking. At this level there is an intuitive sense of the meaning of sets of dualities. This mode of theory generation is not to polarize and handle dualities as related alternatives as at level 4 but to transcend duality, using it and even generating it as a resource for the construction of theory.

With each increasing level of complexity the context of action is extended, becoming more abstract and better able to encompass wider temporal and spatial horizons. The range and meaning of each component is also extended by integration with other components at each successive level so that the 'practitioner' components of level 2 and level 5, while at core the same, have a very different potential in abstract terms because of the differences in the complexity of the context in which they operate.

The complexity of the dimensions of a person's context for action appears to reflect the way in which he relates what he intends to do – the future, more abstract dimensions of his context – with what he remembers – the more concrete, past dimensions – into a pattern which defines what he is doing – his dominant mode of orientation.

At each level all the components or modes are theoretically available to the person but, in practice, as we have shown, one is nearly always dominant. While the dominant mode sets the tone for the whole field the other modes are also fully active. This preferred mode defines the style of present action, while the others, some concrete, some more abstract, contribute to the construction of the context. The total field is thus active in the present with the dominant mode colouring the tone of the context and the other components contributing concrete and abstract, past and future, dimensions to the flow of behaviour within it.

At level 3, for example, if the preferred or dominant mode is mode 2, then mode 1, the more concrete component, contributes to the present awareness of the past and mode 3, the more abstract, contributes to the present awareness of the future. It is interesting to note that, because of the implicit duality, an implicit future dimension emerges at level 3. Similarly, at level 4, a person's dominant mode may be mode 2; the more concrete mode 1, since it is the most firmly rooted, represents the past experience dynamically available in the present for the construction of the context, while modes 3 and 4 provide the abstract dimensions of the future aspect of the context for action. The emergence of an explicit future at level 4 is of particular significance.

The emergence of an implicit future component at level 3 and an explicit future component at level 4 can be linked directly to E. Jaques' model of Levels of Abstraction, and particularly to the time-span dimension of his theory. He has shown that a planned awareness of the future emerges at the third level of his model which he calls 'conceptual scanning', but that the critical move from the concrete to the abstract takes place at the fourth level where the time-span extends to five years. The emergence of an explicit, structural future component in the personal capacity which is expressed at level 4 could explain the nature of this very important shift from the capacity to handle the concrete at levels 1, 2 and 3, with the emergence of an implicit future at level 3, to the handling of true abstraction in an explicit future context at level 4.

The work in this chapter provides the psychological content for a hierarchically organized model of the development and expression of personal capacity. This capacity can be defined as that quality in a person which enables him to create a context of meaning for his action from interaction with his environment. His type of capacity will define the way in which he takes from the total environment those elements which he deems relevant to the construction of his context of action. His level of capacity will define the time and space horizons of that context.

18

Five Levels of Mental Handicap

Ian Macdonald

The assessment of the level of function of mentally handicapped individuals has been a perennial problem. This chapter describes how in practical work with nurses, doctors and others concerned with the problem, a practical assessment scheme was developed comprising a system of five discrete levels of functioning. These five levels bear marked similarities to the five discrete levels of logical dualities arising from the truth table analysis in Chapter 9. This intuitively sensed coincidence contributed to the development of the idea of the possible existence of a hierarchy of contexts within which the basic logical levels can function as mentioned in Chapter 2 (p. 23).

Assessment in the field of mental handicap raises particular difficulties in relation to the preferred model of mental handicap, the question being whether the mentally handicapped people are, in the now discarded term, 'retarded' (i.e. follow normal mental processes, but slowly) or whether the understanding of their behaviour and development of capacity requires totally different theoretical constructs. These questions are not only of theoretical interest. Indeed the impetus for the research reported here came from staff at Leavesden Hospital wishing to look directly at the way they worked on wards. However, as theoretical implications emerged, it has become possible to link the findings of this research to other work which has been and is going on independently, some of which is described in earlier chapters.

The social analytical research methodology,[1] made possible by the staff initiative, meant that the problem could be examined in depth without having to deal with complex

[1] See Rowbottom, R. W. (1978): *Social analysis;* London, Heinemann and Jaques, E. (1965): 'Social analysis and the glacier project', in Brown and Jaques, *Glacier project papers;* London, Heinemann.

problems of access: the staff had identified a problem, the resulting framework for understanding the problem could be seen and felt to be a product of the collaborative research relationship (in this case, with staff at Leavesden Hospital, Ealing, Harrow and Hillingdon Social Services Departments). Initial work, including unstructured interviews and semi-structured interviews with staff from wards within the hospital, began to identify the areas for study. The formal methods included (WISC & WAIS) IQ scores, the Gunzburg Progress Assessment Chart and various *ad hoc* charts constructed by staff themselves. The IQ score is not reliable in predicting areas of social competence although it could more reliably indicate areas of incompetence. These scores were not of practical use to staff other than in a very general way. There were certainly no real points of differentiation of stratification which would allow staff confidently to correlate, for example, level of super-vision and IQ scores. The Gunzburg Chart is a highly devel-oped aid to charting observation but as far as the staff were con-cerned it over-emphasized the outcome of behaviour and varies in the extent to which discretion is specified, i.e. the extent to which the initial decision is made by the staff or by the patient.

The discussions and interviews elicited two major points: first, that staff were concerned that the measuring instrument should portray 'significant changes' in behaviour as well as 'gradual improvement'; second, that the concept of 'super-vision' was crucial but was too clumsy to represent their mean-ing. It seemed that they were suggesting a qualitative repre-sentation of a scale of supervision which would emphasize more than just outcome of behaviour. Further the corollary to the word 'supervision' is 'initiative' and 'independence' which also depends upon the level of opportunity allowed to a person. The staff also wanted to express their intuitive assessment as to the capacity of the handicapped person whatever the level of opportunity or actual behaviour.

The major work began by examining what the staff meant by 'significant change' and 'gradual improvement'. They described a developmental process whereby skills could be taught and improvement noted but what they pointed out was the need to be able to express stages when a person totally restructured the way he or she perceived the problem and consequently acted to solve it. There seemed to be a number of these stages: described as gradual improvement, leading (almost paradoxically) to anxiety, followed by a complete change in coping with the world, sometimes with the result that the outcome of behaviour might even objectively deteriorate. Therefore these stages were not just measurable in terms of an equal interval scale of improvement of outcomes.

The two main issues, then, were to identify and describe these stages and secondly, simultaneously to distinguish between outcomes of behaviours (the achievement of a *goal*) and the process involved to achieve it (the *plan*).

The concern of the staff was with the ability of a person to live an independent life, and the stages in their view described total changes that a handicapped person went through on a progression towards this independence. These stages also reflected in a very practical way the extent to which the staff needed to take responsibility for the handicapped person. This responsibility was related to the handicapped person's capacity to appreciate the existence of problems, how they might be solved; and crucially, how handicapped people and staff reacted and coped with frustration or failure in plans and goals.

Practical field study led to the identification of five stages or levels of development towards independence. The five stages have been built into the assessment procedure, and the staff are at present testing them in assessment situations. These five stages emerged as an analytic statement in response to the descriptions given by staff (as mentioned above). To date (after just over two year's testing) the staff use these five stages in their assessments, and there does not as yet appear to be any need for more or fewer. The existence of five stages does not mean there is an expectation for all handicapped people to progress through all stages.

In the first, or most dependent stage, a person cannot achieve any goals; i.e. his own goals are possibly so fragmented or transitory that for all objective purposes they do not survive long enough for a plan to be operated. There is no independence: activity is dependent upon external assistance in the form of staff aids: the goal and plan must be externally set. This is hypothesizing the lack of ability to form a coherent image *and*, as important, the lack of ability to hold an image even if it has been formed. Such a person may perceive the world with both certainty and total uncertainty. That is everything is as it is *now*, but the 'now' may be a fraction of a second. Identity is dependent not only upon the concrete existence of objects but also upon their precise location in space. Learning is at best a process of exact repetition, imitation, following magic rituals; examples are echolalia and echopraxis. Each time a task is taught it has to be 'retaught' unless all the components are exactly as they were before.

In the second stage, the person can carry out plans which are his own but only if someone else formulates the goal. The hypothesis here is that the 'goal' image is fragmented but can be cohered by an outside request or demand. Once this suggestion has been made the person can then affect a pathway to that goal (although some monitoring may be needed). The difference from stage one is that the plan is not an exact repetition of previously taught behaviour but contains some slight variation sensitive to the external situation. Here some creative and initiative behaviour is possible. The plan is not necessarily rigid.

The third stage is where the person is able to set his own goals and plans. To this extent he is for the first time potentially in possession of, or owns, his action from conception to completion. If the goal is achieved he can 'claim' it as his. It can then become an expression of his potency: his ability to carry out a complete act. At this level, therefore, there is an ability to conceptualize a goal and a way of achieving it at the same time. The characteristic of this level is the inflexibility of both goal and plan. That is, the goal image *must* be actualized *and* in a specific way. It is superficially, typically obsessional. However, unlike the persecutory anxiety state (where other options are rejected out of fear) this level precludes other options being considered at the same time through an inability to change a rigidly set plan. That is, the consideration of another possibility is an interference, a confusing intrusion which can only be accommodated by replacing the original goal/plan sequence altogether. Therefore there is no allowance for other people, if their needs or wishes do not coincide. In this way this level is both a progression towards independence but a regression in terms of coping with frustration. The person in stage 3 will be less amenable than in 2 or in 1 but at the same time more capable of action and survival especially in a physical sense. At this stage a sense of identity, a concept of self, has emerged. However, the brittle ego is unable to cope with holding two options at once. Choice is characterized by wholesale total acceptance or rejection of complete goal/plan packages.

The fourth stage is similar to the third in that the person can set and consequently 'own' both goals and plans; however, the plan is flexible. That is, although the goal image must be realized, as surely as in stage 3, the exact timing is flexible, i.e. the goal is seen as not totally conditional on the outcome of a specific plan. Thus at stage 4, negotiation rather than argument or power struggle occurs. It is possible for the person temporarily to suspend the goal by changing the plan. However, the change of plan must be guaranteed to result in the same goal or the frustration is intolerable. That is to say the uncertainty re-emerges, but is no longer about an end state (goal). This stage is particularly recognizable for the beginnings of caring for others, considering their needs. The cut-off point is that if others threaten the eventual outcome, these considerations are then submerged again.

The fifth stage, again, is where the goals and plans are set by the person, but the images of both do not need to be put into reality as crucially as in the two previous stages. This may relate to an inner confidence of ability; the statement of probability is reassurance enough and allows for a flexibility of trying another approach. Although this level is the highest stage of functioning, it can be confused with stage 1 or sometimes even 2 because of the possible lack of immediate outcome. However, the flexibility and capacity to risk the non-occurrence of the desired goal is an active one. It is an active *substitution* of one goal (or even no goal) for another, either because of frustration of various plans or from choice. This is not the 'amenable' person whose goals are changed by whim or the merest suggestion of another person. As in 4, negotiation occurs but there is not a sense of the person 'being easily led'.

It is the development through these stages that the assessment procedure charts. The five stages can also apply to staff behaviour in terms of the direct care they give. If a staff member has a stage 1 relationship with a handicapped person this means that, for one reason or another, he sets the goals and plans for that person. This can be for many reasons: staff shortage, assessed capacity of the handicapped person or staff personality. However, the staff member can be said to be fully accountable for all the actions of the handicapped person, since all the latter's behaviour is under staff direction.

In the second stage goals are set by staff but the handicapped person is then able to work out a method for himself. A third-stage relationship means that whereas the handicapped person may be initiating goals and plans, staff are constantly monitoring and can intervene to bring a stage 1 or 2 response. At stage 4 only the goal is monitored: therefore at stage 3 if a person had decided to have a bath the staff member would constantly check on the water, how the person was washing and in what state he left the bath, etc. At stage 4 the staff member would only check when the person had come out of the bath if he looked as if he was actually cleaner than when he went in. If he was, no questions would be asked as to how he achieved the goal. At stage 5 the staff are providing a resource only. There is no continuous monitoring of goals and plans unless the handicapped person asks for help.

These levels of opportunity afforded by the staff can be charted, along with the actual behaviour of the person and an assessment of the person's capacity. This charting uses certain activities previously chosen by staff as being central to their care programme.

The lists of activities vary in terms of complexity. According to the level of complexity the stages 'change key'. That is, the fifth stage could be in terms of taking a bath or obtaining open employment. The lists are specific to the care situation but the five stages remain the same. At present a 'core' list of activities crucial for social and physical survival is being drawn up which, it is envisaged, will form a generalized basis for such lists. So far it seems that for such a list behaviour and level of opportunity at stage 5 represent the basis for being able to live and cope with our present society. This consequently opens up further areas for a more precise meaning of the term 'mentally handicapped' and perhaps the appropriate provision of resources to those in need. The identification of possible inappropriate levels and labelling can be gained from the resulting charts designed and in use. The profiles obtained give a description of the relationships between staff and patients or residents and also between levels of opportunity, capacity and actual behaviour. If the level of opportunity is 'too high' some neglect may occur. The patient or resident will begin to show signs of anxiety perhaps in the form of aggression, withdrawal or dependency on another patient or resident.

Evidence here is relatively sparse. However, a tentative distinction might be made between an anxiety state due to inappropriate matching of opportunity and capacity, and anxiety due to moving from one stage to another. The latter is distinguished by the higher-stage activity being sought by the handicapped person (although temporarily rejected) rather than by the staff member imposing the activity. If the level of opportunity is below the level of capacity the person will feel over-protected and feel his/her sense of identity threatened.

Here the emphasis is on who sets the context for action. If the hypothesis is that such anxiety is a product of too low a level of opportunity, the raising of that level should significantly reduce the anxiety (this is yet to be substantially tested).

The essential part of the research has been the emergence of the five stages towards independence and the charting of behaviour, assessed capacity and level of opportunity in terms of these stages with reference to specific activities. These stages represent the qualitative changes of orientation which are not susceptible to analysis using only an additive process. They are stages through which a person increases then decreases his or her certainty of the world until the frustration or substitution of a desired outcome can be coped with and such a situation can be tolerated. Eventually the mentally handicapped person can interpret his own needs and consider them at the same time as the needs of others. He will be able to make goals and plans using a dynamic image of himself and those around him and his general context.

The charts are at present being tested in Leavesden Mental Handicapped Hospital and local authority hostels in Ealing, Harrow and Hillingdon, the constant feedback from staff serving constantly to modify and update the assessment charts.

19

Levels of Abstraction in Mental Activity

Elliott Jaques

It has been the theme of this book that it is generally assumed in the social sciences that human characteristics when measured would prove to be distributed in populations in accord with a uni-modal Gaussian distribution curve. The assumption underlying this view is that these characteristics are parameters with single attributes, which appear in single rather than multiple states. It is worth noting that the opposite assumption informs most other sciences; namely, that the parameters in nature are most likely to be multi-attribute, and that changes in quantity in any given parameter will lead at certain critical points to changes in state.

This chapter will present still further evidence to support a multi-attribute theory of the nature of work-capacity; that is to say, that work-capacity is subject to discontinuity and to change in state with change in quantity, and that it is multi-modally distributed in the population. This idea could serve to explain the systematic discontinuities which occur in bureaucratic systems and which create the depth structure of the work-strata which have been described in Chapter 15. The levels in the depth structure of bureaucratic hierarchies follow from the existence of sub-populations each with its own particular state of work-capacity. Moreover, as has been argued, how any two people perceive the same problem or activity will be different according to the differences in their level of abstraction.

Single-attribute Versus Multi-attribute Parameters
If it is the case that there is a universal and uniform depth structure in the form of regular layers and boundaries towards which bureaucratic systems tend – a system of regular stratifica-

tion – then the question arises as to why this phenomenon should occur. There would appear to be two main possibilities: the first would postulate the existence of various lines of stratification in the external social or physical world, the world outside man; the second would postulate facts about the nature of man himself: such qualitative differences in men's capacities or other aspects of their make-up connected with problem-solving and with personal interaction, as to divide them into stratified sub-groups with natural lines of cleavage between. Consideration of these two sets of possibilities has led me to choose the second as the most likely explanation. If this explanation is correct, the consequences would be far-reaching.[1]

The reason I have discarded the first postulate is that I have been able to find no evidence to support it. If there were external causes, they must be either in some inherent quality of social systems or in the properties of tasks. Yet there is no constant class or caste system, or other system of social stratification, whose existence could explain the apparently universal and timeless character of the stratification of the structure in depth of bureaucratic systems.[2]

The almost universal commonsense view is that bureaucratic stratification and hierarchy exist because they are necessary for large-scale work organization. This view is reflected in the functionalist outlook in sociological theory, succinctly expressed, for example, by Kingsley Davis in connection with social stratification generally: 'We said that it came from the fact that every society has to pay some attention to functional importance and to scarcity of personnel (in terms of talent and

---

[1] Melvin Tumin suggests such a possibility in the structure of human motivation as the explanatory principle for the occurrence of social stratification. Finding no evidence, however, for this particular hypothesis, he writes: 'If we cannot rest the case for the inevitability of stratification on inescapable facts about human motivation, we cannot rest it upon anything at all ... We are dealing with something optional in human affairs' (Tumin, M. M. (1967): *Social stratification*). I believe that Tumin's intuition was right in trying to connect social stratification with psychological factors. But he picked the wrong human characteristic for his explanatory conjecture and was then led to a wrong general conclusion.

[2] The Imperial Roman Army, with its centurions and cohorts, manifests the same character of stratification as Str-2 and Str-3 in modern armies and businesses.

training) in filling its positions. In order to satisfy these requirements, differential rewards must be given for different positions – and these differential rewards are precisely what we call stratification.'[3]

Davis does take account of human abilities in his reference to talent, but in terms of scarcity rather than in terms of a hierarchy and stratification of talent. He then uses differential reward synonymously with social stratification. In both these respects his usage expresses the mainstream of sociological thought. We shall find it useful, by contrast, to differentiate between the continuity of inequality in economic differentials and the discontinuity implied by stratification. And we shall take human ability as the key. For the functionalist type of argument that bureaucratic systems are economically efficient and that these systems were established in order to get the necessary work done, is at best incomplete. Social systems cannot endure in the way the bureaucratic system has endured if they are not closely attuned to man's nature. If, for example, all men were equal in work-capacity, the bureaucratic hierarchy would be an impossible social system. It would never have been discovered. Men would have worked together in leaderless groups or in partnerships, or in other types of small face-to-face size associations, but a bureaucratic hierarchy, never!

Nor can the nature of tasks readily explain the phenomenon. For tasks are man-made things. They are products of human desire and aspiration, created by human imagination of the objects to be produced as the output of the task. Any evidence that there might be not only of a hierarchy of tasks but of an inherent discontinuous stratification of tasks, would therefore point to a stratification of populations with respect to the mental functioning of their members.

Discontinuity and Multi-modality in Mental Functioning
The regularities in stratification of bureaucratic hierarchies must surely reflect an equivalent stratification in human populations, otherwise why would bureaucratic hierarchies ever have occurred at all? The postulate to be considered is that with respect to work-capacity people are divided into distinct and separable categories which are hierarchically stratified; that is

[3] Davis, K. (1949): *Human Society*, p. 388; New York, Macmillan.

to say, as work-capacity increases in amount it undergoes changes in state. A parallel case would be if in the case of intelligence as measured in IQ, there were critical points at which a further increase in IQ produced not only a further increment in intelligence, but a change to a different quality, the emergence of a new quality; as though the 110 to 130 IQ group not only had higher IQs than the 90 to 110 group and the 70 to 90 group, but also had a different kind of intelligence, different in some significant quality as steam differs from water. And there would be another significant difference between he 90 to 110 group and the 70 to 90 group as water differs from ice.

If intelligence as measured by IQ in fact had such characteristics, the discontinuities would show up in a multi-modal distribution, in contrast to the uni-modal distribution which is found. Human qualities with discontinuity of this kind would divide populations into discrete groupings. If the quality related directly to competence to carry given levels of work, the discontinuities would show in divisions of the population into hierarchically placed strata.

It is interesting to note that discontinuity theory to some extent has been a part of psychological thinking in connection with levels of abstraction and conceptualization. Ever since Goldstein and Scheerer published their distinction between concrete and abstract modes of thought[4] a qualitative shift between at least these two levels of mental functioning tends to have been assumed. Harvey, Hunt and Schroder, however, illustrate some of the discomfort about making such an assumption, when they take William James's argument for the existence of a continuous stream of consciousness in the individual as a possible argument against the conception of discontinuity between different categories or populations of individuals. 'We shall leave unsolved,' they write, 'the issue of whether concreteness-abstractness is more appropriately viewed as a qualitatively continuous or discontinuous dimension.'[5]

[4] Goldstein, K. and Scheerer, G. (1939): *The organism;* New York, American Book Co.; and Goldstein, K., (1948): *Language and language disturbances;* New York, Grune & Stratton.
[5] Harvey, O. J., Hunt, D. E. and Schroder, H. M. (1961): *Conceptual systems and personality organisation,* p. 28; New York, John Wiley.

More specifically our postulate is that there are discontinuities in the nature of work-capacity at the 3-month level, the 12-month level, the 2-year level, the 5-year level and so on. These changes in state are such as to divide any population into a series of separate modalities with respect to work-capacity, the group up to 3-month capacity forming one normally distributed modality, the group from 3-months capacity to one-year capacity another normally distributed modality, and so on. It is these different modalities in any population which are at the root of the discontinuities in the depth structure of bureaucratic organization. To put the conjecture another way, any human population is stratified with respect to the work-capacity of its individual members as measured in time-span, and the depth structure of bureaucratic systems is stratified in accord with these changes in state in work-capacity.

If the conjecture about qualitative jumps in the nature of human competence in work, and in all goal-directed behaviour, is valid, then there ought to be qualitative differences which can be observed in the way people at different work-strata actually work: differences in their perception of tasks, differences in the planning and organization of their work, differences in how they carry their relationship with the external task in which they are engaged, and, indeed, in the fullest sense, qualitative differences in the way they picture the world in which they are working.

There are such qualitative differences, such discontinuities, and they manifest themselves in many different ways. Two such types of phenomena will be described, and at a number of different levels: the first type is concerned with the relationship between the individual and the physical resources he uses in carrying out his tasks;[6] the second type is concerned with his relationships with people and social systems. This latter theme has been formulated and developed by my colleagues David Billis and Ralph Rowbottom.[7]

The emphasis throughout the description will continue to be

---

[6] B. Bernstein uses a similar criterion: 'The predisposition to form relationships with objects in a particular way is an important perceptual factor.' (1971): *Class, codes and control*, p. 44; London, Routledge & Kegan Paul.

[7] Rowbottom, R. W., and Billis, D., Chapter 16, 'The stratification of work and organizational design'.

upon behaviour, upon action, or as Piaget has described it,[8] 'upon the sensory-motor ability to organize the outer world'. The field of description is thus the individual, in a bureaucratic role system, at a given organization level, interacting with the outside world in connection with a task or tasks which he is employed to carry out.

Each of the discrete levels to be described will be termed level of abstraction. Each shift across a boundary represents a shift in the capacity of individuals to deal with problems in an increasingly abstract way. The observations may contribute to the development of the concept of level of abstraction itself.[9] The similarities with the Gibson and Isaac logical levels derived from the truth table analysis, and with the levels described by Gillian Stamp are exceedingly striking.

A series of examples will be given to illustrate each point. These examples are real. In describing them we must refer to the title of the particular role (for example, typist, supervisor, research investigator, etc.) and to the time-span of each. In doing so, it is *not implied that all other roles with these same titles have the same time-spans*. It is common practice for the same title to be used for roles of very different levels of work.

First Level of Abstraction: Perceptual-motor Concrete
It is a general feature of roles with time-spans below 3 months that the tasks are assigned in concrete terms and are carried out in direct physical contact with the output. The project can be pictured and constructed by means of direct perception of examples of the output to be produced. For example; a copy typist is given a typed memorandum to copy, and works

[8] Piaget, J., (1953): *The origin of intelligence in the child;* London, Routledge & Kegan Paul.

[9] Level of abstraction is often loosely used to refer to the level of generalization at which a person functions. Its more systematic use as a rigorously defined concept has been markedly limited. Goldstein and Scheerer distinguished between two levels only, the concrete and the abstract, an analysis which is much too restricted: see Goldstein, K. and Scheerer, G. (1939): op. cit.; Harvey, O. J., Hunt, D. E. and Schroder, H. M. (1961): op. cit., in their review of the literature were unable to produce a formulation which went much beyond the distinction between concrete and abstract. They do support the present argument in stating the view that there probably exist many discrete levels, but they do not give any indication of what these levels might be.

physically with her machine in doing so; a manual operator is given a drawing from which to carry out a particular operation on a piece of metal either by hand or by a machine; a laboratory assistant is given a particular test to carry out; a clerical officer is given a set of administrative data to search through and check; a supervisor is given a particular group of operators to watch over; a sales assistant is required to give customers the articles they ask for, wrap them and take payment.

If there is no immediate perceptual contact with the output, no work is done at this level. The whole of the task is at hand in a concrete sense. Either the output itself, or the controls of the machine or equipment affecting the output, can be reached out to, touched, manipulated. Words and other abstract data may be used in the instructions for the task, but these abstractions have an immediate reference which can be concretely pointed to – the piece of material to be worked upon, the drawing or sample to be worked from.

The working relationships with people are also concrete in mode in the sense of being prescribed in content. Rowbottom and Billis describe this as 'working towards objectives which can be completely specified (as far as is significant) beforehand, according to defined circumstances which may present themselves; but not expected to make any significant judgments on what output to aim for or under what circumstances to aim for it'.[10]

This view of relationships with clients can also explain why no managerial roles can be found below the 3-month time-span level. Manager–subordinate relationships require that the manager should be able to do much more than react in a prescribed and delimited way to the needs and demands of his subordinates.

The quality of capacity at this level is thus one of concreteness in the sense of needing to be in immediate perceptual contact with the physical output – visual, tactile, kinaesthetic, auditory – and to be able to manipulate it motorically as work progresses and the task is carried out. This concreteness goes along with mechanistically prescribed relations with others as necessary in the work.

The concreteness of work activity at this level connects with the use of very concrete modes of expressive movement, such as

[10] Rowbottom, R. W. and Billis, D. Chapter 16.

hitting or pushing or tapping the other person, as described for example by Miller and Swanson[11] and by Basil Bernstein[12] with reference to working-class communication.

This first level of abstraction may be termed the perceptual-motor concrete, and the population which works in this mode Work-Capacity Group I.

Second Level of Abstraction: Imaginal Concrete
At the 3-month time-span level and up to the 12-month time-span, tasks are characterized by new qualities not found below 3-month time-span. The goal can no longer be completely specified; imagination must be exercised in the construction of the project, although the task is still concrete in the sense that output can be imagined in concrete terms. For example: a ward sister in charge of a ward in hospital had to be able to interpret the doctor's prescriptions and assess the needs of patients where the doctor had not specifically prescribed, she also had to set terms of reference for each of her subordinate nurses in the light of her assessment of the needs and competencies of each one, all within the general planning of activities and priorities which she carried out; a social worker had to interpret the needs of clients with whom she was doing casework, and not just accept at face value what they said was wrong or needed; a civil service executive officer had to decide how to plan a six-month investigation of how to improve the implementation of a piece of departmental policy; a research investigator had to plan and carry through a six-month research programme to examine certain new methods of bonding metals; a foreman had not only to plan the work of his section from week to week, but also to plan and carry out a retraining and development scheme for his operators in preparation for new methods of production which were to be operating efficiently in nine months' time.

[11] Miller, D. R. and Swanson, G. E. (1958): *The changing American parent;* New York, John Wiley.

[12] B. Bernstein links his qualitative distinction between the behaviour of his so-called working-class and middle-class children to time-span as well: 'The school is an institution, where every item in the present is finely linked to a distant future, consequently there is not a serious clash of expectations between the school and the middle class at all. The child's developed time-span of anticipation allows the present activity to be related to a future, and this is meaningful.' (1971): *Class, codes and control,* p. 29; London, Routledge & Kegan Paul.

In none of these tasks are there terms of reference which can be specified completely or pointed to physically, nor can the tasks be carried out solely by perceptual-motor manipulation of the object. They all require the ability to imagine, but to imagine in concrete terms, what requires to be done, to picture it in the mind's eye, and in imagination also to work out and prepare plans and methods for overcoming problems.

Rowbottom and Billis[13] have pointed to the interpretative content of the work of professionals such as social workers in dealing with clients; they have to use their imaginations in getting a picture of underlying needs, and cannot simply deal with things as presented to them in concrete terms. They describe the work as requiring a 'situational response – carrying out work where the precise objectives to be pursued have to be judged according to the needs of each specific concrete situation which presents itself; but not expected to make any decisions, i.e. commitments on how future possible situations are to be dealt with'.

The location of the output is also no longer given in immediate concrete perceptual-motor terms. It is not available for touching and motor manipulation, although it may be possible physically to oversee the whole of the area of responsibility.

The quality of the capacity involved is that of being able to hold the concrete problem firmly in imagination and to work with it mentally, without the support of being able continuously to test judgment and imagination by tactile manipulation of a physical thing. A physical detachment from the field of work is required, but without losing the subjective sense of the output in concrete terms.

This second level of abstraction may be termed the imaginal concrete, and the population which works in this mode Work-Capacity Group II.

Third Level of Abstraction: Imaginal Scanning
At time-span levels of 1 year to 2 years the emergent characteristic of tasks is that it has become impossible physically to oversee or to imagine all at once the whole of a person's area of

13 Rowbottom, R. W. and Billis, D., loc. cit.

responsibility. The scope of activity has become too wide for this, although it is still possible to do so by mentally scanning the whole, one bit at a time. For example: the owner of a small business employing 150 people was not able to look at all that was going on all at once, but he could run over all the activities in his mind and was up to date in his knowledge of existing sales and stock levels, forward order book, profit position, and other aspects of his business; a sales manager with eight level-2 sales subordinates could not picture all at once all the customers for whom he and his subordinates were accountable, but he could run over them one by one in his mind and reconstruct the total sales position; a battalion commander could not picture the whole of the terrain in which his troops were fighting, but he could cover it by riding physically over the whole, and could build up the total picture as he went.

The instructions received at this level tend to be in conceptual terms of load data and programmes, expense variables, indices, ratios, vectors. These conceptually formulated tasks must be translated into an imaginal picture of the tasks controlled. The totality of the duties must be scanned continually so that progress can be tied up with new instructions.

The effect of scale at this level is that the project can never be constructed as a coherent mental picture. The project itself can be pictured only by scanning: it has become more elusive, it cannot be pictured all at once, but only in a series of time slices. The interplay between project and output, therefore, has become qualitatively more complex. Feedback, is in terms of comparing what is happening in various parts of the output region with equivalent parts of the subjective project. The whole has to be bound together in feel rather than by direct perception, feel supported by conceptual data about the whole. The relationship between project and object is still in terms of concrete comparisons, but perceptual part to part rather than perceptual whole to whole as at level 2. The process of scanning is thus one in which a person must be able to sense the interplay of the various parts without the support of being able physically to perceive at one time the various parts making up the whole.

Rowbottom and Billis have conceptualized work at this level in terms of their observation that it always includes system development – systematic service provision – making systematic provision of services of some given kinds shaped to the needs of a continuous sequence of concrete situations which present themselves; but not expected to make any decisions on the reallocation of resources to meet as yet unmanifested needs (for the given kinds of services) within some given territorial or organizational society'.[14]

The third level of abstraction may be termed the imaginal-scanning level, and the population which works in this mode Work-Capacity Group III.

Fourth Level of Abstraction: Conceptual Modelling
At the 2-year time-span capacity level there emerges a profound change in the quality of abstraction used in carrying out tasks: it is a change from the concrete to the abstract mode of thought and work.

When a designer is asked to get out a design (or indeed when anyone is asked to get out any kind of proposal for a new method or procedure or policy), the higher the level of capacity of the designer the more generalized the form of his design will be in the special sense that the less it will be like things that already exist. What is noteworthy is the fact that in the time-span band from 2 years to 5 years, designs (or method, procedure or policy) will frequently require the designer to start from existing designs but to depart from them to produce new ones which are not recognizably like those which existed originally.

In one such case a designer was instructed to design a new large-scale piece of machinery to do the work of an existing machine but to be based upon different principles so that it would be more versatile and less expensive. He had to analyse the existing mechanism and express it completely in abstract terms of force fields, vectors, power, stresses, direction of movement, degrees of freedom. He then had to detach himself from his picture of the existing machine and immerse himself in the manipulation of his abstractions with a temporary suspension of reference to existing machines – while he continued to retain a firm grip somewhere in the back of his mind on the realizable goal of his work, which was to produce a design which could be translated into something concrete which could be constructed.

[14] Rowbottom, R. W. and Billis, D., loc. cit.

Other examples: a civil service assistant secretary and his department were given the task of producing proposals for a new type of service to the community, including an analysis of the organizational changes which would be required, costs, and a practical programme for implementation if agreed; the general manager of a factory employing 1,200 people was instructed to work out and implement a programme of change in the factory such that in $3\frac{1}{2}$ years' time over half the factory would be working on entirely different products for new markets and the other half would be using new methods and equipment which would be introduced during the period and brought up to full productivity; a purchasing manager had four years in which to develop an entirely new supply network to enable the enterprise to stop producing certain components and to have regular supplies on contract to do so instead.

The common feature in all these examples is that the task requires the individual to retain mental contact with what exists, but then at the same time to achieve a detachment from this experience and to work with ideas of things which are different from what exists – which look different, function differently, do different things. The new thing is not a modification or extension of the old; it is a departure from it.

Rowbottom and Billis have referred to this level in the following way: 'making comprehensive provision of services of some given kinds according to the total and continuing needs for them throughout some given territorial or organizational society; but not expected to make any decisions on the reallocation of resources to meet needs for services of different or new kinds'.[15]

The common feature of this same level of work is that the possibility of direct command is lost. Unless the department is very small (say under 50 people), it is unlikely that staff working at this level and above will recognize all the other members of the department. The junior members at the first level will be found to be organizationally very distant. In larger departments there may be up to 1,500 or 2,000 people. The geographical environment is no longer conceivable *in toto* in concrete terms. It is too extended, contains too many departments, too far-flung customers, too many competitors known and

[15] Rowbottom, R. W. and Billis, D., loc. cit.

unknown. The transition is often referred to managerially as 'becoming chairborne'. In military organization the abstract quality is reflected in the emergence of red tabs, oak leaves, and patches at regimental and brigade levels. Such symbols substitute for the direct quality of command based upon individuals' mutual knowledge of each other at lower levels of organization.[16]

The qualitative jump from level 3 to level 4 is that at level 4 neither the output nor the project can be foreseen in concrete terms, even by imaginal scanning. The project cannot be completely constructed. It remains a combination of a conscious subjective picture, incomplete in itself, whose specific total form and content are unconsciously intuitively sensed but cannot quite be consciously grasped. The cross-comparison between project and emerging output is thus a process with much intuitive feel in the early stages as to whether the work is proceeding satisfactorily; as the work proceeds, the project becomes more and more explicitly filled in through perception of the emerging output, until in the finishing stages the final output can be completely projected and completed. In short, at level 4 the construction of the explicit project can be completed only during the process of work itself.

This level is the one at which what is usually referred to as innovation can begin, innovation in the sense of taking existing things or services as a starting point but being able to detach mentally from a picture of those things and to work in this detachment, returning to concrete representation with new ideas different from existing ideas precisely because of the detachment. In the first three levels of abstraction continual reference to the concrete case either perceptually or imaginally is needed and available in order to be able to work. By contrast, from level 4 and higher the ability to work in phases of interrupted perceptual or imaginal contact with real things is the essence of work.

The notion of an abstract mode of work does not simply mean

[16] It is significant that the title 'General' emerges at the 2-year time-span level in military services. In commerce and industry, the same title tends to come into play, although this fact is less recognized because it is used in the adjectival form of General Manager or General Sales Manager rather than as a noun as in the case of Major-General, etc.

thinking in the abstract in the sense of being a 'back-room boy' or an 'academic' thinker; that is to say, it does not refer to 'abstract' as against practical and down to earth. Nor does it imply merely using abstractions whether words, ideas, conceptions, beliefs or even high-level and abstruse mathematics. The central quality is that of detachment; of abstraction in the sense of being able to work at specific and concrete problems without dependence upon mental contact with existing things, and with the ability to contact things without becoming mentally fixed on them.

In short, the transition in capacity from the third to the fourth level of abstraction (the transition to work-capacities above 2 years) is a transition from concrete to genuinely abstract work. This fourth level of abstraction may be termed conceptual modelling, and the population which works in this mode Work-Capacity Group IV.

Fifth Level of Abstraction: Intuitive Theory
It will be apparent that these descriptions of levels of abstraction are descriptions derived from work-in-progress. At the fifth level of abstraction at 5-year time-span and up to 10-year time-span our experience is limited. The roles analysed include a number of chief executives in industry and in the public services, a number of under-secretary roles in the Civil Service and a number of specialist and professional roles in various services.

The central finding from the point of view of qualities in the task which are not to be found at lower level can be illustrated in the following example. A manager operating at 7-year time-span, on being pressed by his subordinates to come to see the latest prototype of a newly developed product, replied that he had already examined the prototype at an earlier stage of its development. He did not have to take another look but would be content with a verbal description of the new development. His subordinates continued to press him to see for himself, but he insisted that he would prefer to get down to examining the figures of performance, available markets, etc., so that necessary decisions could be made. He did not require physical contact with additional examples. In the discussion two different frames of reference – different levels of abstraction – are interacting, the higher level sifting out a decision from the application of intuitively held generalizations requiring only passing contact with the concrete; that is to say, generalizations having the characteristic of an intuitively constructed theory.

At this level of work we are dealing with chief executives, heads of service, managers of enterprises, departments, army divisions, which may be employing five to ten thousand people. There is no possibility whatever of having other than a very limited contact with the concrete reality of the total field of responsibility – contact with a specific detail or datum here or there, but for the most part activities go on without the head knowing anything about what is happening. He must be occupied in fashioning the longer-term future and leave the present to take care of itself in the hands of his subordinates with the policies and plans he had already laid down.

Rowbottom and Billis refer to this level as that of comprehensive field coverage and describe it in the following terms: 'making comprehensive provision of services within some general field of need throughout some given territorial or organizational society; but not expected to make decisions on the reallocation of resources to provide services outside the given field of need'.[17]

The level of abstraction concerned can be described in terms of the relationship between these periodic contacts with some very few details of implementation and the general policies, strategies, plans and statistically co-ordinated bodies of information which are the everyday content of these roles. The relationship is similar to that between a general theory and a specific and detailed point of application of that theory. A good theory applies over a wide range of concrete cases in such a manner that, given the theory and one detailed example of its application, it becomes possible to understand what will happen in other cases similar to the example and covered by the theory.

In similar vein, the fifth level of abstraction is based on the mental possession of intuitive theories built up from experience. Such intuitively constructed theories then allow the person to function with what might be called one-time contact with the concrete. Each specific case or specific problem or specific

17 Rowbottom, R. W. and Billis, D., loc. cit.

example is generalized and absorbed for use as part of a general formulation.

It can be conjectured that the construction of the project has now become a matter of unconscious intuition, with a complex of apparently disconnected facts and figures. These facts and figures are intuitively sorted over. Those intuitively felt most relevant are elevated and elaborated in subjective consciousness, and the intuitively felt irrelevancies are put to one side. New data are sought and sorted over for connections, for pattern, so that an ordered pattern of relevant facts is gradually constructed, and decisions can be taken. Feedback control continues in relation to a largely intuitive and unconscious project, as for level 4, except that to the extent that it becomes conscious it does so in terms of a general policy the concrete details of which are to be filled in by subordinates, rather than in terms of a project in itself eventually specifiable in concrete terms.

This fifth level of abstraction may be termed the level of intuitive theory, and the population which works in this mode Work-Capacity Group V.

Sixth and Seventh Levels of Abstraction
Because of the evidence from bureaucratic organizations that there exist at least two further levels – a level beginning at the 10-year time-span and a level beginning at the 20-year time-span, and perhaps higher levels as well – it may be postulated that new emergents in the qualitative characteristics of time-span capacity would be found to occur towards the 10- and 20-year levels. In very broad terms it can be noted that if the technology allows, there is a shift towards managing in terms of policy setting and away from directing and co-ordinating the activities of subordinates with collateral relations. That is to say, if the technology is light- or medium-scale manufacturing or services (rather than heavy large-scale technology such as in steel or in oil refining where production cannot be broken into small-scale units) then there is a tendency for the enterprise to differentiate into a series of independent trading subsidiaries each managed by a profit-and-loss account chief executive.

This process is consistent with another notable tendency at levels 6 and 7, and that is that the management of institutions

Summary of Strata and Levels of Abstraction

	Stratum	Time-span	Level of Abstraction	Equitable Payment (1975)	Maximum No. of Employees (labour intensive)	Types of Unit — Industry & Commerce	Types of Unit — Military	Types of Unit — Civil Service	Normal Location of Work Facilities	Nature of Group
ABSTRACT Indirect or General Command	VII	20 yrs	?	£70 000	150 000	Corporation	Army	Perm. Sec.	World-wide	?
	VI	10 yrs	Institution creating	£35 000	20 000	Group	Corps	Deputy Sec.	In several nations	?
	V	5 yrs	Intuitive Theory	£18 000	2500	Full D.–M.	Division	Under Sec.	Spread over one nation	?
	IV	2 yrs	Conceptual Modelling	£9000	350	Medium-sized Business	Brigade	Asst. Sec.	Regional	?
CONCRETE Direct Command	III	1 yr	Imaginal Scanning	£4800	50	One-man Business or Unit	Battalion*	Princ'l	50 000 sq. ft	Mutual recognition
	II	3 mths	Imaginal Concrete	£300	1	Section	Company* & Platoon	Asst. Princ'l	5000 sq. ft	Mutual knowledge
	I		Perceptual-Motor Concrete			Supervisors & Shop & Office-floor	NCOs* & ORs	Clerical & Office Supervisors	Supervising up to 500 sq. ft, Shop & Office Floor up to 150 sq. ft	Face-to-face

* This same type of structure applies to the cohort and centurion in the Imperial Roman Army, and to the military organization in China in 1000 B.C.

turns into the creation and establishment of new institutions. These institutions are among the most prolific creators of new bureaucracies. Insufficient observational work has as yet been done at these levels, however, even to attempt to distinguish the qualitative changes in mode of work being assumed. What can be said is that these institutions can employ tens and hundreds of thousands of people, and commonly have working relationships with central governments or are national departments or services employed by central governments.[18]

The table on p. 294, summarizes the scheme of levels of abstraction described.

Time-span, Work-capacity and Information Processing
It is now proposed to develop the analysis of the nature of work-capacity in the light of the discontinuity theory which has been put forward. It has been suggested that the higher the level of abstraction a person can manage, the longer the tasks or projects which he will be able to plan and further in full-time employment. It is this relation which is necessary if time-span in fact measures level of work. It is also the reason why individuals demand time-spans which are consistent with their capacity seen in terms of level of abstraction. For no matter how interesting the tasks, if their general framework is not sufficiently extended in time the individual feels constricted, hemmed in, in the present.

How then may the relationship between time-span and the work-capacity of the individual be explained? It has to do with the organizing capacity of the mind, its capacity to pattern and order, to categorize, to generalize, or in the language of information theory, the capacity to chunk information bits.[19] For it may be apparent that the longer forward the object of the task to be achieved, the greater is the amount of information or detail to be organized, from the very beginning. The longer the task, the more complex it can be, the greater the number of circumstances to be anticipated.

That the longer the task the greater will be the complexity to begin with, can be shown, for example, by the fact that the

[18] In chapter I, these two levels of abstraction are reformulated in terms of their being levels 1 and 2 of the next higher content of logical process.

[19] Cherry, C. (1957): *On human communication;* New York, John Wiley.

greater number of sub-events in a critical path diagram the farther forward the objective event or goal. The 'future', the goal, shows up as a complex field in the present: longer time-spans are reflected in a larger initial field, with a greater information input-load, with more sub-activities to be undertaken, requiring more complex categorization, with the ability to encompass detailed bits of information into sub-categories, sub-categories into categories, categories into larger categories, and so on. In effect, the individual has to be able to take a higher or wider perspective at the start in order to traverse a longer time-span path to a goal.[20]

It is this assumption about categorization or chunking of information bits, which may explain the discontinuity phenomena described. For categorization is a discontinuous process. Take for example the process of definition: four sticks do not define a chair; nor do four sticks and a board; but four legs, a back and a seat do: there is a sudden linking of information bits (themselves each composed of information bits) which pulls the various bits together into a category which can be dealt with as a single chunk containing the several bits. And once the category has been constructed, additional bits of information can be added and thus taken into account in describing many different types of chair, for example, but all still within the same single category. The category chair can then become one bit of information within a wider category; for example, if put together with the categories of table, bed, etc., to constitute the inclusive category, furniture.

It may be noted that a jump or discontinuity occurs each time in moving from each separate item to the new encompassing category. There is, of course, an infinite regress in this process of boundary definition. In one direction, increasingly inclusive categories are discovered – by processes of scientific generalization and theory building, or of artistic creativity; and in the other direction, by increasingly refined and microscopic

[20] This view has an interesting counterpart in the work of Van Lennep and Muller for Shell International. They describe what they call the 'helicopter principle' in assessing individual capacity. They use this phrase to refer to the height from which the individual is able to survey the work situation while still metaphorically keeping his feet upon the ground. The higher the helicopter view a person can take, the greater his capacity.

analysis, and the revealing of the sub-structure of already defined and known things.

It may thus be seen that discontinuity is the essence of definitory categorization and indeed is contained within the meaning of the term definition itself: *de-finire*, to set boundaries around. The relationships are relationships of inclusion, with boundary-defined discontinuities.

The principle involved can be stated in the following general terms. The capacity to manage activity through time is the counterpart of, and depends upon, the capacity to analyse and detail situations, to pattern and order the detail. The capacity to analyse, pattern and order detail depends upon the organizing and conceptualizing capacity of the mind. The wider the span of the hierarchy of concepts a person is capable of manipulating, the greater is the range of detail he is capable of organizing and therefore the greater his work-capacity. Since categorization is a discontinuous process, so too will work-capacity in populations be found to be discontinuous.

There is one further type of support for our theory; namely, its explanatory power. This theory is able to identify and to explain most of the important phenomena associated with the structure and functioning of bureaucratic systems better than existing assumptions.[21]

Activity Versus Level of Work

Meanwhile, one last assumption may be added about the expression of a person's level of abstraction; it is not possible for a person to perceive the world in any and all its aspects other than through glasses coloured by the particular level of abstraction which he possesses. That is to say, there are no problems and activities which are exclusively level 1, level 2, etc., but there are individuals in the first, second, third, etc., levels of abstraction. Some problems may require analysis into so many details as to be beyond the ordering and patterning potentialities of persons of lower levels of capacity; but that does not place the problem at any particular level higher up. Under such circumstances the person feels overwhelmed by the problem, becomes disorganized, and inevitably fails.

But the more interesting case is that of a number of people

---

[21] See Jaques, E., *A general theory of bureaucracy*, loc. cit.

of different levels of abstraction, say capacity group I, II, III and IV, tackling 'the same problem', say one which is within the competence of the group I person; let us say, the task of doing some copy-typing and let us say each is able to type equally well. Each will be able successfully to complete the task in the sense of producing a satisfactory copy. But each will also have been doing a different task in a very significant sense. The person in capacity group I will have perceived the task in the concrete terms of the production of a fair copy. The group II person will have wondered whether it was this particular task which would best fulfil the needs of the person for whom it was being done, and would seek an opportunity to discuss what was really needed. The group III person would take the experience as one example of tasks which could be assigned to Stratum 1, and would get ideas from the experience which would be used as part of the building up of work systems designed to cope with such tasks. The group IV person would react to the experience by wondering why copy-typing had to be done in the manner assigned; he would be able to put the experience together with other observations, and to use it as material for the development of new systems to be invested in, which would eliminate copy-typing altogether.

In effect, it was quite impossible for Newton to perceive falling apples in the way that a group I apple picker would perceive falling apples. Similarly, it was impossible for Sir Alexander Fleming to perceive spoiled bacteriological plates in the same way that they were perceived by his laboratory assistant as he threw them out. Different pictures of the world, based on different levels of abstraction, lead to different accumulations of experience, different patterning and ordering of detail, and different final outcomes.

This particular conclusion, simple enough in all conscience, is a cornerstone of the argument that industrial societies must as an absolute condition of democracy and human freedom provide a range and distribution of levels of work that correspond to the range and distribution of work-capacity in the population – regardless of the so-called demands of technological advance. To require a person of, say, group III capacity, to work in a Stratum-1 role, and to confine his output to the level 1 concrete output is to cage him; its effect would be like that of employing Newton to pick apples, and Fleming to clean up the laboratory, and to force them to keep their ideas about gravity and about bacteriocides to themselves because that was not what they were being employed for.

There is an implicit distinction here which must be made clear and explicit: it is the distinction between the content of an activity and the level of work of the task to which that activity is directed. By activity is meant what a person is actually doing, without reference to his goal in doing it; for example, writing with a pen; using a slide rule or a micrometer; operating a machine tool, or a business calculating machine, or a typewriter; speaking on a telephone; sitting at a desk talking to someone; drawing some designs; walking about; driving a car.

Unfortunately, such activities are often taken to denote the nature of a role, and to indicate its level of work. Examples from the foregoing list of activities would be: machine tool operator; typist; accounting machine operator; telephonist; interviewer; commercial artist. In fact, these denotations of activity can no more give an indication of level of work than describing a judge as a desk-sitter or a chief accountant as a fountain pen operator. Nor can any chain of activities denote the level of work; as, for example, in denoting a managing director as telephonist–pen user–interviewer–letter dictator.

The level of work in a role results not from the activity but (as we have demonstrated) from the time-span of the *goal* of the activity. Level of work, responsibility, derive from the purposes of human activity, from the nature of the output to be achieved. Thus, it cannot be assumed that any two typists, or drivers, or machine operators, or telephonists, are necessarily carrying the same level of work.

But it might be thought that there is a contradiction in our argument. If a person inevitably carries out an activity at the level consonant with his level of work capacity and demanded by it, how is it possible for anyone ever to be under-employed? This apparent contradiction is readily resolved. To be under-employed is not a feature of the activity, it is a feature of the goal of the activity and its time-span. Thus, in our example above, a person with the capacity to work at Str-2 would be under-employed and feel frustrated if given typing to do whose object was simply to make good copies day by day. He would not be under-employed, however, if the object of the typing was to produce copies of long and complex manuscripts, checking for errors, making suggestions for improving the formulations, preparing the bibliography and index, and getting copy ready for the printer – a three- to six-month task in all.

The frustrating effect of under-employment comes from requiring the person-in-action to confine his attention and his activities to shorter-term and less responsible goals than his work-capacity would cope with. As he carries out these lesser tasks, his higher level of capacity inevitably expresses itself, and he experiences the longer-term possibilities, the higher levels of task and output of which he is capable: the possible new methods; the easier ways of doing things; possibly better decisions; the advantages of doing some other investigation in place of the one he is doing; and so on. But he is not allowed to express these ideas. His manager is not interested in these other ideas, but only in getting the assigned tasks done and on time. At best there might be a suggestions scheme to be used, but that calls for work at home and does not get over the soul-destroying eight hours of frustration at work every day.

In short, under-employment is frustrating because it requires an individual to swallow the inexorable expression of his level of work-capacity, to conceal it, to keep it to himself, to throw it away. The measure of that frustration is the discrepancy between the time-span of the person's work-capacity and the time-span of the objectives of his activity. This discrepancy can be shown in its most dramatic form when capacity is constrained by physical imprisonment of the individual, as Farber has shown in the constriction of time perspective in the life-space of men serving long prison sentences.[22] Forced under-employment through lack of availability of adequate levels of work in the bureaucratic sector of industrial societies has effects akin to imprisonment.

[22] Farber, M. L. (1944): 'Suffering and time perspective of the prisoner', in *University of Iowa Studies in Child Welfare*, Vol. 20, pp. 155–227.

Bibliography

BEILIN, H. (1971): 'Developmental stages and developmental processes'. In Green, D. R., Ford, M. P. and Flamer, G. B. (eds.): *Measurement and Piaget*; New York, McGraw-Hill.

BENDIX, R. and LIPSET, S. M. (eds.) (1953): *Class, status and power*; London, Routledge.

BENNETT, J. (1956–66): *The dramatic universe*; London, Hodder & Stoughton.

BERNSTEIN, B. (1971): *Class, codes and control*; London, Routledge & Kegan Paul.

BIERI, J. and BLACKER, E. (1956): *Journal of Abnormal and Social Psychology*.

BILLIS, D. (1975): 'Managing to care', *Social Work Today*, 6, 38–43.

BLOMMERS, P. and LINDQUIST, E. F. (1960): *Elementary statistical methods in psychology and education*; London, University of London Press.

BLOOM, B. S. (ed.) (1956): *Taxonomy of educational objectives*, Book 1; London, Longman.

BOREVICH, Z. I. and SHAFAREVICH, I. R. (1966): *Number Theory*, translated from the Russian; New York, Academic Press.

BROWN, W. (1960): *Exploration in management*; London, Heinemann Educational.

BRUNER, J. (1966): *Toward a theory of instruction*; New York, W. W. Norton & Co.

BURNS, T. and STALKER, G. M. (1961): *The management of innovation*; London, Tavistock.

CHANDLER, A. D. (1963): *Strategy and structure*; Cambridge, Mass., M.I.T. Press.

CHERRY, C. (1957): *On human communication*; New York, John Wiley.

CHILD, J. (1972): 'Organisational structure, environment and performance: The role of strategic choice', *Sociology*, 6, 1, 2–22.

DAHRENDORF, R. (1968): 'On the origin of inequality among men'. *Essays in the theory of society*; London, Routledge.

DAVIS, K. (1949): *Human Society*; New York, Macmillan.

ELKIND, D. (1961): 'The development of quantitative thinking – A systematic replication of Piaget's studies', *Journal of General Psychology*, 1961, 98, 37.

EMERY, F. E. and TRIST, E. L. (1965): 'The causal texture of organisational environments', *Human Relations*, 1965, 18, 21–32.

ENGELMANN, S. E. 'Does the Piagetian approach imply instruction?' In Green, D. R., Ford, M. P. and Flamer, G. B. (eds.): *Measurement and Piaget*; New York, McGraw-Hill.

EVANS, J. S. (1970): Managerial accountability – chief officers, consultants and boards. Unpublished paper, Brunel University.

FARBER, M. L. (1944): 'Suffering and time perspective of the prisoner'. In *University of Iowa Studies in Child Welfare*, Vol. 20, 155–227.

FRENCH, JR., J. R. P. and SNYDER, R. (1959): 'Leadership and interpersonal power'. In Cartwright, D. (ed.), *Studies in social power*; Ann Arbor, University of Michigan, Institute of Social Research.

GIBSON, R. O. (1975): *Value judgements and dualism in geometry and arithmetic*; Ann Arbor, Michigan, Mathesis Press.

GOLDSTEIN, K. (1948): *Language and language disturbances*; New York, Grune & Stratton.

GOLDSTEIN, K. and SCHEERER, G. (1939): *The organism*; New York, American Book Co.

GREINER, E. L. (1972): 'Evolution and revolution as organisations grow', *Harvard Business Review, 50*, 4, 37–46.

HARVEY, O. J., HUNT, D. E. and SCHRODER, H. M. (1961): *Conceptual systems and personality organisation*; New York, London, John Wiley.

HASSELBLAD, V. (1966): 'Estimation of parameters for a mixture of normal distributions', *Technometrics, 8*, 3.

HAYAKAWA, S. (1964): *Language in thought and action*; New York, Harcourt Brace.

HUNT, J. McV. (1961): 'The impact and limitations of the giant of developmental psychology'. In Elkind, D. and Flavell, J. H. (eds.): *Studies in cognitive development*; London, Oxford University Press.

ISAAC, D. J. and O'CONNOR, B. M. (1969): 'Experimental treatment of a discontinuity theory of psychological development', *Human Relations*, vol. 22, 427.

(1973): 'Use of loss of skill under stress to test a theory of psychological development', *Human Relations*, vol. 26, 487.

(1975): 'On a discontinuity theory of psychological development', *Human Relations*, vol. 29, no. 1, 41–61.

JAQUES, E. (1965a): 'Preliminary sketch of a general structure of executive strata'. In W. Brown and E. Jaques, *Glacier project papers*; London, Heinemann Educational.

(1965b): 'Speculations concerning level of capacity', op. cit.

(1965c): 'Social analysis and the glacier project', op. cit.

(1967): *Equitable payment* (2nd ed.); Harmondsworth, Penguin.

(1976): *A general theory of bureaucracy*; London, Heinemann Educational.

JOHN, E. R. (1957): 'Contributions to the study of the problem solving process', *Psych. Mono., 71*, 447.

JOHNSON, E. (1971): *The Journal of Experimental Psychology Monograph No. 90*, pp. 167–96.

KAHN, R. L. and KATZ, D. (1953): 'Leadership practices in relation to productivity and morale'. In Cartwright, D. and Zander, A. (eds.), *Group dynamics*; Evanston, Ill., Row, Peterson.

KOHLBERG, L.: in Mischel, T. (1971): *Cognitive development and epistemology*; London, Academic Press.

LAWRENCE, P. (1958): *The changing of organizational behaviour patterns*; Boston, Graduate School of Business Administration, Harvard University.

LERNER, H. (1948): *Comparative psychology of mental development*; New York, National Universities Press.

LIPPIT, R., *et al.* (1952): 'The dynamics of power'. *Human Relations, 5*, 37.

McGregor, D. (1960): *The human side of enterprise*; New York, McGraw-Hill.

Miller, D. R. and Swanson, G. E. (1958): *The changing American parent*; New York, John Wiley.

Miller, E. J. and Rice, A. K. (1970): *Systems of organisation*; London, Tavistock.

Miller, J. G. (1960): 'Input overload and psychopathology', *Amer. J. Psychiat.*, *116*, 695.

Pask, G. (1975): *Conversation, cognition and learning*; Amsterdam, Elsevier.

Pepper, S. (1970): *The sources of value*; University of California Press.

Piaget, J. (1950): *The psychology of intelligence*; London, Routledge.
  (1953): *The origin of intelligence in the child*; London, Routledge & Kegan Paul.
  (1954): *The construction of reality in the child*; New York, Basic Books.
  (1960): 'The general problems of the psychobiological development of the child'. In Tanner, J. M. and Inhelder, B. (eds.): *Discussion on child development*. Volume IV; London, Tavistock Publications.
  (1971): 'The theory of stages in cognitive development'. In Green, D. R., Ford, M. P. and Flamer, G. B. (eds.): *Measurement and Piaget*; New York, McGraw-Hill.

Pinard, A. and Laurendeau, M. (1969): ' "Stage" in Piaget's cognitive-developmental theory: Exegesis of a concept'. In Elkind, D. and Flavell, J. H. (eds.): *Studies in cognitive development*; London, Oxford University Press.

Rao, C. R. (1948): 'The utilisation of multiple measurements in problems of biological classification', *J. R. statist. soc. B*, *10*, 159.

Rowbottom, R. W. (1973): Organizing social services, hierarchy or...?' *Public Administration*, *51*, 291–301.
  (1978): *Social analysis*; London, Heinemann Educational.

Rowbottom, R. and Billis, D. (1977): 'The stratification of work and organizational design', *Human Relations*, vol. 30, no. 1, 53–76.

Rowbottom, R. W., Balle, J., Cang, S., Dixon, M., Jaques, E., Packwood, T. and Tolliday, H. (1973): *Hospital organization*; London, Heinemann Educational.

Schon, D. A. (1971): *Beyond the stable state*; London, Temple Smith.

Silverman, D. (1970): *The theory of organization*; London, Heinemann Educational.

Social Services Organisation Research Unit (1974): Brunel Institute of Organisation and Social Studies, *Social Services departments: Developing patterns of work and organisation*; London, Heinemann Educational.

Tolman, E. C. (1951) 'Cognitive maps in rats and men'. In *Behaviour and Psychological Man*; University of California Press, 256–9.

Tumin, M. M. (1967): *Social stratification*; Englewood Cliffs, N.J., Prentice-Hall.

Van De Geer, J. P. (1957): *A psychological study of problem solving*; Haarlem, De Toorts.

Vandiver, N., *Trans. Amer. Math. Soc.*, *31* (1929), 613–42.

WERNER, H. (1948): *Comparative psychology of mental development*; New York, International Universities Press.

(1957): *The concept of development from a comparative and organismic point of view*; Minneapolis, University of Minnesota Press.

(1967): 'The concept of development from a comparative and organismic point of view'. In Harris, D. B. (ed.): *The concept of development*; Minneapolis, University of Minnesota Press.

Index

DATE DUE
